Antifascist Humanism and the Politics of Cultural Renewal in Germany

Antifascism is usually described as either a political ideology of activists and intellectuals confronting the dictatorships of Hitler and Mussolini, or as a cynical tool that justified the Stalinist expansion of communism in Europe. Andreas Agocs widens our understanding of antifascism by placing it in the context of twentieth-century movements of "cultural renewal." He explores the concept of "antifascist humanism," the attempt by communist and liberal intellectuals and artists to heal the divisions of Nazism by reviving the "other Germany" of classical Weimar. This project took intellectual shape in German exile communities in Europe and Latin America during World War II and found its institutional embodiment in the Cultural League for the Democratic Renewal of Germany in Soviet-occupied Berlin in 1945. During the emerging Cold War, antifascist humanism's uneasy blend of twentieth-century mass politics and cultural nationalism became the focal point of new divisions in occupied Germany and the early German Democratic Republic. This study traces German traditions of cultural renewal from their beginnings in antifascist activism to their failure in the budding Cold War.

Andreas Agocs is currently Visiting Assistant Professor at the University of the Pacific, California, where he teaches European and world history. His research area is the cultural and political history of Germany and Central Europe during the nineteenth and twentieth centuries.

CAMBRIDGE
UNIVERSITY PRESS

University Printing House, Cambridge CB2 8BS, United Kingdom

One Liberty Plaza, 20th Floor, New York, NY 10006, USA

477 Williamstown Road, Port Melbourne, VIC 3207, Australia

314-321, 3rd Floor, Plot 3, Splendor Forum, Jasola District Centre, New Delhi - 110025, India

79 Anson Road, #06-04/06, Singapore 079906

Cambridge University Press is part of the University of Cambridge.

It furthers the University's mission by disseminating knowledge in the pursuit of education, learning and research at the highest international levels of excellence.

www.cambridge.org
Information on this title: www.cambridge.org/9781108707695
DOI: 10.1017/9781316084106

© Andreas Agocs 2017

This publication is in copyright. Subject to statutory exception and to the provisions of relevant collective licensing agreements, no reproduction of any part may take place without the written permission of Cambridge University Press.

First published 2017
First paperback edition 2019

A catalogue record for this publication is available from the British Library

Library of Congress Cataloging in Publication data
Names: Agocs, Andreas, author.
Title: Antifascist humanism and the politics of cultural renewal in Germany / Andreas Agocs (University of the Pacific, California).
Description: Cambridge, United Kingdom; New York, NY: Cambridge University Press, 2017. | Includes bibliographical references and index.
Identifiers: LCCN 2017003652 | ISBN 9781107085435 (hardback)
Subjects: LCSH: Anti-fascist movements – Germany – History – 20th century. | Humanism – Political aspects – Germany – History – 20th century. | Exiles – Political activity – Europe – History – 20th century. | Exiles – Political activity – Latin America – History – 20th century. | Kulturbund zur Demokratischen Erneuerung Deutschlands – History. | Nationalism – Germany – History – 20th century. | Germany – Politics and government – 1933–1945. | Germany – Politics and government – 1945–1990. | Germany – Cultural policy. | Germany – Intellectual life – 20th century. |
BISAC: HISTORY / Europe / General.
Classification: LCC DD256.7.A35 2017 | DDC 943.087–dc23
LC record available at https://lccn.loc.gov/2017003652

ISBN 978-1-107-08543-5 Hardback
ISBN 978-1-108-70769-5 Paperback

Cambridge University Press has no responsibility for the persistence or accuracy of URLs for external or third-party internet websites referred to in this publication, and does not guarantee that any content on such websites is, or will remain, accurate or appropriate.

Antifascist Humanism
and the Politics of Cultural
Renewal in Germany

Andreas Agocs
University of the Pacific, California

Contents

List of Figures	*page* vii
Acknowledgments	ix
List of Abbreviations	xi
Introduction: Antifascist Humanism and the Dual Legacies of Weimar	1

Part I Defending the "Other Germany"

1	The "Humanist Front": Antifascism and Culture Wars, 1934–1939	23
2	"Otra Alemanias": Antifascist Humanism in the Diaspora, 1939–1944	37
3	The "Other Germany" from Below: Antifascist Committees and National Renewal in 1945	54

Part II Contesting "Other Germanies"

4	Antifascism as Renewal and Restoration: The Cultural League for the Democratic Renewal of Germany, 1945–1946	71
5	Humanism with a Socialist Face: Sovietization and "Ideological Coordination" of the Kulturbund, 1946–1947	107
6	The Limits of Humanism: Cultural Renewal and the Outbreak of the Cold War, 1947–1948	129

7	Mass Organization and Memory: Antifascist Humanism in Divided Germany, 1948 and Beyond	156
	Conclusion: From the Saar to Salamis	178
	Bibliography	187
	Index	201

Figures

1 Portrait of writer and KPD activist Alexander Abusch
(1902–1982) in the 1950s *page* 34
2 Anna Seghers (1900–1983) giving a speech after her
return from Mexican exile, 1947 48
3 Expressionist poet Johannes R. Becher (1891–1958)
in the 1920s 90
4 Kulturbund Poster, Oktober 1945 102
5 Vice Mayor of Berlin Ferdinand Friedensburg addresses
the delegates at the First Federal Congress of the
Kulturbund Berlin, May 20, 1947 113
6 Participants at the First German Writers' Congress
approach the Kammerspiele building, Berlin,
October 1947 138
7 Ricarda Huch (1864–1947) giving the opening speech
at the First German Writers' Congress, Berlin,
October 1947 142
8 Writer and resistance activist Günther Weisenborn
(1902–1969) in 1947 166
9 Portrait of writer and philosopher Wolfgang Harich
(1923–1995) in 1947 171

Acknowledgments

This project began as an attempt to link the histories of the postwar period and of pre–World War II dynamics of fascism and of battles over culture, and I'm grateful for a lot of help and assistance I've received in my research and writing. This book was conceived and took shape under the direction of Bill Hagen, whose intellectual influence did not only guide this project, but was formative for my approach to history and to my self-understanding as a historian. My doctoral committee advisors, David Beale, Edward Ross Dickinson, and John Hall, provided expertise, guidance, and much-needed encouragement throughout the writing process. Many ideas in this book reflect the influences over my years in Davis of the late Dan Brower, Norma Landau, Ted Margadant, Mike Saler, and Clarence E. Walker. Financial support for research and archival travel came from the Smith-Reed Foundation at UC Davis and from UC Berkeley's Institute of European Studies. I'd also like to acknowledge the helpful and well-organized archivists at the SAPMO-Bundesarchiv in Berlin-Lichterfelde, the Akademie der Künste in Berlin, the Institut für Zeitungsforschung in Dortmund, and the Hoover Institution's Visual Collections in Stanford, California.

Many of this book's pages were drafted in an office at UC Davis's Hemispheric Institute, and I want to thank Christina Siracusa for providing a clean, well-lighted place. Paul Schliwa needs to be acknowledged for reading the manuscript during long nights in Sweden. A number of friends and fellow scholars have expressed interest in or shared comments on aspects of this work, among them Lori Clune, Jason Dawsey, Mel Draper, Maria Duarte, Frieder Günther, Barbara Kaszowska, Terry Renaud, Andrea Scionti, Guenther Roth, and Bob Sharlet. The International Conference on New Narratives of the Cold War in Lausanne, organized and hosted by Agnieszka Soltysik Monnet, yielded many inspirational discussions that went into this book. I'd also like to thank Gesine Gerhard, who read and gave helpful comments on portions of my draft, as well as Greg Rohlf and my colleagues at the University of the Pacific's history department, who have been providing a collegial scholarly and teaching environment during my extended visit over the past years. I owe special thanks to Andrew Port, whose careful reading of the whole manuscript, insightful suggestions for improvements, and overall support made this a much better book.

At Cambridge University Press, I thank the two anonymous readers for their helpful comments, and Lew Bateman, who first saw potential in my manuscript. Michael Watson guided the project through its final phases with astute editorial suggestions and decisions, and Fiona Allison and Claire Sissen provided efficient and patient help with many issues. At Newgen I'd like to acknowledge Ami Naramor, who was a perceptive and competent copy editor, and the project management of Kanimozhi Ramamurthy and the late Siva Prakash Chandrasekaran, who will be remembered for his kind professionalism.

Finally, I'm grateful to my mother and brothers in Germany, who during all too short and rare visits had to see me disappear in archives and libraries and still supported me as much as they could. Sometimes lists like this don't do justice to the people who matter most to us. My wife, Victoria, has been by my side with love and support throughout the time it took to write this book. For this and the many more years we've shared together, I'd like to express my most loving acknowledgements and gratefulness. This book is dedicated to her and to our children, Sophie and Noah, who have been growing faster and more gracefully than this project. Although I'm sure that during these years they've had more captivating readings than this book, their unconditional love and patience were essential ingredients in writing it.

Abbreviations

ACC	Allied Control Council
AdK Berlin	Akademie der Künste Berlin
Afa	Antifaschistisches Aktionskomitee
antifa	Antifascist Committee
BFD	Bewegung Freies Deutschland
CDU	Christlich-Demokratische Union (Christian Democratic Union)
Cominform	Communist Information Bureau
Comintern	Communist International
DSV	Deutscher Schriftstellerverband
DVV	Deutsche Verwaltung für Volksbildung
FDKB	Freier Deutscher Kulturbund in Großbritannien (Free German Cultural League in Great Britain)
FRG	Federal Republic of Germany
GDR	German Democratic Republic
Gestapo	Geheime Staatspolizei (Secret State Police)
KGF	Kampfgemeinschaft gegen den Faschismus
KPD	Kommunistische Partei Deutschlands (Communist Party of Germany)
Kulturbund	Kulturbund zur demokratischen Erneuerung Deutschlands (Cultural League for the Democratic Renewal of Germany)
NKFD	Nationalkomitee Freies Deutschland (National Committee Free Germany)
NSDAP	National Socialist German Workers' Party
Pg	Party member of the NSDAP
SAPMO - Barch	Stiftung Archiv der Parteien und Massenorganisationen der DDR im Bundesarchiv
SBZ	Sowjetische Besatzungszone (Soviet Occupation Zone)

SDA	Schutzverband deutscher Autoren (Association for the Protection of German Authors)
SDS	Schutzverband deutscher Schriftsteller (Association for the Protection of German Writers)
SED	Sozialistische Einheitspartei Deutschlands (Socialist Unity Party of Germany)
SMAD	Sowjetische Militäradministration Deutschlands (Soviet Military Administration in Germany)
SoPaDe	Sozialdemokratische Partei im Exil (Social Democratic Party in Exile)
SPD	Sozialdemokratische Partei Deutschlands (German Social Democratic Party)

Introduction: Antifascist Humanism and the Dual Legacies of Weimar

In July 1945, Berlin was in ruins. Only weeks earlier, the capital of the former Reich had experienced the traumatic violence and chaos of the early days of Russian occupation.[1] On Masurenallee, a major thoroughfare that traverses the affluent middle-class borough of Charlottenburg, one block is still taken up by the semicircular broadcast center, the Haus des Rundfunks. Built in 1931, the unadorned, functional design of the structure reflects the Neue Sachlichkeit (New Objectivity) style of the Weimar period's Bauhaus modernism. The center's left-leaning architect, Hans Poelzig, lost his position after National Socialism came to power in 1933.[2] During the war, the building served as the seat of Joseph Goebbels's propaganda radio, the Großdeutsche Rundfunk, yet the compound somehow survived the bombings that laid so much else in the city to waste. The building's turbulent and contested history continued into the early postwar period. Even though Charlottenburg was to become part of the British sector of divided Berlin in early July 1945, the Soviets would hold on to and broadcast from the building at Masurenallee until 1952.[3]

Like so much in Berlin's architectural landscape, the Haus des Rundfunks embodies many of the contradictions, ruptures, and continuities of German history during the middle decades of the twentieth century: the close relationship between the arts and politics; the battle between left-wing and right-wing visions of modernity; and the influence

---

[1] For accounts of the year 1945 in Berlin, see Anthony Beevor, *The Fall of Berlin 1945* (New York: Viking, 2002); Giles MacDonogh, *After the Reich: The Brutal History of the Allied Occupation* (New York: Basic Books, 2007), 95–124; Richard Bessel, *Germany 1945: From War to Peace* (New York: Harper Collins, 2009).
[2] See Matthias Donath, "Poelzig, Hans," in *Sächsische Biografie*, hrsg. vom Institut für Sächsische Geschichte und Volkskunde e.V., bearb. von Martina Schattkowsky, Online-Ausgabe: www.isgv.de/saebi/ (3.8.2014), accessed August 2, 2014. For Poelzig's role in the Weimar period's Neues Bauen (New Building) movement, see Sabine Hake, *Topographies of Class: Modern Architecture and Mass Society in Weimar Berlin* (Ann Arbor: University of Michigan Press, 2008).
[3] Rundfunk Berlin-Brandenburg rbb, Haus des Rundfunks, "Hier spricht Berlin," www.haus-des-rundfunks.de/, accessed December 27, 2014.

of global political power struggles playing out in Germany.[4] In July 1945, most inhabitants of the city probably had the more immediate realities of a lost war, lack of food and housing, and an uncertain future at the hands of the Allies on their minds. Yet on July 4, 1945, approximately 1,500 Berliners filled the Große Sendesaal, the main broadcasting room at Masurenallee, to attend the inauguration of an organization whose main objective was the resurrection of German culture. The Kulturbund zur demokratischen Erneuerung Deutschlands (Cultural League for the Democratic Renewal of Germany) was one of the first organizations that had been licensed by the Soviet Military Administration in Germany (SMAD). Its first president was the expressionist poet and Communist Party of Germany (KPD) member Johannes R. Becher, although the Kulturbund's member- and leadership included antifascist intellectuals from a wide range of political persuasions. The speeches at the inauguration were preceded by music by Beethoven and Tchaikovsky to underscore the theme of German and Russian reconciliation.[5] Becher shared the stage with, among others, a Protestant pastor and several professors and artists. In an emotional address, the Communist writer described the Kulturbund's goal of renewing German culture after the barbarity of the Nazi years. The coalition of antifascist intellectuals represented in the Kulturbund was to "resurrect" the "other Germany" by building on the "rich heritage of humanism, classicism, and the workers' movement."[6]

The ceremonial inauguration of the Kulturbund has been documented and described many times, especially in the historiographical literature of the former German Democratic Republic (GDR). Yet, the event still opens up questions that frame the analysis in the pages of this book. What motivated this heightened emphasis on the role of German culture so shortly after the war, in a defeated city that lacked the most basic material goods? Why did the antifascist intellectuals who staged the event seem to believe that their eclectic vision of German cultural renewal would connect with the masses and create a new, "other" Germany? And how did their project of a regenerated and reunified German culture play out against the context of the brewing Cold War confrontation that made occupied Germany its battleground and ultimately led to the country's division?

Like the building that provided the setting for its inauguration, the Kulturbund ties into many of the turbulent and contradictory themes

---

[4] For more on the relationship of architecture and memory in German history, see Hake, *Topographies of Class*; Rudy Koshar, *From Monuments to Traces: Artifacts of German Memory, 1870–1990* (Berkeley: University of California Press, 2000).
[5] Toby Thacker, *Music after Hitler, 1945–1955* (Aldershot: Ashgate, 2007), 35.
[6] Archiv der Akademie der Künste Berlin, Nachlass Becher, 39/3, Blatt 7, Bl. 8.

in twentieth-century German history. The hopeful atmosphere at the Kulturbund's inauguration does not mark the beginning of the project of Germany's cultural renewal, and neither did the spirit of nonpartisan "antifascist humanism" survive unscathed into the years that followed. Rather, the establishment of the Kulturbund fell amid a period of intense and shifting debates on German identity and culture that played out between the beginning of the twentieth century and the late 1940s. This book traces the attempt by a group of German intellectuals – first in German exile communities, then in occupied Germany – to represent and "renew" a vaguely defined "humanist" German cultural tradition in response to both National Socialist propaganda and the anti-German sentiment that had built up in the world as a result of the war. Meant to heal the wounds and rifts opened by dictatorship, war, and exile, however, the idea of an "other" – and implicitly better and more unified – Germany ended up, after the hopeful speeches at the Kulturbund inauguration, as a rhetorical tool to distinguish the emerging East German state from its Cold War counterpart to the west.

In 1945 and into 1946, three years before the German division, the Kulturbund was still a nonpartisan coalition of antifascist intellectuals, even though the representatives of the KPD were steadily extending the party's influence. The leadership of the early Kulturbund, men such as the Communist Becher or the Christian Democrat vice mayor of Berlin, Ferdinand Friedensburg, embodied the experiences of a generation who had lived through the tumultuous upheavals of the first half of the twentieth century. Transcending their ideological and party differences, they shared a condemnation of fascism and Nazism, an appreciation of classical German culture, and an acceptance of a collective German need to atone for the crimes committed in the country's name. In addition, they believed in the responsibility of intellectuals to mobilize the masses in the cause of a "renewed" German culture, purged from the distortions and perversions of Nazi cultural policy.

The Kulturbund was modelled on the cooperation between bourgeois-liberal intellectuals and Communist Party activists in antifascist exile German "culture leagues" – both inside and outside Europe – since the 1930s. These loose coalitions introduced ideas of cultural renewal into antifascist mass politics, and they gave voice to the idea of an "other Germany" – a distinctive German Popular Front movement claiming to represent the heritage of Johann Wolfgang Goethe, Heinrich Heine, and other classical eighteenth- and nineteenth-century writers. Their broadly defined and eclectic vision also drew from early twentieth-century ideals of pedagogical reform, Marxist materialism, and the rhetoric of Protestant martyrdom. The "classical" heritage of German culture was supposed to be the tonic that would heal Germany from the destructiveness of the Nazi legacy and the divisions it had created since the early 1930s. However, between the early 1930s and the late 1940s, the concept of the "other Germany" experienced multiple conceptual evolutions and intellectual front lines, first between German and Allied interpreters of German history, then, after 1945, between German former exiles and "inner émigrés," and, ultimately, between German intellectuals in the East and those in the West. Not surprisingly, the Kulturbund and its project of antifascist humanism did not survive as a pluralist, "nonpartisan" organization. Even before the foundation of the GDR as a Soviet client state, the Kulturbund would become a "mass organization" under the direction of the communist Socialist Unity Party (SED), which in turn exercised its pressure with the massive support of the Soviet occupation authorities. The pages that follow expose the ironic fractures that led from a movement aimed at restoring unity among German intellectuals to a discourse that entrenched the German division. As it turned out, the idea of an alternative German cultural tradition – born as a response to the Nazi appropriation of national traditions and driven by the need to find common ground between liberal and communist antifascists – was all too perfectly suited for the intellectual confrontation of a nation about to be divided.

At this narrative's center is a diverse cast of characters who shared a common involvement in the Kulturbund. They include the KPD functionary Alexander Abusch, who mediated between exile literary communities and the Moscow-based KPD during the war, and who decisively changed the dynamics of the Kulturbund after his return from Mexico to Berlin; Johannes R. Becher, the expressionist poet and later minister of culture of the GDR; Ferdinand Friedensburg, the leader of the Christian Democratic Union (CDU) in the Soviet Occupation Zone, who surprisingly found much common ground with German communists and the Soviet occupation authorities; Günther Weisenborn, the writer and former anti-Nazi activist, who made it his mission to preserve the legacy of the German resistance; and Wolfgang Harich, the young and provocative Marxist philosopher and journalist, who would become one of the leading dissidents in the early GDR.[7]

Even though the voices of the "other Germany's" male representatives are more prominent in these pages – and in the archival and published sources they are based on – their antifascist humanism was not a movement without influential and vocal women. The antifascist novelist Anna

---

[7] Ernst Niekisch, Georg Lukács, and Ernst Bloch, among others, also played key roles in the concept of socialist humanism but are not discussed in this work.

Seghers was part of the KPD circle around Abusch in Mexico as well as of the early Kulturbund, and she became an icon of the official GDR memory culture. The poet Ricarda Huch embodied many of the tropes of the "other Germany" even though she spent the Nazi years in "inner exile." A further study is needed to do justice to the role of women in the "other Germany and to its gendered aspects. But whether male or female, many of the intellectuals portrayed here combined a keen, even militant desire to redress the mistakes of Germany's past with a sense of cultural nationalism and, in some cases, shrewd political calculations and tactics. The unintended consequences and moral ambiguities of these individuals' project to represent a "better nation" offer a human perspective on the dramatic ruptures and subtle continuities in mid-twentieth-century European politics and culture.

Arguments and Themes

The narrative sketched thus far sets the stage for a number of interrelated arguments about twentieth-century German and European history. The first line of argument involves a new perspective on and assessment of antifascism. The widespread condemnation and demystification of antifascism was a necessary and perhaps inevitable outcome of the end of the Cold War in the early 1990s. As a result, for leading historians since the fall of the Berlin Wall, antifascism has been little more than a cynical smokescreen served to further Stalin's objective of binding intellectuals to his cause and expanding the power of Moscow-centric communist parties. According to the French historian François Furet, to name one of the most influential voices, the Soviet Union's model of communism "prolonged its tenancy thanks to anti-Fascism."[8] For Furet, antifascism – much like Marxism itself – was the misguided belief of sometimes well-meaning but ultimately naïve intellectuals in the utopian political vision of a united left, a blindness that Stalinist puppet masters in Moscow all too easily exploited.

---

[8] François Furet, *The Passing of an Illusion: The Idea of Communism in the Twentieth Century*, trans. Deborah Furet (Chicago: University of Chicago Press, 1999), 24. Cf. Enzo Traverso, "The New Anti-Communism: Rereading the Twentieth Century," in Mike Haynes and Jim Wolfreys, eds., *History and Revolution: Refuting Revisionism* (London and New York: Verso, 2007), 138–55; idem., *À feu et à sang: de la guerre civile européenne, 1914–1945* (Paris: Stock, 2007). For a comparative study of the attraction of communism in general on Western European intellectuals after the war, see Thomas Kroll, *Kommunistische Intellektuelle in Westeuropa: Frankreich, Österreich, Italien und Großbritannien im Vergleich (1945–1956)* (Köln: Böhlau Verlag, 2007). Also see *Témoigner entre histoire et mémoire. Revue pluridisciplinaire de la Fondation Auschwitz Bruxelles, No104 (July–September 2009): L'Antifascisme revisité. Histoire – idéologie – mémoire* (Paris: Éditions Kimé, 2009).

The rhetorical use and political function of antifascism in the GDR – a state that did not merely experience a "regime change," but disappeared altogether – became the subject of particular scrutiny; its official antifascism is usually seen as indicative of the shaky and flawed premises of the state's foundation. In his study of the founding of the GDR, Gareth Pritchard has demonstrated "how effective Stalinism proved at manipulating, exploiting and eventually neutralizing the idealism of the German Left."[9] Antifascism was, as Corey Ross sums up the interpretive findings since 1989, "nothing other than a propaganda coup that prevented internal criticism, encouraged a selective view of history, created and sustained a culture of enemy-hatred, prevented any genuine confrontation with the Nazi past, and that belittled or obscured 'communist crimes' such as the party purges or the incarceration of alleged 'political enemies' in the Soviet 'special camps' after the war."[10] Few scholars would completely discard the notion that antifascism was "a cynical attempt to create an alibi for the brutal Stalinization of East Germany [and other countries behind the Iron Curtain], and for an ongoing program of human rights abuses."[11] But pointing out that antifascism constituted a more complex, fractured, and dynamic phenomenon over the course of several decades is not the same as excusing or denying its use for the oppressive ends of twentieth-century communist dictatorships; after all, antifascism's failure is easier to diagnose for contemporary historians than for intellectuals whose experience of twentieth-century fascism's often murderous dynamics was direct and visceral.

While KPD ideology and the strategies of the Communist International (Comintern) provide important contexts, this book emphasizes antifascism's role as a *cultural* movement. Its political thrust intertwined

---

[9] Gareth Pritchard, *The Making of the GDR, 1945–1953* (Manchester: Manchester University Press, 2000), 229.

[10] Corey Ross, *The East German Dictatorship: Problems and Perspectives in the Interpretation of the GDR* (London: Oxford University Press, 2002), 178. Antonia Grunenberg, *Antifaschismus: Ein deutscher Mythos* (Reinbek: Rowohlt, 1993); Manfred Agethen, Eckhard Jesse, and Ehrhart Neubert (eds.), *Der missbrauchte Antifaschismus. DDR-Staatsdoktrin und Lebenslüge der deutschen Linken* (Freiburg: Herder, 2002); Dan Diner, "On the Ideology of Antifascism," trans. Christian Gundermann, "Legacies of Antifascism," *New German Critique* 67 (Winter 1996): 123–32. Cf. Mary Nolan, "Antifascism under Fascism: German Vision and Voices," *New German Critique* 67 (Legacies of Antifascism) (Winter 1996): 33–55. See also Josie McLellan, *Antifascism and Memory in East Germany: Remembering the International Brigades 1945–1989* (Oxford: Clarendon Press, 2004); Christiane Wienand, "Remembered Change and Changes of Remembrance: East German Narratives of Anti-fascist Conversion," in Mary Fulbrook and Andrew I. Port, eds., *Becoming East German: Socialist Structures and Sensibilities after Hitler* (New York: Berghahn, 2013), 99–118.

[11] Anthony Glees, Untitled review of *Divided Memory: The Nazi Past in the Two Germanys* by Jeffrey Herf, *The Journal of Modern History* 72, 1 (March 2000): 274–6.

with and intervened in debates on German culture that were part of the country's experience of twentieth-century modernity. As a host of historiographical works have shown, the desire for culture to give unity to a diverse nation – paired with anxieties triggered by the rising influences of popular and commercialized mass culture – led to intense discussions of the proper definition and role of German culture in the Wilhelmine Empire.[12] By the end of the First World War, German culture was arguably split into three distinct manifestations: the "high culture" that served as the fundament of the nationalist-liberal or conservative educated upper-middle class; the popular mass entertainment industry, increasingly borrowing from American mass culture; and the extremely politicized cultural public sphere of Weimar democracy, with its class- and party-based versions of "agitation and propaganda" (agitprop). As Jost Hermand has shown, National Socialism, at least for some of its early adherents, was itself an expression of and attempt at overcoming these cultural divisions.[13]

However, as this book argues, by the 1930s and with the rise of fascism to power, concepts of "restoring cultural unity" or "renewing German culture" after a period of perceived degeneration were no longer exclusive projects of the reactionary political right. Rather, under the circumstances of European – and indeed global – politics in the first half of the twentieth century, a version of antifascism emerged among German exile intellectuals that rested less on the establishment of a utopian new social or economic order and more on the restoration and renewal of cultural ideals of a more tolerant and cosmopolitan, "humanist" German past. In other words, the antifascism that emerges in these pages was less revolutionary than restorative, which explains the sometimes strangely sounding evocations of both Karl Marx and Martin Luther, which characterized antifascist rhetoric before the war as well as in the postwar GDR. The concept of the "other Germany" implied the "resurrection" of a vague notion of eighteenth- and nineteenth-century humanist Germany, as well as of a more concrete pre-Nazi state of cultural and intellectual unity – a unity that had probably always been more wishful projection than tangible fact.

German intellectuals in exile – usually amidst great economic hardship and under constant threat of Goebbels's agents – organized writers'

---

[12] See Fritz Stern, *The Politics of Cultural Despair: A Study in the Rise of the Germanic Ideology* (Berkeley: University of California Press, 1961).
[13] See Jost Hermand, *Culture in Dark Times: Nazi Fascism, Inner Emigration, and Exile*, trans. Victoria W. Hill (New York: Berghahn, 2013), xi–xv, 122–40. See also Lutz Koepnick, "Culture in the Shadow of Trauma?" in Helmut Walser Smith, ed., *The Oxford Handbook of Modern German History* (New York: Oxford University Press, 2011), 711–13.

8 Introduction

congresses in Paris, discussed Heine and Lessing in Great Britain, and staged Schiller plays in Mexico. For these intellectuals – communists, liberals, and conservatives – Hitler's defeat would lead to a "rebirth" of German culture based on an always vaguely defined "antifascist humanism": an awkward mixture of classical Weimar culture, Marxism, and a Protestant rhetoric of martyrdom and national reformation. This centrality of culture in the rhetoric of German antifascism seems to confirm a long-held and only recently refuted image. In a tradition going back to the early twentieth century, German intellectuals, especially from nationalist or conservative backgrounds, have described themselves as "unpolitical," in a supposed marked contrast to their counterparts in Britain and France.[14] Taken up and reinforced by the Allies during World War II, the image of the German intellectual – more interested in *Kultur* than in politics, and more influenced by the antidemocratic cultural criticism of Friedrich Nietzsche than by the liberal thought of John Stewart Mill or the public engagement of Emile Zola – became a staple in the historiography after 1945 and the cultural component of what became to be known as the German "special path."[15] Though many of the assumptions of the *Sonderweg* have been refuted, assumptions of a special German emphasis on aesthetics and *Innerlichkeit* (inner life) persist.[16]

German antifascism's turn toward "cultural renewal" took up older debates and discussions, but this was not a manifestation of an allegedly deep-seated German obsession with culture going back to the Romantic

---

[14] The classical and still influential works on this subject are Stern, *The Politics of Cultural Despair*; Fritz K. Ringer, *The Decline of the German Mandarins: The German Academic Community, 1890–1933* (Cambridge, MA: Harvard University Press, 1969); George L. Mosse, *The Crisis of German Ideology: Intellectual Origins of the Third Reich* (New York: Grosset & Dunlap, 1964).

[15] For the classical *Sonderweg* interpretation, see the first four volumes of Hans-Ulrich Wehler's seminal *Deutsche Gesellschaftsgeschichte. Band 1: Vom Feudalismus des alten Reiches bis zur defensiven Modernisierung der Reformära, 1700–1815* (München: C. H. Beck, 1987); *Band 2: Von der Reformära bis zur industriellen und politischen "Deutschen Doppelrevolution," 1815–1845/49* (München: C. H. Beck, 1987); *Band 3: Von der "Deutschen Doppelrevolution" bis zum Beginn des Ersten Weltkrieges, 1849–1914* (München: C. H. Beck, 1995); *Band 4: Vom Beginn des Ersten Weltkriegs bis zur Gründung der beiden deutschen Staaten, 1914–1949* (München: C. H. Beck, 1995). For the most influential critique of the *Sonderweg*, see David Blackbourn and Geoff Eley, *The Peculiarities of German History: Bourgeois Society and Politics in Nineteenth-Century Germany* (Oxford: Oxford University Press, 1984). For a summary of the *Sonderweg* debate, see William W. Hagen, "Master Narratives beyond Postmodernity: Germany's 'Separate Path' in Historiographical-Philosophical Light," *German Studies Review* XXX, 1 (February 2007): 1–32. Cf. Helmut Walser Smith, "When the Sonderweg Debate Left Us," *German Studies Review* XXXI, 2 (May 2008): 225–40.

[16] See, for example, Wolf Lepenies, *The Seduction of Culture in German History* (Princeton, NJ: Princeton University Press, 2006); cf. Sean A. Forner, "Reconsidering the 'Unpolitical German': Democratic Renewal and the Politics of Culture in Occupied Germany," *German History* 32, 1 (March 2014): 53–78.

period. The emergence of culture at the forefront of German antifascism is tied to the rise and failure of the Europe-wide *Volksfront* (Popular Front) as political mass movement. As Jean-Michel Palmier has shown, after the successes of fascism in Europe in the mid-1930s, the struggle for and defense of culture became a project that drew participants among intellectuals from all European countries as well as the United States. Events like the International Congress for the Defence of Culture in Paris in 1935, for example, had their "roots in a cultural and political movement that developed steadily in France from the 1920s on."[17] The fascist threat to European culture was also a prime concern for the multinational pro-Republican participants in the Spanish Civil War a few years later.[18]

Yet, while part of larger transnational processes, German antifascism evolved in the context of more localized events. The first concrete test for the political effectiveness of the German Popular Front failed to win the Saar referendum in 1935 – the antifascist coalition's overwhelming political defeat meant that henceforth the struggle for German culture became the main front. In addition, for German opponents of the National Socialist regime, the identification with a vague concept of German humanism enabled communists, socialists, and liberals to define their positions while avoiding potentially conflicted discussions about a post-Nazi political and economic order. In an era when fascism claimed ownership of all aspects of society, cultural debates were immensely political, not only as a common ground that enabled coalitions between liberals and communists, but also as a tool that contested the claim of the Nazi regime to represent a racially and ideologically purified national culture.[19]

Initially, it was bourgeois liberal intellectuals such as Thomas Mann who called for the defense of the "other Germany" – the "humanist," i.e., tolerant and cosmopolitan culture embodied by the German Enlightenment (Kant, Lessing, Herder) as well as the "Weimar classics," Goethe, Schiller, and Hölderlin.[20] The emergence of the Popular Front expanded this list to include the mid-nineteenth-century democratic-revolutionary tradition

---

[17] Jean-Michel Palmier, *Weimar in Exile: The Antifascist Emigration in Europe and America*, trans. David Fernbach (London: Verso, 2006), 333.
[18] Ibid., 336–8.
[19] Whether fascism ever made good on its claim to "totalitarian" intrusion of the state into society is, of course, a matter of historiographical debate; see Robert O. Paxton, *The Anatomy of Fascism* (New York: Vintage, 2004). For Nazi conceptions of culture, including the role of the "Weimar classics," see Hermand, *Culture in Dark Times*, 15–45.
[20] For a recent reevaluation of cosmopolitanism as a trait in German cultural history, see Franz Leander Fillafer and Jürgen Osterhammel, "Cosmopolitanism and the German Enlightenment," in Smith, ed., *The Oxford Handbook of Modern German History*, 119–43.

of Heine and Marx. Given the vast range and diversity of this catalog, the exact contours of this antifascist humanism were never very concretely defined, except as a collage of everything German that was not explicitly National Socialist. Perhaps because of its vague definition and its broad range, the antifascist so-called humanist front survived even after the end of the Popular Front movement that set in with the Hitler–Stalin Pact of 1939; as these pages will show, it also continued in occupied Germany after 1945, where its dynamic shaped and was shaped by the emerging Cold War tensions in the occupation zones.

But the concept of culture espoused by the wartime "humanist front" was not only open-ended in its definition and vague in its content. It also made for an uneasy marriage of the "dual legacies of Weimar," which had seemingly contradicted each other before 1933: the bourgeois-liberal ideal of traditional "high culture" – with the "Weimar classics," Goethe and Schiller, as its foundation – and the leftist demand for a politically engaged art, which characterized much of the mass culture of the Weimar republic. As I argue in this book, the result was a peculiar and politically volatile mixture of nineteenth-century cultural nationalism and twentieth-century politics of mass mobilization.[21] The demand for the humanist restoration of classical Weimar culture blended with calls for the "total mobilization of art" – a term nationalist right-wing author Ernst Jünger used in the 1920s, as did left-wing dramatist Erwin Piscator at the antifascist congress in Barcelona in 1936.[22] It also finds echoes in the rhetoric and the programs of antifascists after 1945, from the Kulturbund inauguration to the First German Writers' Congress in October 1947.

Another line of argument in this work involves the period in Germany after 1945 and the consolidation of Communist rule in the Soviet Occupation Zone. Much of the recent scholarship on twentieth-century Germany has complicated the notion of 1945 as a "zero hour" (*Stunde Null*). Without denying the ruptures that occurred with the German capitulation in May 1945, this study emphasizes the transitional character of the years between the early 1940s and early 1950s.[23] This book

---

[21] See Detlev J. K. Peukert, *Die Weimarer Republik: Krisenjahre der klassischen Moderne* (Frankfurt a. M.: Suhrkamp, 1987). See also James M. Diehl, *Paramilitary Politics in Weimar Germany* (Bloomington: Indiana University Press, 1977). For the central role of mass mobilization in the first half of Europe's twentieth century, see also Mark Mazower, *Dark Continent: Europe's Twentieth Century* (New York: Vintage, 1998). For the mobilization of the German middle classes, see Peter Fritzsche, *Rehearsals for Fascism: Populism and Political Mobilization in Germany* (New York: Oxford University Press, 1990).

[22] See Palmier, *Weimar in Exile*, 54, 163.

[23] See Stefan-Ludwig Hoffmann, "Germany Is No More: Defeat, Occupation, and the Postwar Order," in Smith, ed., *The Oxford Handbook of Modern German History*, 593–614; Jeffrey K. Olick, *In the House of the Hangman: The Agonies of German Defeat*,

embarks on its narrative with the militant cultural movements and the highly politicized debates on culture that characterized Weimar and Nazi Germany. The very names of organizations such as Nazi ideologue Alfred Rosenberg's Kampfbund für deutsche Kultur (Militant League for German Culture) expresses this understanding of the function of culture.[24] If the Nazis, as Lutz Koepnick argues, were "seeking to fuse the political and the aesthetic, power and art, into one mobilizing dynamic," a similar thing could be said of the antifascist idea of a militant humanist front.[25] In the second half of the twentieth century, this idea of mass mobilization under the umbrella of cultural-political movements arguably gave way to the rise of a consumer-oriented "culture industry" – with its roots in Weimar – in the postwar Federal Republic of Germany (FRG).[26] At the same time in the GDR, the Kulturbund – born as a cultural movement for a "militant democracy" (*kämpferische Demokratie*) – evolved into a largely depoliticized SED mass organization entrusted "to incorporate and direct hobby groups and lay artistic circles in East Germany."[27] It is the aim of this study to show how the political conflicts

---

1943–1949 (Chicago: University of Chicago Press, 2005). Much of the (re)assessment of 1945 in the context of enduring continuities is owed to the research into the memory of everyday experiences (*Alltagsgeschichte*) spanning the National Socialist period and the postwar years, especially Lutz Niethammer, ed., *Lebensgeschichte und Sozialkultur im Ruhrgebiet 1930 bis 1960, Band 1: "Die Jahre weiß man nicht, wo man die heute hinsetzen soll." Faschismuserfahrungen im Ruhrgebiet* (Berlin: Verlag J. H. W. Dietz Nachf., 1983), *Band 2: "Hinterher merkt man, daß es richtig war, daß es schiefgegangen ist." Nachkriegs-Erfahrungen im Ruhrgebiet* (Berlin: Verlag J. H. W. Dietz Nachf., 1983), *Band 3: "Wir kriegen jetzt andere Zeiten." Auf der Suche nach der Erfahrung des Volkes in nachfaschistischen Ländern* (Berlin: Verlag J. H. W. Dietz Nachf., 1985). For the continuities and ruptures of twentieth-century German history, see also Paul Betts and Greg Eghigian, eds., *Pain and Prosperity: Reconsidering Twentieth-Century German History* (Stanford, CA: Stanford University Press, 2003); Konrad Jarausch and Michael Geyer, *Shattered Past: Reconstructing German Histories* (Princeton, NJ: Princeton University Press, 2003).

[24] For the Kampfbund für deutsche Kultur and Alfred Rosenberg's role, see Hermand, *Culture in Dark Times*, 35, 38, 55.

[25] Koepnick, "Culture in the Shadow of Trauma?" 711.

[26] For general surveys of postwar (especially West) German cultural history, see, e.g., Hermann Glaser, *The Rubble Years: The Cultural Roots of Postwar Germany, 1945–1948* (New York: Paragon, 1986). The German original was published in two volumes as *Kulturgeschichte der Bundesrepublik Deutschland. Band 1: Zwischen Kapitulation und Währungsreform, 1945–1948* (München: Hanser, 1985), *Band 2: Zwischen Grundgesetz und großer Reform, 1949–1967* (München: Hanser, 1986); Jost Hermand, *Kultur im Wiederaufbau: Die Bundesrepublik Deutschland, 1945–1965* (München: Nymphenburger, 1986); for an analysis of American and Soviet impacts on their respective client states, see Konrad Jarausch and Hannes Sigrist, eds., *Amerikanisierung und Sowjetisierung in Deutschland, 1945–1970* (Frankfurt: Campus, 1997); for discussions of "Americanization" and 1950s *Alltagskultur*, see Hanna Schissler, ed., *The Miracle Years: A Cultural History of West Germany, 1949–1968* (Princeton, NJ: Princeton University Press, 2001).

[27] Esther von Richthofen, *Bringing Culture to the Masses: Control, Compromise, and Participation in the GDR* (New York: Berghahn, 2009), 3. Cf. Jan Palmowski, *Inventing*

12   Introduction

between liberalism, fascism, and communism tied in with these larger historical shifts in the understandings of cultural practice.

The analysis of the complicated relationship between antifascism and postwar memory in the two German successor states to the Nazi empire builds on a vast literature on German attempts to cope with the National Socialist past (*Vergangenheitsbewältigung*).[28] Jeffrey Herf, for example, has called attention to the Mexican KPD colony's role in the formation of the memory culture of the later GDR.[29] For the West German case, Dirk A. Moses has sought to overcome the polarities of the German memory debates, which oscillate between the narrative of "linear progress or transformation in [West Germany's] collective memory," and the "moralistic tone in some of the secondary literature" that diagnoses the republic's failures – especially in its early decades – to adequately memorialize its past and acknowledge its responsibilities.[30] Focusing on the political language that participants in debates on national identity have employed, Moses defines post-1945 West German democracy as a "*discursive* achievement" – a "value consensus [that] emerges incrementally out of contested struggles over collective memory."[31] Like Moses's work, these pages pay close attention to political language, treating terms such as "cultural renewal," "antifascism," and "socialist humanism" as shifting discursive patterns, rather than fixed entities. In addition to a clearer understanding of the continuities of pre- and post-1945 Germany, a deeper analysis of the intellectual evolutions and political uses of these concepts revises what Clare Flanagan has called the "political myth" of

---

a Socialist Nation: Heimat and the Politics of Everyday Life in the GDR, 1945–1990 (Cambridge: Cambridge University Press, 2009).

[28] Seminal examples of the literature on Germany's "coming to terms with the past" are: Charles Maier, *The Unmasterable Past: History, Holocaust, and German National Identity* (Cambridge, MA: Harvard University Press, 1988); Mary Fulbrook, *German National Identity after the Holocaust* (Cambridge: Cambridge University Press, 1988); A. Dirk Moses, *German Intellectuals and the Nazi Past* (New York: Cambridge University Press, 2007); Peter Reichel, *Vergangenheitsbewältigung in Deutschland: Die Auseinandersetzung mit der NS-Diktatur in Politik und Justiz* (München: Beck, 2001).

[29] See Jeffrey Herf, *Divided Memory: The Nazi Past in the Two Germanys* (Cambridge, MA: Harvard University Press, 1997). Cf. Jürgen Danyel, ed., *Die geteilte Vergangenheit: Zum Umgang mit Nationalsozialismus und Widerstand in beiden deutschen Staaten* (Zeithistorische Studien, Vol. 4) (Berlin: Akademie Verlag, 1985).

[30] Moses, *German Intellectuals and the Nazi Past*, 5. See also Robert G. Moeller, "Germans as Victims?: Thoughts on a Post–Cold War History of World War II's Legacies," *History & Memory* 17, 1/2 (2005): 147–94; Bill Nivens, ed., *Germans as Victims: Remembering the Past in Contemporary Germany* (Houndmills: Palgrave, 2006); Robert G. Moeller, *War Stories: The Search for a Usable Past in the Federal Republic of Germany* (Berkeley: University of California Press, 2001). For an overview of more contributions to the "memory debate" of the early 2000s, see Alon Confino, "Telling about Germany: Narratives of Memory and Culture," *Journal of Modern History* 76 (June 2004): 389–416.

[31] Ibid., 14.

"German silence," an alleged "failure of Germans to respond to their situation."[32]

The discussions of the Kulturbund board, the debates in its publications, and the unresolved disputes between exiles and "inner émigrés" fit into what Andrew I. Port has identified as the early postwar decades' pattern of "forgetting *and* coming to terms with the past," and they confirm that "no subsequent period witnessed as much *Vergangenheitsbewältigung* as the early years of the two new German states – depending, of course, on how one defines that term."[33] As this work illustrates, the experiences of Nazi dictatorship and German collective responsibility were not suppressed but at the foreground of postwar intellectuals' concerns. At the same time, explicit allusions to the Holocaust were rare (though not completely absent), a fact that doesn't seem to do justice to the monstrosity of this event – and to the problems it would pose for postwar German identity for decades to come.[34] Still, the Kulturbund's vision of cultural renewal was neither a purely political exploitation of the "antifascist myth" – even though this was undoubtedly part of it – nor was it simply a reductionist and morally questionable emphasis on German victimhood. Rather, the antifascist voices portrayed in these pages combine an emphasis on German suffering and national martyrdom *and* expressions of atonement for an – often vaguely defined – collective national responsibility over the sins of Nazism and war.

This book is also part of a more recent trend to take a closer look at the debates among intellectuals and the processes of cultural and democratic renewal in early postwar Germany. Sean A. Forner, for example, has traced the concepts of democratic politics among intellectuals in all four occupation zones that envisioned alternatives to both the parliamentary models of the Western Allies and the party-state of the Soviet model.[35] This

---

[32] Clare Flanagan, "Political Myth and Germany 1945–1949," *German Life and Letters* 57, 1 (January 2004): 124. See also Frank Biess, *Homecoming: Returning POWs and the Legacies of Defeat in Postwar Germany* (Princeton, NJ: Princeton University Press, 2009), 6–7.

[33] Andrew I. Port, "Democracy and Dictatorship in the Cold War: The Two Germanies, 1949–1961," in Smith, ed., *The Oxford Handbook of Modern German History*, 615.

[34] See Moses, *German Intellectuals and the Nazi Past* for West Germany. For the centrality of the Holocaust in the "post-Sonderweg" historical imagination, see Walser Smith, "When the Sonderweg Debate Left Us." For Germany's post-unification identity, see also Jan-Werner Müller, *Another Country: German Intellectuals, Unification and National Identity* (New Haven, CT: Yale University Press, 2000).

[35] See Sean A. Forner, *German Intellectuals and the Challenge of Democratic Renewal: Culture and Politics after 1945* (Cambridge: Cambridge University Press, 2014). For the postwar concepts of the more prominent German intellectuals Thomas Mann, Bertolt Brecht, Karl Jaspers, and Friedrich Meinecke, see Mark W. Clark, *Beyond Catastrophe: German Intellectuals and Cultural Renewal after World War II, 1945–1955* (Lanham, MD: Lexington Books, 2006).

investigation highlights the often overlooked continuation of religious and nationalist concepts and tropes in the speeches and writings of intellectuals whose professed aim it was to correct and resurrect German national traditions. The rhetorical and interpretative framework for this understanding of the nation's post-Nazi "resurrection" was provided by the Protestant Reformation. Speeches at events such as the Kulturbund inauguration and the First German Writers' Congress were strikingly rich in religious language and Protestant tropes, thereby mixing Marxist and socialist tenets with one of the key ingredients of traditional German nationalism. In a wider sense, therefore, this study tries to untangle the complex strands that clashed and combined in the first postwar years under the circumstances of Allied occupation, and which included twentieth-century ideology, Protestant rhetoric, cultural nationalism, and concepts of mass mobilization. In a fractured way, they accompanied Germany's stormy transition from the first half of the twentieth century into its divided later decades.

Of course one of the major developments that complemented this transition was the "Stalinization" of the countries behind the Iron Curtain, which by 1947 included the Soviet Occupation Zone (SBZ) of Germany. In contrast to the hagiographic official historiography of the GDR, Western historical scholarship has traditionally embedded the early years of the Kulturbund in the narrative of the Stalinist takeover.[36] Undoubtedly, the gradual demise of the Kulturbund's pluralist, nonpartisan antifascism and its only thinly disguised manipulation by first KPD and then SED were part of a transnational development that cemented the rule of Soviet-controlled Communist parties in the countries occupied by the Red Army.[37] Yet, as Norman Naimark points out, "Stalinism was

---

[36] For the official GDR version of the early Kulturbund's history see Karl-Heinz Schulmeister, *Auf dem Wege zu einer neuen Kultur: Der Kulturbund in den Jahren 1945–1949* (Berlin [East]: Dietz Verlag, 1977); Gerhard Schmidt, *Der Kulturbund zu Frieden und Demokratie in den Jahren 1948/49: Ein Beitrag zur Vorgeschichte der Gründung der Deutschen Demokratischen Republik. Teil 1 and Teil 2* (Berlin [East]: Kulturbund der DDR, 1984). For Western accounts, see Wolfgang Schivelbusch, *In a Cold Crater: Cultural and Intellectual Life in Berlin, 1945–1948*, trans. Kelly Berry (Berkeley: University of California Press, 1998); Norman M. Naimark, *The Russians in Germany: A History of the Soviet Zone of Occupation, 1945–1949* (Cambridge, MA: The Belknap Press of Harvard University Press, 1995), 400–8; David Pike, *The Politics of Culture in Soviet-Occupied Germany, 1945–1949* (Stanford, CA: Stanford University Press, 1992). German-language accounts are in Gerd Dietrich, *Politik und Kultur in der Sowjetischen Besatzungszone Deutschlands (SBZ), 1945–1949. Mit einem Dokumentenanhang* (Bern, Switzerland: Peter Lang, 1993); Magdalena Heider, *Politik – Kultur – Kulturbund. Zur Gründungs- und Frühgeschichte des Kulturbundes zur demokratischen Erneuerung Deutschlands 1945–1954 in der SBZ/DDR* (Cologne: Verlag Wissenschaft und Politik, 1993).

[37] A recent attempt at comparing this process in Poland, East Germany, and Hungary is Anne Applebaum, *Iron Curtain: The Crushing of Eastern Europe, 1944–1956* (New York: Doubleday, 2012).

too complex a phenomenon to be reduced to a matter of politics and the mailed fist alone."[38] Even though the Kulturbund shared the fate of many organizations and institutions in what would become the European Eastern Bloc, this book reminds us that postwar "Stalinization," often portrayed as a rather monolithic and generic blueprint, had distinct local and national roots and manifestations.[39] It is one of the assertions of this work that the Cold War and the process that led to the German division in the years from 1947 to 1949 did not emerge in a vacuum, but were fed by a diverse range of historical threads and traditions. Visions of cultural renewal, projects of national atonement and resurrection, and beliefs in mass mobilization and collective reeducation shaped and influenced the cultural-political dynamics in the SBZ and the early GDR in often unpredictable and contradictory ways. By tracing the postwar Kulturbund back to early twentieth-century cultural reform projects and organizations of exile intellectuals, this book establishes a distinct German strand of antifascist humanism and German cultural nationalism that interjects the traditional Cold War narrative of the clash of liberal and totalitarian systems.

Last, with its timeframe spanning the years from 1945 to 1948 in the Soviet Occupation Zone, this book opens up a new perspective on the "prehistory" of the GDR. Although the focus in recent scholarship seems to have shifted from the GDR's early years to its later decades of relative "normalization" and the various aspects of East German *Alltagsgeschichte* (everyday culture), for most historians, the evaluation of the GDR is still closely tied to the history of its foundation.[40] As a result, this work is located at the periphery of a number of lively debates on the character and legacy of the "workers' and peasants' state."[41] Does the GDR have

---

[38] Naimark, *The Russians in Germany*, 6.
[39] For the classical model of "Sovietization," see Hugh Seton-Watson, *The East European Revolution*, third ed. (New York: Frederick A. Praeger, 1956); cf. Introduction to *Stalinism Revisited: The Establishment of Communist Regimes in East-Central Europe*, ed. Vladimir Tismaneanu (Budapest: Central European University Press, 2009); see also John Connelly, *Captive University: The Sovietization of East German, Czech, and Polish Higher Education, 1945–1956* (Chapel Hill: University of North Carolina Press, 2000).
[40] For an emphasis on the interpretation of the subjective experiences of the GDR, see Mary Fulbrook, *The People's State: East German Society from Hitler to Honecker* (New Haven, CT: Yale University Press, 2005). Cf. Konrad H. Jarausch, ed., *Dictatorship as Experience: Towards a Socio-Cultural History of the GDR* (New York: Berghahn, 1999). For recent approaches to physical and psychological aspects of GDR history, see Fulbrook and Port, eds., *Becoming East German*.
[41] For useful summaries and evaluations of the debates surrounding GDR research, see Ross, *The East German Dictatorship*; Jürgen Kocka, ed., *Historische DDR-Forschung: Aufsätze und Studien* (Berlin: Akademie Verlag, 1993); Konrad H. Jarausch, "Beyond Uniformity: The Challenge of Historicizing the GDR," in *Dictatorship as Experience*, 3–16; Fulbrook, *The People's State*, 1–20; Peter Grieder, *The German Democratic Republic* (Basingstoke: Palgrave Macmillan, 2012); Andrew I. Port, "The

to be described as a "totalitarian" regime in Stalin's likeness, or was it from the beginning a "participatory dictatorship," in the words of Mary Fulbrook, which enjoyed considerable popular support in combination with harsh techniques of repression?[42] As many scholars have argued, the GDR's claim to represent the antifascist "other Germany" remained one of the SED regime's longest-lasting sources of allegiance not only among the general population, but especially among intellectuals, many of whom struggled until 1989 to reconcile their oppositional stance with their belief in the legitimacy of the state's attempt to write a new chapter in German history.[43] This book means to unearth the long and knotted roots of these claims and conflicts, roots that, as I argue, reached back well before 1933.

Famously dismissed by Hans-Ulrich Wehler as a "Russian satrapy," the GDR was conceived in the image of its Soviet patrons, yet it needs to be interpreted within the larger contours of German history.[44] The traditional leftist and communist historiography usually provides these contours in the form of the larger development of the German workers' movement and the German left.[45] Alternatively, many historians, notably the proponents of the special path theory, stress an alleged continuity of antiliberalism and authoritarianism in German history, which links the SED dictatorship to its Nazi predecessor in a seemingly straight line. By synthesizing the diverse strands of arguments outlined earlier, this book offers a new perspective on the larger influences that shaped Germany's conflicted twentieth century, with its authoritarian and repressive as well as its emancipatory and democratic elements. The antifascist humanism that tried to represent an "other Germany" constituted a distinct tradition of cultural nationalism that took up early twentieth-century arguments as well as wartime exile agendas. It aimed to "renew" German culture

Banalities of East German Historiography," in Fulbrook and Port, eds., *Becoming East German*, 1–30.

[42] For a defense of totalitarianism theory in the context of the GDR, see Grieder, *The German Democratic Republic*; for a critique of this approach, see Port, "The Banalities of East German Historiography."

[43] For the lasting appeal of antifascism in the East German populace, see Ross, *The East German Dictatorship*, 177–82; see also John C. Torpey, *Intellectuals, Socialism, and Dissent: The East German Opposition and Its Legacy* (Minneapolis: University of Minnesota Press, 1995). Cf. Andrew I. Port, *Conflict and Stability in the German Democratic Republic* (Cambridge: Cambridge University Press, 2007); Palmowski, *Inventing a Socialist Nation*.

[44] Quoted in Ross, *The East German Dictatorship*, 156. Cf. Wilfried Loth, *Stalin's Unwanted Child: The Soviet Union, the German Question and the Founding of the GDR* trans. Robert F. Hagg (New York: St. Martin's Press, 1998).

[45] For a general history of the left in Europe and its contribution to democracy, see Geoff Eley, *Forging Democracy: A History of the Left in Europe, 1850–2000* (New York: Oxford University Press, 2002).

Introduction 17

with a vaguely defined blend of bourgeois high culture and concepts of mass mobilization. Under the circumstances of the Cold War and occupation it ultimately failed to overcome its own contradictions and unresolved conflicts, thus the other, humanist Germany became a propaganda tool in the German division rather than a political reality that would make for an alternative to the new Germanies in East and West.

Sources and Organization

The concept of antifascist humanism that is the subject of these pages was never more than vaguely delineated. Rather, it constitutes a tradition that was *claimed* more than it was intellectually defined. Accordingly, this study focuses less on philosophical and theoretical writings on humanist doctrines and more on the political debates that took place in published writings as well as in internal conversations and discussions among intellectuals. By combining the analysis of printed sources with archival material, especially the minutes of the internal meetings of the Kulturbund from 1945 to 1947, this investigation reconstructs the winding path of a concept whose very openness made it possible for a wide variety of historical actors to claim it. Therefore, this book also resorts to the methods of *Alltagsgeschichte* ("history from below") in an endeavor to show that some of the tropes of antifascist humanism extended to short-lived grass-roots antifascist committees (antifas) that sprang up during the last months of the war. With this range of sources, I attempt to underline the complexity of antifascist thought and activism in Germany in the decades between 1930 and 1950 in both its political and cultural aspects. It is one of this book's underlying assumptions that the study of twentieth-century Germany needs to pay closer attention to the nexus between politics and culture in order to shed light on the apparent discrepancies and contradictory interpretations that often result from an exclusive emphasis on either political or cultural and intellectual histories. This work straddles the borders between political and intellectual history, aiming to expand the scope of both. Such an approach, which combines empirical, archival research with the hermeneutical interpretation of intellectuals' and artists' writings, could be seen as an example for a new intellectual history, which, in the words of Alexander Gallus, integrates "hard" political history with "soft" cultural and intellectual historical scholarship.[46]

---

[46] See Alexander Gallus, "'Intellectual History' mit Intellektuellen und ohne sie: Facetten neuerer geistesgeschichtlicher Forschung," *Historische Zeitschrift* 288, 1 (2009): 139–50. Cf. Daniel Wickberg, "Intellectual History vs. the Social History of Intellectuals," *Rethinking History* 5, 3 (2001): 383–95.

Antifascism in Germany began as a political mass movement and became a project of cultural renewal. The first chapter traces this development back to 1935, the year of the unsuccessful Popular Front referendum campaign against the Saar's annexation to Nazi-ruled Germany. After this defeat, the antifascist battleground shifted from an attempt to influence voters to struggle for the representation of German culture. The chapter shows how exiled and resistance intellectuals, basing themselves on the concept of a nonpartisan Popular Front of working-class and bourgeois intellectuals, revived conservative early twentieth-century reform ideas and claimed a "humanist" German tradition to counter the National Socialist construction of a German culture cleansed along racial and ideological lines. As Chapter 2 shows, with the military demise of the National Socialist regime, and the increasing public exposure to its unprecedented crimes, the antifascist construction of the "other Germany" also served exiles as a defense against sweeping Allied condemnations of German national character ("Vansittartism"). The chapter focuses particular attention on the Communist and non-Communist exile community in Mexico City during the war, and the role and ideas of Alexander Abusch, the editor of the exile publication *Freies Deutschland/Alemania Libre*. Abusch would later become a key figure in the Kulturbund, as well as in the cultural-political establishment of the GDR. The chapter thus establishes the continuity between debates among antifascist intellectuals before 1945 and in the postwar SBZ. Chapter 3 concludes the first part of this book by looking at the unsuccessful attempt at reviving antifascist mass politics in the form of the antifascist committees, which emerged in the last days of the war in Germany. The chapter shows that this popular antifascism employed many of the tropes of the exile intellectual discussion circles, including the ideas of a better Germany that needs to be distinguished from the Nazi version of national identity. Allied and Soviet prohibitions of the antifas ended this strand of antifascism that unsuccessfully tried to combine paramilitary mass politics and cultural renewal "from below."

In the second part of this book, the focus turns to the Kulturbund as one of the key cultural institutions in early postwar Germany. Chapter 4 reconstructs the foundation of the Kulturbund in Berlin in June 1945, but unlike earlier accounts of this event, links it closer to the ideas and intellectual activities of some of its key founders before 1933. The Kulturbund in this analysis emerges as an organization that takes up multiple strands of reform ideas, cultural movements, political attitudes from communism to nationalism, and a heavy dose of Protestant reformatory rhetoric. The poet Johannes R. Becher, the group's influential first president, combines almost all of these strands in his own biography. Thus, the chapter argues, the Kulturbund, often described as little more than a Stalinist front organization, embodies a movement of restoration – of pre-1933 German cultural ideals – as much as a movement for renewal. This is reflected as well in the organization's attitude toward representatives of the "inner emigration," a specific German condition that further complicates the idea of the "other Germany."

The fifth chapter describes the gradual decline of the pluralist nonpartisanship of the Kulturbund. While this is a story that has been told before, the chapter focuses on the dynamics between the KPD/SED representatives Becher and Abusch and the Christian Democrat Ferdinand Friedensburg, a key liberal member of the early Kulturbund. By analyzing debates within the Kulturbund's board as well as in its journal, *Aufbau*, the chapter illustrates how communists as well as liberals such as Friedensburg shared a vision of centrally led cultural renewal and popular mobilization; at the onset of the Cold War, these demands could only play into the hands of the KPD, who placed Abusch as "ideological coordinator" on the Kulturbund board. The contradictions and political-moral conflicts inherent in a project that called for a massive reeducation attempt made the concept of cultural renewal in post-Nazi Germany both a necessary step toward confronting the past and a pretext for an authoritarian future.

In the sixth chapter, this book analyzes how the political context of the Cold War figured in intellectuals' attempts to simultaneously realize the ideals of the "other Germany" and to prevent the (renewed) cultural division of Germany in the wake of its political rift. At the center of this chapter are the debates and conflicts during the First German Writers' Congress in 1947, an event that tragically failed in its attempt at bringing intellectuals in East and West together to overcome the impeding division. However, as the chapter shows, the congress not only underscored the East–West divisions, but also highlighted other unresolved issues such as the moral status of the inner émigrés and the attempt to describe German Nazism as part of a larger, Europe-wide crisis of modernity. Specific German discussions among the congress's participants did not cause the Cold War, but they fed into it and shaped some of its dynamics.

By 1947 and 1948, the discussions surrounding the "other Germany" and the legacy of the recent Nazi past were not only affected by the impeding German division, but also by the new cultural directives emanating from the Soviet Union in the context of the "anti-cosmopolitan" and "anti-formalist" campaigns. Chapter 7 delineates some of these new conflicts and the way they affected representatives of the "other Germany," such as writers Alfred Kantorowicz and Günther Weisenborn.

Born around 1900, these intellectuals made up a "generation unit" who experienced its intellectually and politically formative years before the Second World War.[47] In other words, more than just a political ideology or a tactical ploy, despite its contradictions by the late 1940s, antifascism and German cultural unity were hard to let go because they gave meaning and identity to a generation who failed in its attempt to overcome either the old or the new divisions among German intellectuals.[48] In the end, the chapter argues, the way had been paved for an instrumentalization of the "other Germany" in the terms of the two German states' claims to political and moral superiority. At the same time, the antifascist cultural renewal that the early Kulturbund had envisioned ended up a largely depoliticized organization managing petty bourgeois cultural activities under close control of the SED and divorced from the political and social concerns of the East German working class that erupted in 1953.

A conclusion sums up the findings and places this book's themes into a larger context. All in all, the intellectuals in these pages were not only interested in "another Germany." Their concepts of "cultural renewal" and "socialist humanism" also denoted the belief in a different modernity, one that led straight from Goethe and Lessing to the late twentieth century, without the disastrous "detour" of nationalist mass politics and technological mass murder that characterized European and especially German history in the first half of the twentieth century. In their particular historical moment, the protagonists of these chapters thus offer differing answers to the wider question of the relationship between modernity, culture, totalitarianism, and the role of intellectuals.[49] This book is the story of their vision's potential as much as of its failure to overcome the politics of the twentieth century with the culture of the eighteenth and nineteenth centuries.

---

[47] Karl Mannheim's classical sociological definition of "generation units" includes "vehicles of formative tendencies and fundamental integrative attitudes" that enabled individuals to identify themselves "with a set of collective strivings." Karl Mannheim, "The Problem of Generations," in Kurt H. Wolff, ed., *From Karl Mannheim*. Second expanded edition (New Brunswick, NJ: Transaction Publishers, 1993), 380.

[48] For the generation of men born around 1900 as a "superfluous" generation, see Detlev J. K. Peukert, *Die Weimarer Republik: Krisenjahre der klassischen Moderne* (Frankfurt a. M.: Suhrkamp, 1987), 30.

[49] For an overview of German thought on modernity, see John P. McCormick, ed., *Confronting Mass Democracy and Industrial Technology: Political and Social Theory from Nietzsche to Habermas* (Durham, NC: Duke University Press, 2002).

Part I

Defending the "Other Germany"

1 The "Humanist Front": Antifascism and Culture Wars, 1934–1939

In May 1933, three months after the National Socialist (NS) seizure of power, the already retired philosopher Edmund Husserl was forced to sever his ties to Freiburg University – now administered by his former student and new rector Martin Heidegger, who infamously saw an "inward truth and greatness" in Nazism.[1] As a man with deep nationalistic ties to Germany, Husserl wrote: "The future alone will judge which was the true Germany in 1933 and who were the true Germans – those who subscribe to the more or less materialistic-mythical racial prejudices of the day, or those Germans pure in heart and mind, heirs to the great Germans of the past whose traditions they revere and perpetuate.... For the moment I am, so to speak, a refugee from Germany."[2] It was the Nazis' racial ideology and Husserl's Jewish background rather than his philosophical ideas that were the grounds of his dismissal – after all, Heidegger himself acknowledged that his own phenomenological thought was deeply influenced by Husserl.[3] But Husserl's statement was surely correct in placing his fate in the context of a conflict between two diverging visions of German culture.

Although the cultural "coordination" and the racial and political purges in 1933 constituted an early climax in this conflict, its roots went farther back. One of the demands of a National Socialist German Workers' Party (NSDAP) program in 1920 called for "the legal prosecution of all tendencies in art and literature of a kind likely to disintegrate our life as a nation."[4] What the Nazi program, with characteristic hyperbole, attacked were the modernist, expressionist, Dadaist, pacifist, and leftist tendencies in the literature and the arts of the Weimar period, but arguably

---

[1] Hugo Ott, *Martin Heidegger: A Political Life*, trans. Allan Blunden (New York: Basic Books, 1993), 135.
[2] Ibid., 185.
[3] Ibid., 181. For the relationship of some aspects of Heidegger's philosophy and National Socialism, see Emmanuel Faye, *Heidegger: The Introduction of Nazism into Philosophy in Light of the Unpublished Seminars of 1933–1935*, trans. Michael B. Smith (New Haven, CT: Yale University Press, 2009).
[4] Quoted in Richard J. Evans, *The Coming of the Third Reich* (London: Penguin, 2003), 413.

the Nazi project – much like its fascist counterparts in Italy – aimed at a much wider goal of cultural renewal. Nazi ideologues such as Alfred Rosenberg envisioned an ideological and racially purified communal culture based on class-transcending *völkische* principles, which would not only purge German culture from its undesirable leftist and Jewish elements, but also would be a culture "in which a split into high and low was no longer possible and where all of the volk comrades would be moved by the same volkish exhilaration in the realm of culture."[5] The name of the organization that Rosenberg founded in 1928, the Kampfbund für deutsche Kultur (Militant League for German Culture), left no room for doubt that for Nazi theorists, as well as their opponents, the representation of German culture was a struggle that had to be fought with the same militant rhetoric and organizational means as the political fights on the streets and in the beerhalls of the Weimar Republic.

Ultimately, it would be not Rosenberg, but Joseph Goebbels who would shape the Nazi approach to culture after the movement came to power in 1933. Under the more pragmatic Goebbels, the Nazis crafted and sponsored a highly effective mass entertainment industry while "at the same time they laid claim as 'ancestors' of their movement and values to such figures as Luther and Nietzsche, Goethe, Schiller and Hölderlin"[6] – or in Husserl's words, the same "great Germans of the past" who "had been the domain of Germans pure in heart and mind." This made the resistance and struggle against the new fascist order in Germany also a war for the representation of German cultural heritage. Driven into exile, by the mid-1930s, the use of the term "humanism" became common among Nazi opponents to emphasize that "the classical German heritage was indissociable from those values now trampled on by the Nazis: a certain belief in freedom, justice and democracy."[7] In 1928, the liberal writer Thomas Mann had voiced a demand for "an alliance and pact between the idea of a conservative culture and the idea of a revolutionary society.... Germany would find its true self, the day that Karl Marx reads Friedrich Hölderlin."[8] By the mid-1930s, under the influence of the *Volksfront* cooperation of Nazi opponents, communist intellectuals, such as Johannes R. Becher and Georg Lukács, who had formerly criticized "bourgeois" culture, began to praise "Hegel, Schiller,

---

[5] Jost Hermand, *Culture in Dark Times: Nazi Fascism, Inner Emigration, and Exile* (New York: Berghahn, 2013), 39; see also 35/36.
[6] Jean-Michel Palmier, *Weimar in Exile: The Antifascist Emigration in Europe and America*, trans. David Fernbach (London: Verso, 2006), 290–1. See also Hermand, *Culture in Dark Times*, 122–40.
[7] Palmier, *Weimar in Exile*, 290.
[8] Quoted in ibid., 290.

and Hölderlin." In 1935, during a conference of antifascist intellectuals in exile in Paris, Thomas Mann's son Klaus coined the term "socialist humanism" for this synthesis of bourgeois high culture and socialist politics that would enable the cooperation of communist and liberal antifascists.⁹

This chapter explores the question of how pre–World War II ideas of humanism, originally a bourgeois pedagogical concept that dealt with classical learning rather than with contemporary politics and that aimed at the education of man to become human ("*die Bildung des Menschen zum Menschen*") became a militant doctrine of antifascist resistance and the rhetorical centerpiece in the construction of an "other Germany." This chapter will show that the failure of antifascist mass politics intensified cultural debates and shifted the battleground from politics to the representation of German culture. In the longer term, the redefinition of humanism created the notion of an "other Germany" as well as the institutional and rhetorical foundations for debates on cultural-political renewal after 1945.

The Saar Struggle and the Failure of Mass Politics

The first instance of a German antifascist coalition occurred from 1934 to 1935 in the Saar region. The Saar plebiscite in January 1935 was a product of the Versailles Treaty from 1920, according to which the industrialized southwestern German region was to be administered by the League of Nations for fifteen years to compensate for French World War I damages. Thereafter, a popular referendum would give the population the choice to be returned to Germany, to be incorporated into France, or to maintain the status quo, an administration by the League of Nations. Throughout the 1920s and early 1930s, communists as well as Social Democrats, along with all other major German parties demanded the return of the Saar to Germany. However, the assumption of Hitler to power in January 1933 boosted the NSDAP influence in the Saar. While the Nazi regime consolidated its power in the rest of Germany, the Saar underwent a process of "(self)-coordination" [*(Selbst)-Gleichschaltung*] On July 14 – the date was a deliberated provocation to the French – most of the Saar's conservative, Catholic, and nationalist parties and organizations joined the NSDAP in a "German Front" coalition for the union of the Saar with Nazi-Germany.¹⁰

---

⁹ See James D. Wilkinson, *The Intellectual Resistance in Europe* (Cambridge, MA: Harvard University Press, 1981), 21.
¹⁰ See Andreas Merl, "'... sich selbst auf dem Altare des Vaterlandes zu opfern' – Zum vorauseilenden Gehorsam der Saarländer 1933 bis 1935," in Hans-Christian Herrmann

The formation of the German Front, as well as the sobering realization that Hitler's regime did not collapse after a few weeks, triggered a change in politics on the working class left. In August 1933, the Saar Social Democratic chairman Max Braun endorsed the "status-quo" option in the upcoming referendum rather than seeing the Saar join Nazi-ruled Germany. It took a few months longer for the Communist Party of Germany (KPD) to adopt the same position. The other important change was the first antifascist coalition of the former bitter enemies. Against the wishes of the Social Democratic Party in Exile (SoPaDe) leadership in Prague, and almost a year before the Communist International's (Comintern's) official adoption of 'popular front' politics, communists and Social Democrats in the Saar entered a Unity Front (*Einheitsfront*) against the advance of fascism.[11]

The antifascist Unity Front, however, was unable to stem the tide of German nationalism that swept the Saar. When the results of the referendum were announced on January 15, 1935, more than 90 percent of the voters had voted for the return to Germany, while the Unity's Front's campaign for the status quo had swayed only 8.8 percent, or fewer than 47,000 voters. The Unity Front and neutral observers had expected a result of around 40 percent of votes for the status quo. This assumption might have been based on the impression of antifascist mass rallies, especially at Sulzbach in August 1935.[12] Another mass rally by the Unity Front at the last weekend before the vote gathered 150,00 participants. More than twice as many people, however, spent the same weekend attending the Nazi directed Unity Front rally, for which 350,000 Saar citizens took to the streets.[13]

Mary Nolan has argued that the antifascist movement "saw Nazism in terms of production, class relations, and exploitation, not in terms of consumption, social rationalization, and new forms of mass culture."[14] Antifascists' disappointment in mass politics is evident in the sober reactions to the left's defeat in the Saar plebiscite. A disillusioned Norbert

---

and Ruth Bauer, eds., *Widerstand, Repression und Verfolgung. Beiträge zur Geschichte des Nationalsozialismus an der Saar* (St. Ingbert: Röhrig Universitätsverlag, 2014), 128.

[11] See Joachim Heinz, "Sozialdemokratie und Kommunisten 1933 bis 1945 im Saarland. Ein Überblick," in Hermann und Bauer, eds, *Widerstand, Repression und Verfolgung*, 190-194; Ralph Schock, ed., *Haltet die Saar, Genossen! Antifaschistische Schriftsteller im Abstimmungskampf 1935* (Berlin: J.H.W. Dietz Nachf, 1984), 9–12. Influential German postwar politicians for whom the Saar struggle was a formative experience include the West German SPD politician Herbert Wehner and the last general secretary of East Germany's Socialist Unity Party (SED), Erich Honecker.

[12] See Heinz, "Sozialdemokratie und Kommunisten," 194.

[13] Merl, "Zum vorauseilenden Gehorsam der Saarländer 1933 bis 1935," 147

[14] Antifascism under Fascism: German Vision and Voices," in "Legacies of Antifascism," *New German Critique* 67 (Winter 1996): 55, 51.

Mühlen, for example, wrote: "We know today that a new, triumphant ideology will not emerge out of the movement, out of the struggle of the masses. In the age of fascism, the masses are not the bearers of ideas [*keine Ideenträger*]."[15] Equally pessimistic was the analysis of Willi Schlamm, the editor of the *Europäische Hefte*:

> An era has ended in which it seemed that the reason and the insight into their own life situation could steer the social masses to rise by themselves. In reality, the function of the masses as builders of society has vanished. The masses have shown themselves to be completely malleable, without consciousness, and able to adjust to any power and any misdeed. They have no historical mission. In the twentieth century, in the century of tanks and radio ... the masses have been eliminated from the process of social formation.[16]

While the lack of antifascist mass appeal was discouraging, many intellectuals were convinced of the potential for a broad-based cultural-intellectual resistance to Hitler. The Saar plebiscite had been preceded by a pitched propaganda battle between Goebbels and a large number of German and European intellectuals and writers who tried to use their influence and literary voices to bring about a vote for the status quo. These efforts culminated in a joint appeal (*Aufruf*) to the Saar Germans against Nazi Germany. The "Aufruf," published on September 21, 1934, in the Social Democratic organ *Volksstimme*, was signed by twenty-eight renowned members of the antifascist cultural scene, including writers Heinrich and Klaus Mann, Lion Feuchtwanger, Ernst Toller, Johannes R. Becher, and Anna Seghers; the general secretary of the communist-influenced exile Association for the Protection of German Writers (Schutzverband deutscher Schriftsteller ([SDS)]), Alfred Kantorowicz; as well as theater director Erwin Piscator and theater critic Alfred Kerr. But the signatories also included non-leftists, such as painter and journalist Prinz Max Karl zu Hohenlohe and the then-editor of the Catholic nationalist paper *Das Reich*, Hubertus Prinz zu Löwenstein (in his later years in U.S. exile known as the "red prince").[17] Though ultimately politically unsuccessful, the *SaarAufruf* provoked a "fierce counter-reaction" in the form of a propaganda campaign in the Nazi paper *Völkischer Beobachter* and the *Angriff*, the organ of Goebbels's ministry. In November 1934, the twenty-eight signatories of the *Aufruf* had their German citizenship revoked by the NS government.[18] Antifascist intellectuals were now officially no longer representing a German state – making the question of

---

[15] Schock, ed., *Haltet die Saar, Genossen*, 237.
[16] Ibid., 242.
[17] Ibid., 123, 350.
[18] Ibid., 37–41.

who would represent German culture all the more pressing and politically relevant.

The Saar had also been a battleground in the war of publishing policies waged between Goebbels and the later Comintern activist Willi Münzenberg, whose "Editions de Carrefour" series of exile publications in Paris were a main conduit for antifascist literature.[19] Münzenberg published the anti-Nazi journal *Gegenangriff* (*Counterattack*), a response to Goebbels's *Angriff*. The ministry of propaganda responded by applying not only the intellectual, but the economic resources of the Third Reich. The Journalist and author Norbert Mühlen vividly described Goebbels's strategy of silencing one of the most fervent anti-Nazi papers, *Westland*, by buying the paper as a secret bidder.[20] According to Mühlen, one of *Westland*'s editors, the action led to an expensive defeat for Goebbels as the editorial staff of the paper left and founded a new publication under the name *Grenzland*. This episode would become representative of the cultural battles between the ministry of propaganda and exile and antifascist publications, especially after 1939, when Goebbels amplified his efforts to quell the exile press and its negative effect on international opinion of the Nazi regime.[21]

The Birth of the "Other Germany"

The antifascist Unity Front did not prevail in the Saar, but it did play a role in Stalin's "sensational reorientation," which, according to German communist Babette L. Gross, "did not come in response to a belated recognition of political realities but as a result of the altered requirements of Soviet foreign policy."[22] After years of denouncing socialist and Social Democratic movements as "social fascism" or "fascism's twin brother," the success of fascism in Italy and Germany as well as its increasing political appeal in France and Spain led Stalin to lift his ban on the cooperation between Moscow-controlled organizations and other socialists, and even liberals and Catholics.[23] The result was the decision at the VII. Comintern Congress in Moscow in July and August 1935 for the

---

[19] See Gerd R. Ueberschär, *Für ein anderes Deutschland: Der deutsche Widerstand gegen den NS-Staat 1933–1945* (Frankfurt/Main: Fischer, 2006), 79.
[20] Schock, ed., *Haltet die Saar, Genossen*, 117–18.
[21] See Hermann Haarmann, ed., *Heimat, liebe Heimat. Exil und innere Emigration (1933–1945)* (Berlin: Bostelmann und Siebenhaar, 2004), 44ff, 70.
[22] Milorad M. Drachkovitch and Branko Lazitch, eds., *The CominternHistorical Highlights: Essays, Recollections, Documents* (New York: Frederick A. Praeger, 1966), 121.
[23] See Kevin McDermott and Jeremy Agnew, *The Comintern: A History of International Communism from Lenin to Stalin* (Houndmills: Macmillan, 1996), 125. The classical account of the Comintern and the Popular Front is E. H. Carr, *Twilight of the Comintern, 1930–1935* (New York: Pantheon, 1982). See also Paolo Spriano, *Stalin and the European Communists*, trans. Jon Rothschild (London: Verso, 1985); Gerd-Rainer

"the creation of a 'broad antifascist front.'"[24] Under the coordination of the Bulgarian Comintern general secretary Georgi Dimitrov, so-called Popular Front coalitions were formed between 1935 and 1939 to counter fascist parties in elections from France to Spain to Chile. However, ideological and tactical differences between communists and socialists flared up again with the Hitler–Stalin Pact of 1939, which meant that the Popular Front movement ultimately remained a short-lived ideal.[25]

Attempts at creating a German popular front centered initially on reviving the Saar's Unity Front of KPD and SPD. Negotiations between representatives of the two working-class exile organizations in Prague in November 1935 failed, however.[26] The SoPaDe leadership in Prague had not forgotten the communists' vicious attacks before 1934, and the KPD was unwilling to give up its claim for the leadership of the working class.[27] But the Saar defeat also led to an exodus of Nazi opponents and therefore contributed to the number of exiled Germans in Europe. In Paris, the communist efforts at creating a popular front were more successful than in Prague – they did not lead to an antifascist mass movement that challenged Nazi power, though, but to the efforts of writers and intellectuals to counter the Nazis' representation of German culture.

In addition to the SDS in Paris, Münzenberg's "Committee for the Creation of a German Popular Front," established in February 1936, won the support of the numerous exiled German writers and intellectuals in the French capital, among them Heinrich and Klaus Mann, Lion Feuchtwanger, and Ernst Toller, all of whom had been active in the Saar propaganda struggle. The novelist Heinrich Mann played "an active part" in formulating the "Manifesto of the 118," the Committee's assertion of liberal freedoms of speech, belief, and worship, and its demand for "a Germany characterized by peace and freedom, morality, integrity, and lawfulness, blessed with a strong, self-assured, and energetic democracy." The manifesto's very first sentence emphasized that the resolution had "been adopted by more than a hundred representatives of the liberal German bourgeoisie and the German working class of all political tendencies."[28] The Popular Front Committee joined a multitude of German exile organizations and publications that transcended the party boundaries of the Weimar political landscape to form what former Hamburg

---

Horn, *European Socialists Respond to Fascism: Ideology, Activism, and Contingency in the 1930s* (New York: Oxford University Press, 1996).
[24] See Palmier, *Weimar in Exile*, 344.
[25] Ibid.
[26] Drachkovitch and Lazitch, eds., *The Comintern*, 124.
[27] McDermott and Agnew, *The Comintern*, 121.
[28] Drachkovitch and Lazitch, eds., *The Comintern* 125–6.

literature professor Walter A. Berendsohn called a "humanist front" against Nazi Germany.[29] At an antifascist conference in Paris in 1935, Klaus Mann had coined the term "socialist humanism" as the basis for the Popular Front alliance between Communists and liberals in the cultural contest with the NS regime.[30] By the outbreak of the war, his father Thomas's leisurely image of a Hölderlin-reading Marx had evolved into the concept of a "humanist front" that both vehemently opposed but in some respects also echoed the militant link between culture and politics expressed in Rosenberg's right-wing Kampfbund für deutsche Kultur in the Weimar days.

Humanist Culture from *Bildungsideal* to Militant Antifascism

The concept of German humanism had come a long way from its early twentieth-century roots in academic debates over secondary and higher education. After the end of World War I, educators and scholars of ancient culture, such as Werner Jaeger and Eduard Spranger, were the initiators of a "neo-humanist revival." The teaching of classical Greek and Latin, especially at the secondary institutions of higher learning (*Gymnasien*) aimed at the "education of man to be human" (*Bildung des Menschen zum Menschen*) and to address the perceived crisis of spiritualism and culture, especially among the middle classes, after the First World War.[31] As Jaeger formulated it in a speech in 1925, humanist education would reintroduce exhausted Europeans to the roots of their own culture and revive the damaged Western value system:

> We are deeply alienated from the meaning and the origin of [this] culture.... We fussily grope into the caches of Asiatic wisdom for surrogates ... because we have lost faith in the worth of our own European culture. While Rabindranath Tagore in Peking announces the rebirth of the Asian soul to the packed crowds of yellow students at his feet, we [Europeans], reeling from world war and cultural crisis, gaze at the fashionable theory of the "decline of the West."[32]

The emphasis on the legacies of classical Greece and Rome, as it was conceived by eighteenth- and early nineteenth-century scholars such as

---

[29] Walter A. Berendsohn, *Die humanistische Front: Einführung in die deutsche Emigranten-Literatur. Erster Teil: Von 1933 bis zum Kriegsausbruch 1939* (Zürich: Europa Verlag, 1946; reprint 1978).

[30] See Wilkinson, *The Intellectual Resistance in Europe*, 21.

[31] Werner Jaeger, "Antike und Humanismus," Rede zur Eröffnung der Tagung "Das Gymnasium," Berlin, April 1925; reprinted in Hans Oppermann, ed., *Humanismus* (Darmstadt: Wissenschaftliche Buchgesellschaft, 1970), 20.

[32] Ibid., 19.

Johann Joachim Winckelmann and Wilhelm von Humboldt, and continued by Goethe, Hölderlin, and the Weimar classics, would stem the tendencies of fragmentation and spiritual hollowness in twentieth-century Europe.

Some humanist scholars differentiated sharply between a general "Western" cultural heritage and a specific German humanist tradition. Archaeologist Ludwig Curtius, for example reminded his audience that the chain of thinkers that embodied humanist ideals in German culture did not include "Montaigne, Ronsard, Racine, Voltaire, Anatole France, Valery, not Hobbes, Shaftesbury, John Stuart Mill, and Herbert Spencer, but Winckelmann, Lessing, Herder, Goethe, Hegel, Hölderlin, Jacob Burckhardt, Fr[iedrich] Nietzsche."[33] With these nationalistic inflections, the interwar humanist debate seemed to stand squarely in the tradition of German anti-modernist cultural criticism and apolitical "Mandarin" ideals.

No wonder that most humanist scholars had little to say about the rise of fascism in Europe and Germany in the 1920s and 1930s. The humanist ideal of scholarship and instruction in Latin and ancient texts lent itself to political disengagement and emphasis on the inner life (*Innerlichkeit*). Scholar Julius Stenzel, therefore, understood humanism in 1928 as a "counterweight against the general dangers of modern thinking."[34] The danger emanated from the growing influence of existentialist ideas since the publication of Martin Heidegger's *Sein und Zeit* (1925), a radical attack on the Western metaphysical tradition. For humanist intellectuals like Stenzel, the threat to Western civilization came from the antihumanist ideas of Heidegger and Nietzsche, rather than the political doctrines of inhumanity propagated by Hitler and Goebbels.

By 1932, however, the debate on the humanist tradition could no longer ignore the politics of its time. Literary scholar Ernst Robert Curtius – no relation to Ludwig Curtius – warned against the appropriation of humanist ideals by communism and fascism. Humanism was to refrain from propaganda and sermon. At the same time, Curtius realized that the scholarly humanist ideals went beyond a narrow focus on education and that they were gravely threatened by the political tendencies in the late Weimar Republic:

If today, in the second third of the twentieth century, humanism is to live again, it can only be a *total humanism*: one that is sensual and spiritual, philological and

---

[33] Ludwig Curtius, "Die Antike Kunst und der Moderne Humanismus," *Die Antike* 3 (1927), reprinted in Oppermann, ed., 52.

[34] Julius Stenzel, "Die Gefahren Modernen Denkens und der Humanismus," *Die Antike* 4 (1928), reprinted in Oppermann, ed., *Humanismus*, 109.

musical, philosophical and artistic, religious and political. When, however, the ignorance of the times, the misgivings of those in power, or the coarseness of the rabble prevents such a new existence in the light of day, then the scattered and nameless [adherents of humanist ideals] will find each other and work in secrecy.[35]

Like many scholars and academics of his persuasion, Ernst Robert Curtius tried to live his humanist ethical ideals in "inner exile" after 1933.

While the ideals of humanism seemed to invite a retreat into private scholarship and the conditions of inner emigration, it was taken up by the left, especially when the KPD's Popular Front policy necessitated the search for common ideological principles with the liberal and bourgeois Nazi opposition. Communist intellectuals such as Alexander Abusch and Alfred Kurella set out to forge a synthesis between Goethe's and Schiller's humanism and Marxist materialism. After the writers' congress in Paris in 1935 had introduced the term "socialist humanism," the KPD functionary Kurella, a member of the communist exile organization in Moscow, the National Committee for a Free Germany (Nationalkomitee Freies Deutschland, NKFD), noted that the "defense of humanist culture had become the positive substance of the antifascist struggle," and tried a more specific definition of humanism.[36] Kurella described Goethe, Schiller, Herder, and Winckelmann as initiators of a German emancipatory tradition and adherents of the ideals of the French Revolution. However, the failure of political revolution, combined with bourgeois class interests, had distorted this tradition to a "general opposition between politics and humanity (as inner life [*Innerlichkeit*])." The Popular Front, on the other hand, would give rise to an "antifascist humanism, or better: to the real overcoming [*positive Auflösung*] of … humanism's contrast between humanity [*Menschlichkeit*] and politics."[37]

The KPD functionary and writer Alexander Abusch would become the most influential example for the marriage of the "dual legacies" of Weimar: the appropriation of classical German culture and the mid-twentieth-century ideal of leftist mass mobilization. Abusch was born in 1902 in Kracow to an Austrian Social Democratic scrap metal dealer and a Jewish mother. He spent his childhood and early youth in Nuremberg in a lower-middle-class milieu of Social Democratic workers, Jewish shopkeepers, and militarist schoolteachers, thus experiencing

---

[35] Ernst Robert Curtius, *Deutscher Geist in Gefahr* (Stuttgart: Deutsche Verlagsanstalt, 1932), 129–30.
[36] Alfred Kurella, "Verfall und Triumph des Humanismus" (1936) in *Der Mensch als Schöpfer seiner Selbst: Beiträge zum sozialistischen Humanismus* (Berlin [East]: Aufbau, 1961), 11.
[37] Ibid., 14.

early on the contradictions and tensions of the Wilhelmine Empire. (In the first part of his memoirs, published in 1984, Abusch wrote that a revisiting of Nuremberg in the 1970s revealed "what might be the essence of West German capitalism" because his childhood streets had been turned into a "sort of ghetto for Turkish and Greek guest workers.")[38] His early exposure to classical literature and the leftist political agitation of the pre–World War I years influenced him more than the rudimentary Jewish instruction he received in Hebrew school. As he wrote in his memoirs, he didn't realize at the time "how much Biblical history matters to a historical materialist" and that learning a foreign language – even Hebrew – provided "a humanistic education even for an atheist." Like many Jewish-born communists, he severed his "inner connections" with Judaism, yet the writings of Moses Mendelsohn, "the friend of Lessing," in the Jewish library "brought him closer to classical German literature."[39]

As for so many intellectuals of his generation, the Spartakus uprising in 1919 and its tragic and brutal defeat were key experiences for Abusch, who became a communist at the same time that he began to write and publish his first "militant proletarian poems [*proletarische Kampfgedichte*]."[40] In 1921, as a nineteen-year-old member of a communist youth organization, Abusch envisioned the end of capitalism as a state where culture and the arts sought and found "a deeper foundation among the masses."[41] As Willi Stoph, the president of the German Democratic Republic (GDR), said about his later minister of culture: "Always at the frontlines, he knew how to use his close cultural connections to make the arts an effective weapon of class struggle."[42]

Abusch's dual interests in literature and radical politics predisposed him to become the KPD's mediator between the cultural and political forces of the Weimar years. Under the pseudonym Ernst Reinhardt, he gathered experiences in illegal publishing as editor of the KPD organ *Rote Fahne*, first in Jena, then in Berlin. During his time in Berlin, he also became friends with poet Johannes R. Becher (see Chapter 4).[43] When the Nazis took power in 1933, Abusch fled to France, where he became a close associate of Comintern functionary Willi Münzenberg

---

[38] Alexander Abusch, *Der Deckname: Memoiren* (Berlin [East]: Dietz, 1984), 14.
[39] Ibid., 17–18.
[40] Ibid., 29–37; see also Alexander Abusch, *Entscheidung unseres Jahrhunderts. Beiträge zur Zeitgeschichte, 1921 bis 1976* (Berlin [East]: Aufbau, 1977, 15–31.
[41] Ibid., 33.
[42] Willi Stoph, "Ein Kämpfer für die gerechte Sache der deutschen Arbeiterklasse," in *Alexander Abusch: Bildnis eines Revolutionärs. Freunde und Genossen über ihre Begegnungen mit Alexander Abusch in fünf Jahrzehnten* (Berlin [East]: Aufbau, 1972), 10.
[43] Abusch, *Deckname*, 166–91.

Figure 1 A portrait of writer and KPD activist Alexander Abusch (1902–82) in the early 1950s. Abusch was a key figure in the shifting dynamics of the "other Germany." His trajectory from editor of KPD exile publications in Paris and Mexico City to Kulturbund functionary to GDR minister of culture also personifies the marriage between politics and culture that characterized antifascist humanism. Photo by Abraham Pisarek/Ullstein bild via Getty Images.

and of communist literary representatives such as Anna Seghers and Bertolt Brecht.⁴⁴ Like Kurella, Abusch made the defense of German literary classics a centerpiece of antifascist rhetoric. In 1937, as editor of the illegal *Die rote Fahne*, he wrote: "It would be a grave mistake for antifascists to say: 'Leave Schiller to the Nazis!' This would be giving up an important part of our struggle for freedom."⁴⁵ The mission of antifascist publishing was "not to leave one word, one sound, one color of German culture to the fascists ... Where there were communists, there was the true German culture, the *other* Germany."⁴⁶

By the time Abusch took on his crucial role, the battle over the "true German culture" was conducted all over Europe, and reverberated even in exile groups and journals in North America.⁴⁷ The NS regime tried economical as well as political measures to undermine the activities of exile publications and organizations. In June 1936, in a move that echoed previous maneuvers in Germany and at the Saar, the German propaganda ministry succeeded in gaining control over the financially struggling anti-Nazi émigré paper *Pariser Tageblatt*. In return for Goebbels's financial backing of the struggling paper, the *Tageblatt*'s publisher, Wladimir Poljakow, fired the paper's editor, Georg Bernhard, and agreed to a less confrontational course for the restructured publication.⁴⁸ Operatives of the German embassies also kept a close watch on the émigrés and, as a Gestapo letter on Walter Berendsohn's activities in Denmark indicates, kept pedantic records of their public comments and their potential damage to the NS regime's image abroad.⁴⁹ However, until the outbreak of the war, the NS propaganda officials could not prevent émigré efforts to represent "the other Germany." In September 1937, for example, in response to an exhibition in Copenhagen by the German propaganda ministry on "The German Book," the émigré community in Denmark

---

⁴⁴ Ibid., 324ff.
⁴⁵ Alexander Abusch "Weder Schiller noch ein anderes Stück von Deutschland," Leitartikel der *Roten Fahne*, 2, 1937, reprinted in Alexander Abusch, *Literatur im Zeitalter des Sozialismus: Beiträge zur Literaturgeschichte 1921 bis 1966* (Schriften, Band II) (Berlin [East]: Aufbau, 1967), 224–6; see also Alexander Abusch, *Ansichten über einige Klassiker* (Berlin [East] and Weimar: Aufbau, 1982).
⁴⁶ Alexander Abusch, "Vorwort," in Volker Riedel, *Freies Deutschland. México 1941–1946*. With a preface by Alexander Abusch (Berlin [East]): Aufbau Verlag, 1975), 11, emphasis in the original.
⁴⁷ See, for example, exile author Walter Schonstedt's article "Illegal Periodicals in Germany," *The American Mercury* (January 1935), and "Anti-Nazi "Papers: Illegal Publications Which Attack the Hitler Régime Are Circulating in Germany," *MacLean's Magazine Toronto* (March 1935). University of California, Shields Library, Special Collections, D-26 Walter Schönstedt Collection, Box 1, scrapbook.
⁴⁸ See *Pariser Tageszeitung* 1, 1 (June 12, 1936), page 1.
⁴⁹ Reprinted in an appendix to Walter A. Berendsohn, *Die humanistische Front: Einführung in die deutsche Emigranten-Literatur. Zweiter Teil: Vom Kriegsausbruch 1939 bis Ende 1946* (1949; Worms, Germany: Verlag Georg Heintz, 1976), 226–7.

organized a counter-exhibition under the title "the German Culture War (*Der deutsche Kulturkampf*)," featuring books that were burned and prohibited by the Third Reich.[50] With the outbreak of the war, not only NS propaganda activities, but also German weapons had to be countered by a "militant humanism," whose tone could even approach the rhetorical lows of Nazi language in its "first contemptuous, then increasingly distorting demonization of the NS regime's protagonists and the masses that cheered them."[51] Even though the exile opposition had temporary successes in its "culture war" against Hitler and Goebbels, by 1940, the editorials of émigré papers and exhibitions of anti-Nazi art would prove powerless against German tanks invading Western Europe.

[50] Berendsohn, *Die humanistische Front, Erster Teil*, 66.
[51] Haarmann, ed., *Heimat, liebe Heimat*, 35.

2 "Otra Alemanias": Antifascist Humanism in the Diaspora, 1939–1944

Even after the Moscow-directed Popular Front policy fell apart with the Hitler–Stalin Pact in 1939, during the 1940s, the Communist Party of Germany (KPD) initiated a commission and "action program" for a postfascist Germany. The program envisioned a "bloc of the militant democracy [*Block der kämpferischen Demokratie*] which would unify all productive forces of the German people ... across any ideological and political differences."[1] The doctrine of socialist humanism, coined in the heyday of the Popular Front in 1935, was to become the cornerstone for a vision of cultural renewal that would bind communist and liberal antifascist forces together in cultural leagues during the war. The cultural leagues in the exile communities were representative of antifascist cultural associations under communist dominance but built on wide-ranging alliances between working-class movements, liberal opposition, and intellectuals. The Freier Deutscher Kulturbund (Free German League of Culture [FDKB]) in Great Britain, for example, was initially under the leadership of another former Saar plebiscite activist, the theater critic Alfred Kerr.[2] Among the communist founding members was the later German Democratic Republic (GDR) historian of the working class, Jürgen Kuczynski. But with its large number of non-Communists in leading positions – Kerr himself did not belong to any party – and its mixture of political presentations and apolitical cultural events, the league was typical for the antifascist consensus that developed during the war. More than concrete political or socioeconomic conceptions, the FDKB emphasized a general identification with the tradition of German "humanism," especially the German Enlightenment thought of Immanuel Kant and Gotthold Ephraim Lessing and the "Weimar

---

[1] Quoted in Magdalena Heider, *Politik – Kultur – Kulturbund. Zur Gründungs- und Frühgeschichte des Kulturbundes zur demokratischen Erneuerung Deutschlands, 1945–1954 in der SBZ/DDR* (Cologne: Verlag Wissenschaft und Politik, 1993), 16/17.

[2] For the history of the FDKB, see Charmion Brinson and Richard Dove, *Politics by Other Means: The Free German League of Culture in London, 1939–1946* (London: Valentine Mitchell, 2010).

Classics," Johann Wolfgang Goethe, Friedrich Schiller, and Friedrich Hölderlin.³

According to the FDKB's introductory bulletin, membership had grown to 1,000 members by the end of 1939, after starting out with four people a year earlier. The text lists the various events – art exhibitions, cabaret performances, and presentations by German artists as well as by British writers such as Wickham Steed, Kingley [sic] Martin, and J. B. Priestley.⁴ The FDKB headquarters in the London suburb of Hampstead was the hub of a network of similar German cultural leagues in Liverpool, Manchester, Edinburgh, and Bristol. It also established connections with an "Anglo-German-Austrian-Czech Friendship Club" in Leeds, which organized readings of Heine translations for the British members of the club.⁵ The emphasis on the contributions of non-German artists to the German exile organizations and on the interest of the British public in the FDKB-sponsored events is a sign of the attempt by German intellectuals to counteract the growing cultural isolation of official, i.e., NS-approved, German culture from the Western (modernist) cultural mainstream. The goal of all these organizations was obviously the establishment of an alternative to Goebbels's cultural policies.

Besides organizing educational events, the FDKB also fulfilled the role of a publisher of fiction that would have been prohibited in Germany itself. The league's publications included literature, for example, Theodor Plivier's thematizations of the German war in the East, as well as selections of Thomas Mann's radio addresses to the German people. As in all exile communities, a German-language journal with news and commentaries for the League's members played a central role. The first edition of the *FDKB Nachrichten*, published in London on December 4, 1939, presented the organization's goals and its program under the title "The Free German League of Culture. What it can do, what it is, what it wants."⁶

The publishers of the *FDKB Nachrichten*'s initial edition felt it necessary to clarify that their organization was "neither a harmless [*unverbindliche*] tea party nor a political group." Rather, the FDKB's members saw themselves as "antifascists, the sworn enemies of the Hitler system," and as "activists" who tried to "keep the German spirit of the past awake in the present and to preserve it for the future."⁷ With these objectives, the FDKB emphasized that it was not a party organization, even if "these days nothing happens in the vacuum of 'pure art' or 'pure science.'"⁸

---

³ Heider, *Politik – Kultur – Kulturbund*, 21–2.
⁴ *FDKB Nachrichten*, Vol. 1, No. 1 (December 4, 1939), page 1 (title page).
⁵ Ibid., page 3.
⁶ Ibid., page 1.
⁷ Ibid., page 2.
⁸ Ibid., page 1.

The close working relationship between communist and liberal members of the FDKB and their common emphasis on classical German cultural heritage became increasingly strained after 1943/44, when the KPD leadership demanded greater "politicization." Social-democratic authors who were discontent with the communist influence in the FDKB had found refuge since 1939 in an alternative organization, the Gruppe Unabhängiger Deutscher Autoren (Group of Independent German Authors).[9]

England provided thriving conditions for bourgeois-democratic organizations such as the FDKB, which offered the émigrés the opportunity to hold on to the traditions and lifestyles of the German-Jewish educated middle class (*Bildungsbürgertum*). According to West German historian Werner Röder, the participation of the KPD was mere "camouflage" by a party isolated from its political mass base.[10] But such an interpretation underestimates the political character of the FDKB's cultural offerings. The FDKB's literary publications included overtly political literature, for example, the pamphlet *Women under the Swastika*, which compiled ten short literary vignettes and poems on German women's resistance against the Third Reich's interrelated war and gender policies.[11] Moreover, the FDKB officials' contention that nothing was untouched by politics in the Europe of the 1930s and 1940s needs to be taken seriously. The emphasis of exile organizations on the preservation of German culture was not only part of maintaining the broad Popular Front consensus between working-class and bourgeois political doctrines, but also an inevitable result of NS ideology and practice. Activities such as the FDKB's public readings of Lessing and Hölderlin do not seem very political in the context of post-1945 liberal Western Europe, but become highly political and oppositional if one considers the radical nature of National Socialism, which did not only aim to reshape German politics and society, but to create a new national culture. The fact that exile opposition groups such as the FDKB formed around the idea of cultural resistance, rather than political programs, lends support to the argument that NS totalitarianism fundamentally differed from other twentieth-century authoritarianisms in its emphasis on a radical cultural "cleansing" along racial and ideological lines. Thus, it was the nature of NS ideology and practice that contributed to the

---

[9] Werner Röder, *Die deutschen sozialistischen Exilgruppen in Großbritannien 1940–1945. Ein Beitrag zur Geschichte des Widerstandes gegen den Nationalsozialismus.* [Schriftenreihe des Forschungsinstituts der Friedrich-Ebert-Stiftung, Band 58] (Bonn-Bad Godesberg: Verlag Neue Gesellschaft, 1973), 87.
[10] Ibid., 85.
[11] *Women under the Swastika* (London: Free German League of Culture in Great Britain, 1942). University of California, Davis, Shields Library Special Collections, P-004 89:33.

exile groups' emphasis on cultural activities. The "war" over the "true" representation of German culture, especially abroad, was an essential part of opposition activities and led to a continuation of the rhetoric of cultural renewal after the war.

Alemania Libre: The Free Germany Movement in Mexico

The more pluralist dynamics of exile opposition organizations, and their conceptions and uses of "humanist" German culture, were also to be found in the German exile communities in Latin America, especially the communist group in Mexico. Because of their geographical distance, the Latin American exile circles that formed after the fall of France in capitals such as Montevideo, Buenos Aires, and Mexico City had relatively little influence on events or opinions in Germany during the war. Yet it is here that continuities not only of historical actors, but also of rhetorical strategies, ideas, and social practices can be observed from WWII-exile to post-1945 projects of cultural renewal.

More than in France or Great Britain, exile circles in Latin America had to take into account the politics of their host countries. While opposition activity against Hitler was generally allowed – unlike in, say, Switzerland – radical left-wing rhetoric had to be toned down to prevent censorship or crackdowns by the local authorities. Under these circumstances, a focus on cultural issues rather than on revolutionary politics seemed to be the safer way to maintain the host countries' welcome. But, just as in Europe, cultural institutions and publications also provided the common denominator between adherents of the various political doctrines that congregated under the concept of "antifascism."

An example for the wide range of German-language exile publications was *Das Andere Deutschland/La Otra Alemania*, which was published monthly in Buenos Aires, Argentina, from 1937.[12] The paper's content and rhetoric were representative of similar publications by German exiles in Uruguay, Mexico, and Brazil, which contained an assortment of brief articles about the ongoing war, essays, short stories, and poems, either written by German authors on site or sent in by authors exiled in other European countries. Detailed accounts of the politics in the Latin American host countries were rare. Characteristic were not only the appeals to political antifascism, but also the keen attention paid to the Nazi regime's attempts to represent German culture on the European

---

[12] For an in-depth study of *Das Andere Deutschland*, see Germán C. Friedmann, *Alemanes antinazis en la Argentina* (Buenos Aires: Siglo ventiuno, 2010).

continent. The edition of *La Otra Alemania* from March 1942, for example, contained an article by "an associate in Switzerland" about a "poets' conference" (*Dichtertagung*) held by the Nazis in Weimar. The anonymous author quoted the Nazi-controlled *Bodensee-Rundschau*'s official summary of the event: "The hour of the European spirit ... where poets from fourteen nations made a spontaneous, firm commitment to the Reich as the guardian and creator of a new European intellectual life." Naturally, the correspondent not only points out the political agenda of this claim, he also disparages the artistic and moral values of the "coveted" Norwegian and Finnish poets, as well as of the "illiterates from the Balkans." The German writer Hans Carossa, an "inner exile" whose work before 1933 was celebrated by the Nazi regime, is depicted as "enormously conceited and craving for accolades" (while a Goebbels speech is seen as "smart and logical").[13] Initially barred from NS organizations because of his liberal views, Carossa had made his peace with the regime, and in 1941 Goebbels made him president of the European Writers' Association, an organization aimed at binding artists in German-controlled Europe to the Third Reich.[14] The attack on Carossa – especially compared to the almost flattering portrait of Goebbels – testifies to the acrimony between exiles and the "inner émigrés," a conflict that German intellectuals took to other continents and that they would carry over into the postwar period.

Overall, the correspondent at the NS-sponsored poets' meeting was "disgusted" by the Nazis' ambitions to be "the successors and heirs of the great intellectual minds of Weimar and to lead and control the intellectual life of Europe; they want to have it all and be it all, these delusions of grandeur will ultimately destroy Germany." However, the article was not exclusively interested in poetry and the Nazis' cultural diplomacy. The author also recounts his conversations with German officers during the conference. Like many exiles, the correspondent seemed surprised and shocked by the radicalization that had occurred in Germany since the 1930s:

I heard more than once that the Russian POWs were knowingly and intentionally left to slowly starve, just as everybody else who isn't needed at the moment and who doesn't belong to the predestined master race. I was shocked at how widespread this principle had become: they had become used to considering only the Germans as humans in the actual sense of the word. ... What was said

---

[13] "Dichtertreffen in Weimar," *Das Andere Deutschland/La Otra Alemania* (Buenos Aires), March 1942.
[14] See Ernst Klee, *Das Kulturlexikon zum Dritten Reich. Were war was vor und nach 1945* (Frankfurt a. M.: S. Fischer, 2007), 94.

about the conditions in Poland was so unspeakably horrible, it is almost impossible to believe.[15]

Reports from Europe like this one not only testify to the extent of information about German atrocities that was available even in Latin America, they also reinforced the exile intellectuals' conviction that their cultural activities, such as the performance of stage productions, played concrete political roles. In an issue of *La Otra Alemania* from September 1942, the director of the "Free German Stage" in Buenos Aires, P. Walter Jacob, wrote: "There is one question that is being asked over and over again: 'How much sense does it make to preoccupy oneself with matters of the arts and the theater, at this moment of world-historical bloody conflicts and decisions which are likely to shape human communities for the next centuries?'" Jacob's answer was the standard argument of the "other Germany":

> Especially in times like ours, when powerful and ruthless propagandists attempt to distort the historical facts – even in the realm of culture; when they are about to destroy what has grown organically over centuries ... especially in a time like this, it is the duty of everyone who still has the opportunity to freely engage in the arts to fight against the forces of destruction and to preserve for a new era all that is threatened by cultural vandalism and violent, mad ignorance.[16]

However, a brief comment by Hans Jahn also implies that politicizing the stage could challenge the taste of German-speaking ticket buyers in Buenos Aires: "When serious, critical, and 'tendentious' plays leave the house half empty, while it is packed when trivial comedies are performed, then the actors, who depend on this for their living, might be forced to choose a path that they rather wouldn't go." Future assessments of the exile theater's impacts "will also judge that part of the emigrant community that constituted its audience."[17]

A look at the pages of journals such as *La Otra Alemania* reveals that exile publications and discussion circles formed a transnational network of antifascist correspondence and activism. Issues of the journal usually contained a summary of the activities of other "anti-Hitler" communities in Latin America and Europe, as well as from groups in China and South Africa, complemented with greeting messages of solidarity ("*Grußworte*"). During the war, the journal *Freies Deutschland/Alemania Libre* (*Free Germany*), published in Mexico between 1941 and 1946, became one of

---

[15] "Dichtertreffen in Weimar."
[16] P. Walter Jacob, "Freies Deutsches Theater – Heute," *Das Andere Deutschland/La Otra Alemania* (September 1942), 20–1.
[17] Hans Jahn, "Das Emigrantentheater und sein Publikum," *Das Andere Deutschland/La Otra Alemania* (September 1942), 22.

the most influential antifascist publications. In many respects a model for the postwar journal *Aufbau* in Berlin, *Freies Deutschland* was openly communist, yet it exemplified the pluralist dynamics of exile institutions and their continuation in the postwar political-cultural scene. The antifascist organization in Mexico continued the work of the Popular Front committee in Paris, whose members had to flee after the German occupation in 1940, and combined it with the kind of bourgeois-intellectual focus on "humanist" German culture that characterized the Free German Cultural League in Great Britain.

Between 1939 and 1941, the left-populist Mexican government under Lazaro Cárdenas made Mexico City a refuge for Nazi opponents fleeing occupied France, leftist participants defeated in the Spanish Civil War, and refugees leaving their previous exile in the United States, where the political climate since the Hitler–Stalin Pact had become more hostile toward communist activists.[18] In 1941, startled by the German attack on the Soviet Union, the KPD leadership in Mexico organized the Free Germany Movement (Bewegung Freies Deutschland [BFD]) to coordinate resistance activities in Latin America. The BFD's monthly publication, *Freies Deutschland*, and its cultural institution, the Heinrich-Heine Club, constituted a forum for the German-speaking antifascist community in the Latin American country. Although initiated by the KPD, both journal and club addressed not only communists, but anybody "with an interest in humanist culture."[19] In Mexico City this meant above all communist and non-Communist Party-affiliated refugees; members of the Jewish exile community that had existed since 1933; and even the so-called German colony (*Deutsche Kolonie*), the descendants of earlier German emigrants and plantation owners, whose institutions had largely been undermined by NS organizations.[20]

The founding of *Freies Deutschland* as well as the Heinrich-Heine Club was the result of an influx of communist intellectuals from the German exile community in Paris. At the end of 1941 and the beginning of 1942, the communist and non-communist intellectuals and artists in Mexico were joined by KPD functionaries on their flight from Spain and France to the Soviet Union; the Japanese attack on Pearl Harbor, in the meantime, had blocked the passage to Russia via the Pacific.

---

[18] For Mexican foreign policy during the 1930s, see Friedrich Schuler, *Mexico Between Hitler and Roosevelt: Mexican Foreign Relations in the Age of Lázaro Cárdenas, 1934–1940* (Albuquerque: University of New Mexico Press, 1999). See also Alexander Abusch, "Vorwort," in Volker Riedel, *Freies Deutschland. México 1941–1946*. With a preface by Alexander Abusch (Berlin [East]): Aufbau Verlag, 1975), 5.

[19] Ibid., 6.

[20] Ibid.; Wolfgang Kießling, *Alemania Libre in Mexico. Band 1. Ein Beitrag zur Geschichte des antifaschistischen Exils (1941–1946)* (Berlin [East]: Akademie Verlag, 1974), 29ff.

Many functionaries of the KPD's illegal leadership, such as Paul Merker and Alexander Abusch, stayed in Mexico and applied their experience in political organization to the BFD and its institutions.[21] The novelist and KPD member Anna Seghers, who had written her novel *Das Siebte Kreuz* (*The Seventh Cross*) in exile in Paris, became the Heinrich-Heine Club's first president. As in the FDKB in Great Britain, the Heinrich-Heine Club – the decision to name the club after the nineteenth-century Jewish-German exile poet was highly symbolic – offered readings and performances of NS-censored art, political education, and presentations of classical German humanist culture. A chronicle of its events from 1941 to 1945 lists, for example, lectures on Hölderlin's *Hyperion* – "from a political and military perspective" – followed by first readings of works by Egon Erwin Kisch and Johannes R. Becher and concerts of the works of Beethoven.[22]

An issue from December 1941 provides an example of the eclectic pool of influences from which the German antifascists in Mexico drew inspiration. Under the heading "Deutsche Meister ueber Mexico [German Master Thinkers on Mexico]," a full page presents thoughts and comments related to Mexico by Goethe, Friedrich Engels, Bismarck, Nietzsche, and Heine. The opposite page of the spread contains an indictment of the Nazis' racist view of the Mexican people.[23] Even though articles such as this one strove to connect German culture with the exiles' host country, the Heinrich-Heine Club's efforts to educate its patrons in the history and language of Mexico seemed to encounter much less interest among the German community than the offerings on German humanist culture. In a diary entry from 1945, BFD president Ludwig Renn noted the small attendance of a lecture on Maya mythology by the "very good" Mexican literary scholar Ermilo Abreu Gómez: "The audience was much too small. This shows again how dull-minded the German colony is. Of course the refugees from Europe wouldn't attend something like this because they don't understand enough Spanish."[24] Renn's comments indicate that the members of the Heinrich-Heine Club did not conceive of exile as a permanent situation, but lived in the hope of returning to a postfascist Germany. On the other hand, Renn's judgment hardly portrays the

---

[21] Kießling, *Alemania Libre in Mexico. Band 1*, 58ff.; Abusch, "Vorwort," in Riedel, *Freies Deutschland*, 6f.

[22] *Alemania Libre in Mexico. Band 2. Texte und Dokumente zur Geschichte des antifaschistischen Exils 1941–1946*, ed. Wolfgang Kießling (Berlin [East]: Akademie Verlag, 1974), 185–95.

[23] *Freies Deutschland/Alemania Libre*, Nr. 2 (15 December 1941), 16/17.

[24] Quoted in Kießling, *Alemania Libre in Mexico. Band 1*, 116.

German expatriates as fervent participants in mass mobilization and revolutionary action.

Merker, who had transitioned from an ardent foe of social democracy to an influential partisan of the Popular Front ideal, plays a central role in Jeffrey Herf's analysis of the Mexican émigré community. Merker seemed to be an exception among high-ranking communists because he emphasized the central role of antisemitism in NS ideology and practice, and thereby transcended the orthodox communist "master narrative" of fascism.[25] For Herf, Merker's position illustrated that the exile situation "could bring to the fore elements of Communist traditions which had remained in the background in Europe and in Moscow exile."[26]

There is little mention of these deviations from the official Communist Party line in the East German historiography of the Free Germany Movement in Mexico. Published in East Berlin in 1974, Wolfgang Kießling's literary history of the exile communist group did not mention Merker's reflections on the Jewish question and the responsibilities of a postfascist Germany. Instead, Kießling reiterated the broad pluralist appeal of the Heinrich-Heine Club, whose members were made up of "communists, Social Democrats, and bourgeois democrats; they were atheists, Christians, and Jews." However, "Zionist ideas, towards which some members and guests of the club were leaning, had no influence on the activities of the cultural association."[27] Against any exaggerated or romanticized conceptions of the influence of artists and intellectuals on the antifascist struggle, Kießling's account emphasizes the leading role of the political, as opposed to the cultural, activists: "As the core of the movement *Freies Deutschland*, the organized communist group could not be replaced, not even by the creative, political, and ideological capabilities of individual authors ... [The German authors in Mexico] were [only] able to serve as representatives of German cultural life because they linked their work with the ideology and organization of the KPD."[28]

While Kießling's account shows how the relatively less dogmatic ideological climate in the Mexican communist colony was downplayed by an East German regime portraying itself as the legitimate successor to the antifascist activists, there can be little doubt that culture was very much

---

[25] Jeffrey Herf, *Divided Memory: The Nazi Past in the Two Germanys* (Cambridge, MA: Harvard University Press, 1997), 40–68."
[26] Ibid, 40. See also Paul Merker, "Über die Bewegung 'Freies Deutschland' in Lateinamerika," in Heinz Voßke, ed., *Im Kampf bewährt. Erinnerungen deutscher Genossen an den antifaschistischen Widerstand von 1933 bis 1945* (Berlin [East]: Dietz Verlag, 1977), 440.
[27] Kießling, *Alemania Libre in Mexico. Band 1*, 103. See also Merker "Über die Bewegung 'Freies Deutschland' in Lateinamerika," 435.
[28] Kießling, *Alemania Libre in Mexico. Band 1*, 12.

the focus of the German communist movement in Mexico. The crucial link between communist politics and humanist culture was forged by Abusch, whose position as chief editor of the illegal KPD organ *Die rote Fahne* from 1933 to 1939 had given him extensive experience in the publishing of communist underground literature.[29] In exile in Paris, Abusch had been the "liaison" between the party leadership and the communist and left-leaning writers in the French capital.[30] In Mexico City, upon assuming the editorial functions of *Freies Deutschland*, Abusch seemed to have resumed this function as coordinating instance between party bureaucracy and antifascist intellectuals.

After September 1942, *Freies Deutschland* was published in a circulation of 3,300 to 4,000 copies, most of them "going from hand to hand."[31] In his preface to Volker Riedel's history of *Freies Deutschland*, Abusch states that the publication's task was to "operate culturally and politically according to the ideas of a broad popular front that had begun in France." The basis of this cultural and political popular front "under the foreign sky of Mexico" was to be the "defense and conservation of German humanist culture, in constant struggle with fascist ideology."[32] In a telegram to Cárdenas's successor as Mexican president, Manuel Avila Camacho, Abusch and the coeditors of *Freies Deutschland* described their publication as representing "the German mind's best humanist traditions of Goethe, Herder, Kant, Heine and Marx in the irreconcilable fight against Hitlerism."[33] The editors and contributors to the journal also frequently linked their efforts to the humanist and cosmopolitan ideas of early-nineteenth-century traveler to Latin America Alexander von Humboldt.[34] Even though he asserted the primacy of the party over the ideas of intellectuals, Kießling summarizes the central question behind these activities thus: "Humanist German traditions – who will continue them?"[35]

In May 1943, the leadership of the BFD organized the first countrywide congress of the movement in Mexico City before more than 100 participants, including representatives of the Mexican government.[36] The congress commemorated the tenth anniversary of the Nazi seizure

---

[29] Ibid., 311.
[30] Abusch, "Vorwort," in Riedel, *Freies Deutschland*, 7. See also Chapter 1 of this work.
[31] Ibid., 17.
[32] Ibid., 7.
[33] Quoted in *Alemania Libre in Mexico. Band 2*, 84.
[34] Abusch, "Vorwort," in Riedel, *Freies Deutschland*, 10; Kießling, *Alemania Libre in Mexico. Band 1*, 35 and passim.
[35] Kießling, *Alemania Libre in Mexico. Band 1*, 34.
[36] See *Unser Kampf gegen Hitler. Protokoll des Ersten Landeskongresses der Bewegung "Freies Deutschland" in Mexico* (Mexico City: Alemania Libre, 1943), 9.

of power and the first anniversary of the German sinking of the Mexican steam tanker *Portrero Del Llano*, which had led to Mexico's entry into the war on the side of the Allies. Among the official goals of the participants was the German exile community's declaration of solidarity with the Mexican war effort. A more tangible and practical objective was the discussion and clarification of the legal status of the German antifascists, who were now officially nationals of an enemy country. Accordingly, the BDF's Erich Jungmann prefaced the conference's protocol with the emphatic assertion that "no decent German would want to be associated with the Nazi big shots [*Nazibonzen*], Gestapo agents, and soldiers who murder, plunder, and rob in the occupied countries."[37] This emphasis on the difference between Nazis and "decent" Germans – by now a standard trope in antifascist speeches and writings – was confirmed by the attending Mexican government officials. For José Muñoz Cota, who gave an address as a representative of Defense Minister Cárdenas, the congress stood in the tradition of the "German intellectual realm of the great philosophers, the great artists, the great liberating ideas embodied by Marx, Engels, Goethe, and Heine." In contrast to this group of "immortal" thinkers stood "the ambitions of an abnormal being, who relied on the selfish philosophy of Nietzsche, and who aimed at shackling not only the freedom of Germany but of the whole world."[38]

The speeches by other participants at the congress in Mexico City also anticipated a number of other tropes and themes that would characterize the rhetoric of cultural renewal after the war. Paul Merker issued a declaration on the German people's shared responsibility for Hitler's atrocities, at least "until [the German population] openly rejects Hitler's fascism and joins the fight of Allies in an armed uprising." He also added a condemnation of antisemitism, which he defined as a "subordinate" part of the larger Allied effort against fascism. Nevertheless, Merker stressed that a "free democratic" Germany, if its economic situation allowed for it, had to compensate for the damages done to the Jews.[39] While Merker appealed to Jews to join the struggle of the "other Germany," Ludwig Renn tried to reconcile the leftist exile antifascists and the "German colony," the earlier German immigrant community whose members generally opposed the Allied war against a country to which they still felt a strong allegiance. The BDF president argued that "it would be a mistake to dismiss them all as Nazis. It is our task to unite the democratic elements among them."[40] Renn's reconciliatory and

[37] Ibid., 6.
[38] Ibid., 14.
[39] Ibid., 24/25.
[40] Ibid., 29.

Figure 2 Novelist Anna Seghers (1900–83) giving a speech after her return from Mexican exile, 1947. Seghers's political activism and artistic status made her an iconic figure of the German left and of antifascist humanism during the war and later in the GDR.
Photo by Ullstein bild via Getty Images.

inclusive tone would be echoed after the war in the similarly conflicted relationship between returning exiles and "inner émigrés," the intellectuals and artists who had stayed in Germany and compromised with the regime to different degrees.

If Renn's speech was reconciliatory, Anna Seghers's opening address listed the names of some of the prominent and non-prominent individuals who had perished during the Nazi tyranny, and who joined the "mass of the Jewish population whom Hitler had condemned to extermination." But for Seghers, the remembrance of martyrdom was not enough: "In their eternal, silent agreement, our nation's dead demand more from us than mere remembrance, historical discussions, or poetic mystification." Seghers ended her appeal to militant resistance – which she saw "growing by the hour" in German factories – with Ricarda Huch's translation of a poem by Italian revolutionary Giuseppe Mazzini: "Woe to him who didn't recognize the flag/who, after suffering and sacrifices have passed/and after the victory flame has been lighted/hides away and says, 'I was not a part of it.'"[41] Seghers's

[41] Ibid., 18/19.

adoption of a poem by Mazzini reflects how much the antifascism of the "other Germany" blended the militant activism of the 1930s and 1940s with the cultural and cosmopolitan nationalism of the nineteenth century. The BDF congress in 1943 was part of German intellectuals' struggle to wrest the meaning of German culture and national identity from the Nazis' claims to it since the early 1930s. As Abusch had written in 1937, as editor of *Die Rote Fahne*, "The German popular front is the true executor of the living legacy of the two greatest German poets, Schiller and Goethe."[42] However, by the early 1940s, Goebbels and his NS propaganda ministry no longer provided the only competing interpretation of the legacy of German culture.

Antifascism and Definitions of Cultural Identity

During the course of the war, the belief in other countries that the German nation had fallen into the hands of a small criminal leadership had given way to accusations and condemnations of the German people as a whole. The gradual exposure of German atrocities, especially since the beginning of the Russian campaign, and the lack of a salient resistance and opposition to Hitler in Germany itself, raised questions of the continuity of the Nazi regime with the larger trajectory of German history. It also led to widespread beliefs in the culpability of German culture in the spectacle of inhumanity that the Nazi aggression had unleashed on Europe. Among historians and politicians in Allied countries – but also in the views and writings of the bourgeois German exile writer Thomas Mann – a rhetoric emerged that seemingly drew a "straight line" from the inner-worldly idealism of German romanticism to the militarist adventurism of the Second Empire and the irrational and cruel fanaticism of NS ideology.[43]

The conflation of fascism and German identity – according to which "the German nation and Nazism were identical, fascism was rooted in the German national character, and there were no German antifascists"[44] – became associated with the name of the undersecretary

---

[42] Alexander Abusch, "Weder Schiller noch ein anderes Stück von Deutschland," Leitartikel der *Roten Fahne*, 2, 1937, reprinted in Alexander Abusch, *Literatur im Zeitalter des Sozialismus: Beiträge zur Literaturgeschichte 1921 bis 1966* (Schriften, Band II) (Berlin [East]: Aufbau, 1967), 224–6; see also Abusch, *Ansichten über einige Klassiker* (Berlin [East] and Weimar: Aufbau, 1982).

[43] See Thomas Mann's speech "Warum ich nicht nach Deutschland zurückgehe (1845)," in Eberhard Rathgeb, ed., *Die engagierte Nation: Deutsche Debatten 1945–2005* (Munich: Hanser, 2005), 20–4.

[44] Kießling, *Alemania Libre in Mexico. Band 1*, 126.

in Churchill's foreign office, Lord Robert Vansittart, who since 1940 had propagated an anti-appeasement "hard line" toward Germany.[45] In his radio-transmitted propaganda speeches and their 1942 publication under the title *Black Record,* Vansittart claimed that the essence of German national character rested on the three features of envy, self-pity, and cruelty: all three "proceed from the average German's callous egotism, his utter indifference to the feelings and interests of others." In his autobiographical essays, Vansittart even alluded to Goethe's *Faust* to illustrate his belief in an "endemic and incurable" German militarism: "There has never been the slightest variation in choice, because the German nation has always been animated by the Spirit of Assent to Evil, *der Geist der stets bejaht,* if I may reverse one of its own most famous quotations."[46] Even the German labor movement, from August Bebel to the Social Democratic parliamentary faction of 1933, stood in the tradition of the militarist and aggressive German national character traits.[47]

The British diplomat was by no means the only one who tried to convince the Allied governments that the war had to be conducted not just against the Nazis, but against the *Germans*. In the United States, German émigrés Friedrich Wilhelm Foerster and Emil Ludwig pressed for a "hard peace," while American fiction writer Rex Stout called for hatred of Germany and portrayed "Hitler as the culmination of a deeply rooted mental and nervous disease afflicting the German people."[48] By 1942, however, Vansittart's name had been firmly ingrained in the German exile communities as representing a position that did not distinguish between Nazis and Germans and that viewed National Socialism as the inevitable outcome of deeply rooted developments of German history. Predictably, "Vansittartism" drew fierce rebuttals from German exiles. Anti-Nazi activist Heinrich Fraenkel, in a tract for the Fabian Society in London, called Vansittart's theses "grist for Goebbels' mill."[49] In a similar rebuttal, London-based exile publisher Victor Gollancz claimed

---

[45] See Röder, *Die deutschen sozialistischen Exilgruppen in Großbritannien,* 143f; Merker, "Über die Bewegung 'Freies Deutschland' in Lateinamerika," 456; Nolan, "Antifascism under Fascism," 52.

[46] The Rt. Hon. Lord Vansittart, *Lessons of My Life* (New York: Knopf, 1943), 197; the allusion of course is to the *Faust* character Mephistoles, the devil, who always says "no" (and not "yes").

[47] Röder, *Die deutschen sozialistischen Exilgruppen in Großbritannien,* 143f.

[48] Marjorie Lamberti, "German Antifascist Refugees in America and the Public Debate on 'What Should Be Done with Germany after Hitler,' 1941–1945" *Central European History* 40, 2 (June 2007), 291.

[49] Heinrich Fraenkel, "Vansittart's Gift for Goebbels: A German Exile's Answer to the Black Record," in *Fabian Tracts, Volume 7 (Nos. 223–261), 1928–1944* (Nendeln/Liechtenstein: Kraus Thomson, 1969), 545–60.

that the *Black Record* "plays into the hands of Dr. Goebbels."[50] With the military tide increasingly turning against the Nazi regime, the "culture war" over the meaning of German humanism had opened a new front.

The KPD group in Mexico and the BDF activists also reacted against Vansittart's polemics, especially since the conservative British lord did not distinguish between Hitler's and Stalin's extremism, or between German fascists and antifascists. BDF president Ludwig Renn, who had spent time in a Nazi concentration camp, argued that ideas of an inherently evil German nature were equivalent to the application of Nazi theories; therefore, he proclaimed that "we are defending the German nation against the charge of being cruel by nature, but we also declare without reservations that it is [the German people's] historical guilt to admit Hitler to power, and that this guilt can only be restituted by the German people themselves."[51] German exile intellectuals had reasons to reject the idea of a historically predetermined collective guilt for Nazism. For Paul Merker, the problem was that, as Herf puts it,

if the causes [of National Socialism] were found so far in the past, and if all of German history was merely the prehistory of Nazism, then the proximate issues of human agency and moral responsibility during the end of Weimar and in the Nazi era would be lost under the weight of retrospective historical determinism. Those who denounced German history, and the Germans in general, made it impossible to affix individual guilt and responsibility.[52]

For the KPD, the thesis of a collective German guilt predetermined by centuries of historical development posed concrete political challenges. On the one hand it did not explain how the antifascist Germans – with the KPD as their vanguard – somehow "broke out" of the historical cycle. Antifascism, too, had to be rooted in German traditions. On the other hand, if the communists were to take power in a postwar Germany, the radical break with the past, especially with the political and economic trajectories that had led to the Nazi reign, had to be justified with deep-seated historical defects in German society. The pages of a journal such as *Freies Deutschland*, representing the "other Germany" and its humanist tradition, could not be unaffected by these discussions, which "were dominated by the question of the German people's guilt for the atrocities committed by the Hitler gang." According to its editor, Abusch, the journal confronted attempts "to prove that the course of German history and the development of the German mind had necessarily led to Hitler's

---

[50] Victor Gollancz, *Shall Our Children Live or Die? A Reply to Lord Vansittart on the German Problem* (London: Victor Gollancz, 1942), 3.
[51] Kießling, *Alemania Libre in Mexico. Band 1*, 130f.
[52] Herf, *Divided Memory*, 54.

imperialism and barbarism [*Ungeist*]." Against these ideas, and with the Nazi regime on the defense, the mission of *Freies Deutschland* had changed. The journal now was to "provide the historical evidence of the existence of humanist and socialist forces within the German people ... At the same time the Nazi opposition's shared responsibility for their inability [to prevent fascism] had to be presented in a differentiating manner and combined with unswerving lessons for a truly democratic future."

In a 1943 issue, Abusch responded to an official Washington government publication that denounced representatives of classical German philosophy and literature as "precursors of Nazism." The publication, which aimed to explain National Socialism's "basic principles" and warn against "the use of Germans abroad for Nazi aims," mentioned Johann Gottfried Herder, Johann Gottlieb Fichte, Wilhelm von Humboldt, and even Social Democratic founder Ferdinand Lassalle as early proponents of the *völkisch* nationalism of Nazi ideology. Abusch fiercely rebuked this interpretation and defended thinkers whose "humanist outlook in reality made them German precursors of democracy," and who "represented the sharpest contrast to the anti-democratic, reactionary, and uncultured Nazism."[53] In a later article, Abusch referred to the German officers who had defected and fought alongside the Soviets in the antifascist National Committee for a Free Germany (Nationalkomitee Freies Deutschland [NKFD]) as "the true descendants of Stein, Gneisenau, Scharnhorst, Clausewitz, and the intellectual heirs of Fichte and Kleist."[54] With the defeat of Goebbels and the NS regime imminent, Abusch and his journal were not willing to concede the interpretation of German culture to the postwar planners in Washington and London. And against sweeping condemnations of the German nation, Communist and non-communist antifascists responded with appeals to nineteenth-century nationalist traditions.

The volatile and politically unsuccessful Popular Front ideal of a broad, pluralist coalition of antifascist forces survived on the level of the intellectual confrontation over German culture. Unsuccessful in mobilizing masses of voters against Germany's annexation of the Saar region, antifascism evolved in tight-knit circles of intellectuals and political functionaries. The conspiratorial and semi-elitist character of the exile opposition movements, with their emphasis on classical "humanist"

---

[53] Alexander Abusch, "Herder, Fichte, und die fünfte Kolonne in Amerika" (1943) in Alexander Abusch, *Entscheidung unseres Jahrhunderts. Beiträge zur Zeitgeschichte, 1921 bis 1976* (Berlin [East]: Aufbau, 1977), 299–303.
[54] Alexander Abusch, "Nachfahren der Stein und Clausewitz" (1943) in Abusch, *Entscheidung unseres Jahrhunderts*, 327.

culture, blended with and often replaced the mobilizing rhetoric that had characterized the interwar period. Thus, the debate over the role of the humanist tradition on Germany did not subside with the end of the Nazi regime. Rather, the postwar public sphere of political-literary journals and discussion groups was a logical continuation of the intense politicization of interpretations of German culture, especially the contested claim on the "humanist" heritage. Many of the articles in the exile journal *Freies Deutschland* were republished in the postwar publications *Aufbau* and *Weltbühne*, thus establishing continuities between the wartime publication activity in Mexico and the postwar journals in Berlin. In Mexico, Alexander Abusch also began work on his book *Der Irrweg einer Nation* (*A Nation's Errant Path*), published in 1946 in Berlin and a counterargument to both "Vansittartism" and Friedrich Meinecke's *Die deutsche Katastrophe* (*The German Catastrophe*). While Germans after the war seemed content to leave the retribution against Nazi individuals to the Allies, German intellectuals in East and West, schooled in the "culture wars" against Goebbels and Vansittart, were ready to pass judgment on German culture themselves.

3 The "Other Germany" from Below: Antifascist Committees and National Renewal in 1945

While in faraway places such as Mexico, communist intellectuals shaped antifascism into a militant project of cultural renewal, Allied troops advancing into German territory during the last days of the war were often greeted by representatives of antifascist grassroots organizations and committees (antifas). During the chaos of the Nazi dictatorship's breakdown, these groups had taken over local power structures in many places and had begun to "cleanse" positions in the local governments and economies of Nazi Party members and officials. Thus, when U.S. troops entered Leipzig in May 1945, they did not encounter the expected Nazi "Werewolf" insurgents, but members of the National Committee for a Free Germany (Nationalkomitee Freies Deutschland [[NKFD]). Although dominated by the resurfaced Communist Party of Germany (KPD), the committee, which claimed to have more than 6,000 members, was based on a broad pluralist appeal. In its drive to recruit members, an NKFD leaflet emphasized its open definition of antifascism: "This movement is neither a party nor a club [*Verein*] but a spiritual connection [*geistige Bindung*] that encompasses all antifascists regardless of their religious or political confessions."[1] As this chapter will show, the antifa activism that flared up briefly in the first postwar months showed some of the same preoccupation with German identity and national renewal as the intellectual discussion groups of antifascist exiles.

Like the exile cultural leagues discussed in the previous chapter, the antifa movement rested on the Popular Front ideal of broad antifascist alliances that transcended the traditional party boundaries not only among the working-class parties, but also among liberal-bourgeois and national-conservative opposition movements. As noted before in this work, after 1934, these coalitions had survived mainly in exile circles of oppositional intellectuals, but not in the form of antifascist "grassroots" movements in Germany itself. In the spring and summer of 1945 – for

---

[1] National Komitee "Freies Deutschland" in Leipzig, SAPMO – BArch, SgY 26/1 G125/1, Blatt 11 and Blatt 27.

the first time again after the unsuccessful Saar referendum – the antifa movement represented a resurrected Popular Front antifascism that complemented and went beyond the relatively small, conspiratorial circles of émigré intellectuals or exiled communist functionaries discussed in the previous chapter. According to standard historical accounts of the immediate postwar period, they also constituted the "first and only political initiative with revolutionary potential" in the defeated and occupied Reich.[2] Unlike in other European countries, though, the domestic German Popular Front resistance that emerged at the end of the war in the form of loosely organized leftist committees reflected the desperate situation of a militarily defeated Third Reich, rather than an overwhelming popular opposition to the NS regime before 1945. The antifas never became true mass movements, and therefore were never a seriously considered political alternative to the Allied occupation regimes or the reestablishment of German parliamentary politics. The political goals and organizational forms of *rätedemokratische* (council democratic) Popular Front groups did not only face opposition by Allied and German plans for postwar Germany. They also ran against the grain of political activism after 1945, when interwar mass mobilization and class agitation gave way to parliamentary politics by consensus-based *Volksparteien* (mass-based parties) and interest groups. As a result, antifascism never became a political force "from below" in either the eastern or western half of postwar Germany.

The NKFD in Leipzig was one of the largest of these antifascist groups. The name derived from the resistance groups that the Soviets had formed in Moscow out of the ranks of German communists and POWs.[3] The foundation of the NKFD in Moscow followed in the footsteps of Popular Front exile organizations such as the Free Germany Movement (BFD) in Mexico, which was discussed earlier in this work. After the Red Army's military success at Stalingrad, the NKFD was the Soviet Union's attempt to create an indigenous German military resistance from the ranks of German communists and POWs. It appealed to the prospect of a KPD-led reconstruction of Germany, but also to hopes among national-conservative Wehrmacht officers for more favorable peace terms if Germany liberated itself and avoided occupation.[4]

---

[2] Theodor Eschenburg, *Geschichte der Bundesrepublik Deutschland, Band 1. Jahre der Besatzung 1945–1949* (Stuttgart: Deutsche Verlagsanstalt, 1983), 107.

[3] Letter of the NKFD Leipzig to the High Command of the Red Army, May 5, 1945, SAPMO – BArch, SgY 26/1, V G125/1, Bl. 5.

[4] For an account of the NKFD in Moscow, see Wolfgang Leonhard, *Child of the Revolution*, trans. C. M. Woodhouse (London: Ink Links, 1979), 240–86; see also Gerd R. Ueberschärr, *Für ein anderes Deutschland. Der deutsche Widerstand gegen den NS-Staat 1933–1945* (Frankfurt a. M.: Fischer Taschenbuch Verlag, 2006), 141–9.

However, the NKFD's efforts to sway German soldiers to defect or the German population to overthrow Nazi authorities never yielded much fruit. The radio transmissions from Moscow reached communists and Social Democrats in Leipzig, who adopted the name NKFD for their illegal group.[5] At the end of the war, with the Red Army deep in German territory, the NKFD and its local antifas were welcomed as temporary assistance to the Russians' advance; they were not seen as political alternatives to the establishment of Soviet occupation authorities. By November 1945, both the Moscow-centered and the local NKFDs were dissolved, to the disappointment of many German leftists and their hopes for a more autonomous socialist reconstruction of Germany.[6]

The Marxist historiography of the German Democratic Republic (GDR) portrayed the antifa groups as "activists of the first hour" who paved the way for the unification of the working-class parties into the Socialist Unity Party (SED) and who harmoniously cooperated with the Red Army on denazification and the setup of new local administrations.[7] It also emphasized the early prohibition of antifas in many localities under Western Allied administration, which were seen – not unjustifiably – as Cold War suppression of communist activities.[8] Standard GDR history textbooks did not mention that Stalin and KPD leader Walter Ulbricht disbanded the antifas in the Soviet Occupation Zone (SBZ) by June 1945 because of the Party leadership's distrust of the "relatively free-floating leftist committees," which usually consisted of broader Popular Front alliances between communists, Social Democrats, trade union activists, and bourgeois Nazi opponents.[9] The GDR historiography also stayed silent on the disappointment some local communist antifa leaders felt

---

[5] Letter of the NKFD Leipzig to the High Command of the Red Army, May 5, 1945, SAPMO – BArch, SgY 26/1, V G125/1, Bl. 5.
[6] See Norman M. Naimark, *The Russians in Germany: A History of the Soviet Zone of Occupation, 1945–1949* (Cambridge, MA: Harvard University Press, 1995), 253; Gareth Pritchard, *The Making of the GDR: From Antifascism to Stalinism, 1945–53* (Manchester: Manchester University Press, 2000), 30–55; Timothy R. Vogt, *Denazification in Soviet-Occupied Germany: Brandenburg, 1945–1948* (Cambridge, MA: Harvard University Press, 2000); Lutz Niethammer, Ulrich Bosdorf, and Peter Brandt, eds., *Arbeiterinitiative 1945. Antifaschistische Ausschüsse und Reorganisation der Arbeiterbewegung in Deutschland* (Wuppertal: Peter Hammer Verlag, 1976), 249–51.
[7] See Institut für Marxismus-Leninismus beim Zentralkomitee der SED, *Geschichte der deutschen Arbeiterbewegung, Band 6: Von Mai 1945 bis 1949* (Berlin [East]: Dietz, 1966), 23–5.
[8] See, for example, the GDR standard history by Rolf Badstübner et al., *Deutsche Geschichte, Band 9. Die antifaschistisch-demokratische Umwälzung, der Kampf gegen die Spaltung Deutschlands und die Entstehung der DDR von 1945 bis 1949* (Berlin [East] and Köln: Pahl-Rugenstein, 1989), 16–21.
[9] Naimark, *The Russians in Germany*, 271; see also Leonhard, *Child of the Revolution*, 318–26.

over the Red Army's conduct in the territories it occupied – especially the widespread and traumatic experiences of rapes committed by Russian soldiers.[10]

In the German Democratic Republic, the existence of the antifas became part of antifascism's official "foundation myth." The existence of the committees legitimized the East German state's self-image as having been built on the shoulders of popular working-class resistance against the Third Reich. In the postwar West, on the other hand, the history of the movement played an almost nonexistent role. While the official memory of anti-Nazi resistance in West Germany has been dominated by the Stauffenberg circle or the student resisters of the "White Rose," the socialist rhetoric of the grassroots antifas made their legacy ill-suited as a foundation for the Federal Republic. Instead, West German histories of the period usually emphasize the antifas' enduring influence on the institution of works councils (*Betriebsräte*) and the concept of co-determination (*Mitbestimmung*) in the Federal Republic's social market economy.[11] Moreover, the legitimacy of those antifas that were regarded as Moscow-controlled through their affiliation with the NKFD were especially controversial: former members of the NKFD who had fought alongside the Red Army against the German military were – like former members of the SS – excluded from the newly created Bundeswehr in the Federal Republic.[12]

Unlike the Soviet Union, the Western Allies, in their fight against Nazi Germany during World War II, never explored the strategy of supporting an armed domestic German resistance. American observer Arthur D. Kahn, who witnessed the end of the war as an officer in the Psychological Warfare Division of the Office of Strategic Studies (OSS), complained bitterly about a Supreme Headquarters of the Allied Expeditionary Forces (SHAEF) directive not to exhort German citizens to rise up against Nazi commands. In October 1944, for example, with American troops closing in on the border city of Aachen, citizens

---

[10] Naimark, *The Russians in Germany*, 85; see also Atina Grossman, *Jews, Germans, and Allies: Close Encounters in Occupied Germany* (Princeton, NJ: Princeton University Press, 2007).

[11] See, for example, Christoph Kleßmann, *Die doppelte Staatsgründung: Deutsche Geschichte 1945–1955* (Göttingen: Vandenhoek & Ruprecht, 1982), 121–6; Eschenburg, *Jahre der Besatzung*, 107. For workers' initiatives and work councils in the Soviet Occupation Zone, see Siegfried Suckut, *Die Betriebsrätebewegung in der Sowjetisch Besetzten Zone Deutschlands (1945–1948): Zur Entwicklung und Bedeutung von Arbeiterinitiative, betrieblicher Mitbestimmung und Selbstbestimmung bis zur Revision des programmatischen Konzeptes der KPD/SED vom "besonderen deutschen Weg zum Sozialismus"* (Frankfurt/Main: Haag und Herchen, 1982).

[12] See Kai P. Schoenhals, *The Free German Movement: A Case of Patriotism or Treason?* (New York: Greenwood Press, 1989), 1.

refused Nazi orders to either evacuate the town or defend it "to the last man." A "regular battle" broke out between revolting civilians – apparently supported by Wehrmacht units – and the Hitler-loyal SA and SS.[13] According to Kahn's assessment, active American encouragement of such revolts could have shortened the war. The SHAEF directive strengthened the Western Allies' position in the budding Cold War by limiting the influence of the reemerging KPD, but it also complicated an indigenous German denazification, and it might have prevented more spontaneous acts of retribution against Nazi functionaries.

Despite the revolutionary potential of militant antifascist groups, defeated Germany did not exhibit the kind of "spontaneous, popular demand for revenge which manifested itself in instant executions, lynchings and public humiliations" and which cost the lives of tens of thousands of real and alleged Nazi collaborators in liberated European countries.[14] The specter of indigenous violent anti-Nazi purges in the immediate wake of the NS regime's breakdown is alluded to in OSS officer Kahn's conversations with the U.S.-appointed German officeholders in occupied Mainz, who were convinced that "if the Western Allies had not imposed restraints, the German people would have conducted a massive denazification on their own." The re-installed Social Democratic police president of Mainz, Jacob Steffan, told Kahn: "The Nazis are grateful … to the Americans. If not for you, there would have been a frightful bloodbath. All the Nazis would have been killed."[15] In fact, however, the breakdown of NS structures seemed to be accompanied by little popular violence by Germans against individual Nazi perpetrators. Acts of retribution by the antifas usually took the shape of coercing former NS officials to perform reconstruction work. In May 1945, former party officials in the Ruhr city of Duisburg, for example, were notified that "Party members, friends, and sponsors of the Nazi clique" had to report to work for the Action Committee for Reconstruction (Aktionsausschuß für Wiederaufbau). If the notified did not show up, the Action Committee flyers threatened, "dismissed political inmates would see to [the former Nazis'] attendance."[16]

---

[13] Arthur D. Kahn, *Experiment in Occupation. Witness to the Turnabout: Anti-Nazi War to Cold War, 1944–1946* (University Park: University of Pennsylvania Press, 2004), 17, 184–5.
[14] See István Deák, Jan T. Gross, and Tony Judt, *The Politics of Retribution in Europe: World War II and Its Aftermath* (Princeton, NJ: Princeton University Press, 2000).
[15] Kahn, *Experiment in Occupation*, 47.
[16] "Mitteilung des 'Aktionsausschuß für Wiederaufbau zur Heranziehung von den Parteigenossen, Freunden und Gönnern der Naziclique zur Wegräumung von Strassensperren," 9. Mai 45. StA DU: OB Akte Weitz 100/39, "Aufrechterhaltung der öffentlichen Sicherheit und Ordnung durch die Militärregierung," Bl. 89.

Antifa leaflets of the last weeks of the war and the early postwar months emphasized the existence of "the other Germany" by reminding the Allies of indigenous efforts at resisting the Nazi regime such as the Freiheitsaktion Bayern (Freedom Action Bavaria [FAB]). The Antifaschistisches Aktionskomitee (Antifascist Action Committee [Afa]) in Munich, for example, expressed concerns that U.S. troops, outraged by the sight of "heaps of dead bodies" at the nearby Dachau concentration camp, would resort to an indiscriminate punishment of the civilian population. The Afa reminded the occupation power of a failed uprising of workers at Dachau – and its tragic crackdown by Nazi-loyal troops – to argue against an anticipated collective punishment.[17]

Both the Kampfgemeinschaft gegen den Faschismus (KGF) in Bremen and the NKFD in Leipzig, in one of their leaflets, explicitly asked, "Are the German people guilty?"[18] The NKFD answered the question with a qualified "no": "Not the German people as a whole, but predominantly the Nazis, the militarists, and the war criminals are guilty." However, similarly to the KGF's publication *Aufbau*, the NKFD leaflet added, "the German people are guilty to the extent that they were not capable of toppling the Hitler regime by themselves." The NKFD also critically confronted those "who claim they didn't know anything." The leaflet called for the population to "report all active Nazis who now suffered from amnesia."[19] "Joy," because of the liberation from National Socialism, and "shame," because Germans had not had the strength to liberate themselves, also mingled in the greetings that the Red Army received from the antifas in Gera and other places in Thuringia.[20]

The antifas felt legitimized to ask for permissive treatment because in many regions of Germany, the activities of antifa committees seemed to have been not only attempts at replacing Nazi leadership structures, but also the earliest form of *Vergangenheitsbewältigung* (coming to terms with the past). In Thuringia, a leaflet of the Anti-Nazi-Komitee Jena proclaimed that the Nazis had "cruelly persecuted and slaughtered the Jews

---

[17] Leaflet of the *Antifaschistisches Aktionskomitee in Munich*, n. d., SAPMO – BArch, SgY 26/2, Bl. 83. The Dachau uprising in April 1945 was linked to the activities of the FAB, a group of Wehrmacht officers and civilians in Munich whose attempt to deliver the city to U.S. troops was crushed by the still functioning NS structures. More than 100 people were killed in retaliatory punishment by the Nazis. See Ueberschär, *Für ein anderes Deutschland*, 236.

[18] *Der Aufbau– Organ der Kampfgemeinschaft gegen den Faschismus*, Nr. 4, July 1945, SAPMO – BArch, SgY 26/4, Bl. 30. For the KGF, see also Peter Brandt, *Antifaschismus und Arbeiterbewegung. Aufbau – Ausprägung – Politik in Bremen 1945/46*. Hamburger Beiträge zur Sozial- und Zeitgeschichte, Band XI (Hamburg: Hans Christians Verlag, 1976).

[19] SAPMO – BArch, SgY 26/1 G125/1, Bl. 20.

[20] Ibid., Bl. 39/40.

at home as well as in occupied countries"; as a result, they had "degraded the nation of poets and thinkers [*das Volk der Dichter und Denker*] into a nation of murderers and henchmen [*Volk der Mörder und Henker*] and desecrated the German name in the whole civilized world. In the eyes of the world we are completely extinguished as a cultural nation [*Kulturvolk*]."[21] In addition to its mention of German atrocities – again restricted to Nazis, not Germans, as culprits – this leaflet conveys how the catastrophe of guilt and defeat was felt to have diminished German high culture and its standing in the rest of the world.

Neither were the appeals to the German humanist heritage and the idea of a nationalist renewal to eradicate Nazism from Germany restricted to exile intellectuals. An illegally distributed communist leaflet during the war was headlined "Der Ruf unserer Ahnen" (Our Ancestors' Call). Underneath the headline, the leaflet featured a quote by the Reformation humanist Ulrich von Hutten: "*Erbarmt euch übers Vaterland,/ihr werten Teutschen, regt die Hand.*"[22] The Hutten quote was printed next to Friedrich Schiller's famous appeal to anti-tyrannical revolt from his play *Wilhelm Tell*: "Where there is no justice to be found for the oppressed/ When the burden becomes unbearable – then he reaches confidently to the skies/and takes hold of his eternal rights." Underneath the quotes, an appeal to resistance against the Nazi regime began with the statement: "Germany can only be saved by Germans!"[23]

Other examples indicate that the activists of the antifa movements were not only engaged in the struggle against fascism, but also participants in the debates around "Vansittartism," the question whether a true German antifascism could exist in a culture that had borne the Nazi regime and ideology after – as this view held – centuries of authoritarian and militarist gestation. Not only their sharp distinction between Germany and Nazism distinguished German antifascists from Vansittartists, but also their different attitudes toward Nazi Party members themselves. The call for a radical, sweeping anti-Nazi purge in the early versions of the U.S. Joint Chiefs of Staff Directive 1067 (JCS 1067) was drafted under the influence of the Vansittartist faction of advisors within the Roosevelt

---

[21] Leaflet of the Anti-Nazi-Komitee Jena, n. d., SAPMO – BArch, SgY 26/1 G125/1/3 Bl. 30.

[22] "Have pity with the fatherland/You noble Germans, raise your hands"); see the image in Ueberschär, *Für ein anderes Deutschland*, 80.

[23] Ibid. The full stanza in Schiller's play is: "Nein, eine Grenze hat Tyrannenmacht:/Wenn der Gedrückte nirgends Recht kann finden,/Wenn unerträglich wird die Last – greift er/Hinauf getrosten Mutes in den Himmel/Und holt herunter seine ew'gen Rechte,/ Die droben hangen unveräusserlich/Und unzerbrechlich, wie die Sterne selbst – /Der alte Urstand der Natur kehrt wieder,/Wo Mensch dem Menschen gegenübersteht/Zum letzten Mittel, wenn kein andres mehr/Verfangen will, ist ihm das Schwert gegeben."

administration.²⁴ For Vansittartists, National Socialism was the manifestation of German national character. Yet even though the antifa stance toward purging society went farther than most Germans – and some among the Allies – were prepared to go, the committees saw their activities as endogenous contribution to the liberation of a country that – in their eyes – had been as much the victim as the perpetrator of Nazism. Consequently, just as for the intellectual combatants in the exile culture wars, with the defeat of Nazi regime the meaning of antifascism shifted. Its focus became the refutation of generalized accusations against German national character while at the same time critically investigating the recent and more distant past. While antifascist intellectuals in their exile publications tried to salvage the German legacy from the rubble heap of the Nazi crimes, the antifascist committees represented "the other Germany" from below.

It is doubtful, however, whether the antifa movement would have had become a long-term force of revolutionary change in Germany even without the presence of Allied occupation. The movement's understanding of direct democracy and its reliance on non-party-based political mobilization went against the grain of the transformation of mass politics and the changed forms of political organization after 1945. Therefore, unlike the new or reestablished parliamentary parties in the Western zones, the antifas' informal grassroots democracy model, and their vaguely nationalistic attempts at making antifascism the basis of a reconstructed socialist Germany, never developed into a nationwide movement. By the end of 1945, individual committees wrote letters "for the purposes of establishing contact" with other groups, but nowhere did this translate into efforts to transform the antifas into a national parliamentary force.²⁵ Instead, many leaflets, such as one by the Afa in Munich, rejected the formation of parties. According to the Afa leaflet, the loss of pluralist, antifascist unity would impede the urgent efforts at mitigating the postwar hardships.²⁶ The antipathy toward party formation, therefore, was not only a result of Allied attempts to control the political reconstruction in their respective occupation zones. The rejection of party politics also reflected the experience of fragmentation during the Weimar period, a sentiment

---

[24] See Lutz Niethammer, *Entnazifizierung in Bayern: Säuberung und Rehabilitierung unter amerikanischer Besatzung* (Frankfurt am Main: Fischer, 1972), 34–47; for a discussion of the conflict within the Roosevelt administration between "Vansittartists," such as treasury secretary Henry Morgenthau, and "outlaw theorists," who held that the Nazi revolution stood outside the realm of German legal norms.
[25] Letter from the Verband der Anti Nazi-Faschisten Bad Godesberg to the Verband der Anti Faschisten Wuppertal, October 11, 1945, SAPMO – BArch, SgY 26/2 Bl. 22.
[26] Leaflet of the Antifaschistisches Aktionskomitee München, n. d., SAPMO – BArch, SgY 26/2 Bl. 83.

that was expressed, for example, in a letter to the Zentralausschuss in Wuppertal: "We have five parties now, but, knowing our dear Germans, soon there will be fifteen." The letter writer urged the Zentralausschuss to "look for and cultivate the common bonds between the parties."[27]

To the *actual* political parties, which started to reappear or establish themselves in the four occupation zones from the end of 1945, the exact purpose and hierarchy structure of the antifas were not always clear. In October 1945, the Zentralausschuss in Wuppertal received a written inquiry by the Christian Democrats as to when the committee was founded and who its carrier was. The Christian Democrats were also wondering "whether the 'democratic popular movement' constituted a new party" and inquired "what the Central Committee's program or goal was, apart from what needs to be done right away for the urgent needs of the population."[28] The Zentralausschuss's reply is not known, but it is likely to have been along the lines of the following declaration in the KGF's *Aufbau* from May 6, 1945. The declaration emphasized that the Kampfgemeinschaft was not a party, but "an alliance between all anti-fascists." Like their equivalent groups in other parts of Germany, the committee in Bremen called for the "intellectual, spiritual, and political process of the German people's self-cleansing [*geistigen, seelischen und politischen Selbstreinigungsprozeß des deutschen Volkes*]."[29]

In spite of the popular sentiment against parliamentary politics, the committees' concept of democracy and political reconstruction presupposed the ability to mobilize and unite masses of people in the name of an antifascism that for most had outlived its purpose with the end of the NS regime. In one of the earliest memoranda to its local cells, the KGF leadership in Bremen urged: "If we are to achieve decisive influence on the emerging new order of all social life, it will mainly depend on the political influence that our organization will gain by mobilizing all antifascist forces." In July 1945, the KGF organ *Aufbau* explained: "Democratic structures and laws are important and necessary, but the practice and the manner of applying democracy are even more critical.... True democracy can only exist if the broad masses are at all times vigilant and prepared to fight for the defense of democratic rights against forces who, under the disguise of democratic speeches and purely formal democratic procedures, pursue dictatorial aims and reactionary politics."[30]

---

[27] Letter from Albert Forthmann to the Wuppertaler Zentralausschuss, November 6, 1945, SAPMO – BArch, SgY 26/2 Bl. 19.
[28] Letter to the Zentralausschuss Wuppertal from October 19, 1945, SAPMO – BArch, SgY 26/2 Bl. 35.
[29] *Der Aufbau – Organ der Kampfgemeinschaft gegen den Faschismus*, Bremen, May 6, 1945, SAPMO – BArch, SgY 26/4 Bl. 8, Bl. 19. Emphasis in original.
[30] Quoted in Brandt, *Antifaschismus und Arbeiterbewegung*, 122, 119.

The appeal to the mobilization of the "broad masses" appears almost quixotic in its attempt to reverse the process of "disintegration and de-idealization" that differentiated the postwar era from the first half of the twentieth century.[31] The repression of the antifas by the Allied authorities seemed to have encountered no protest by the wider population; the U.S. military government in southern Germany claimed a "continuing apathy" of the Germans in their occupation zone.[32] This assessment may have been self-serving, but unquestionably the failure of Weimar democracy, the "reorganization and fragmentation" of the working class under the Nazis, as well as the experiences of mass agitation, total war, and defeat, had created a "strongly reduced mobilization potential" even among workers.[33] Thus, when the Kampfbund gegen den Faschismus in Essen renamed itself Einheitsorganisation der Arbeiterschaft (United Organization of Workers) and developed rudimentary "party-like structures" with formal membership recruitments and collection of membership dues, its appeal to the unity of workers of all confessions and political parties found little resonance. Moreover, even before the prohibitions by the Allied authorities, the remaining Communists in the antifas had begun to abandon the committees to focus on the reformation of the KPD.[34]

Therefore, despite their takeover of factories and the establishment of works councils – on the surface the most revolutionary action of the committees – the antifas did not resume the tradition of the workers' and soldiers' councils of the 1918 revolution.[35] Lutz Niethammer's research among mining workers at the Ruhr showed that the pre-1933 allegiance of most works council members to communist or Catholic working-class organizations was replaced by an almost nearly complete hegemony of the restructured SPD after 1945.[36] After the war, the vast majority of Germans in the Western zones preferred the more consensus-oriented

---

[31] Martin Broszat, Klaus-Dietmar Henke, and Hans Woller, eds., *Von Stalingrad zur Währungsreform: Zur Sozialgeschichte des Umbruchs in Deutschland*. Quellen und Darstellungen zur Zeitgeschichte. Herausgegeben vom Institut für Zeitgeschichte, Band 26 (Munich: R. Oldenbourg Verlag, 1988), xxvii.

[32] Niethammer, *Entnazifizierung in Bayern*, 137.

[33] Nolan, "Antifascism under Fascism," 55; Brandt, *Antifaschismus und Arbeiterbewegung*, 107.

[34] Hartmut Pietsch, *Militärregierung, Bürokratie und Sozialisierung. Zur Entwicklung des politischen Systems in den Städten des Ruhrgebietes 1945 bis 1948*. Duisburger Forschungen: Schriftenreihe für Geschichte und Heimatkunde Duisburgs, 26. Band (Duisburg: Walter Braun Verlag, 1978), 113, 114.

[35] See Brandt, *Antifaschismus und Arbeiterbewegung*, 105. See also Eberhard Kolb, *Die Arbeiterräte in der deutschen Innenpolitik 1918–1919* (München: Ullstein, 1978).

[36] See Lutz Niethammer, ed., *"Hinterher merkt man, daß es richtig war, daß es schiefgegangen ist." Nachkriegs-Erfahrungen im Ruhrgebiet* (Berlin: Verlag J. H. W. Dietz Nachf., 1983), 7, 311–12.

and "managerial" style of the reestablished trade unions and the new *Volksparteien* to the radical and revolutionary politics of the Weimar left.[37]

Instead of reviving the traditions of the 1918 revolution, the antifa version of antifascism seems to be the last remnant of Weimar-era mass politics. The very names for the antifa groups – the plethora of antifascist *Kampfgemeinschaften* (militant associations) or *Aktionsgruppen* (action groups) – imply a conflation of politics and combat that evokes the paramilitary political organizations of the turbulent Weimar democracy rather than the situation in Germany after twelve years of Nazi rule. Thus, antifas such as the KGF still adhered – on a local, rather than national level – to the rhetoric and activist self-understanding of such organizations as the SPD's Reichsbanner or the KPD's Roter Frontkämpferbund. As James M. Diehl argues, paramilitary politics " – which had their Right-wing manifestations in Stahlhelm and SA (the Nazis' 'Storm Division') – became a surrogate for the unresolved civil war that had followed the incomplete revolution of 1918." Moreover, these "combat leagues had continued and radicalized the practice during the Empire of ' blocbuilding' (*Blockbildungen*), the formation of militant 'blocs,' 'cartels,' 'fronts,' and 'movements' designed to mobilize mass support either in favor of or in opposition to the prevailing social and political order."[38]

The "transformation of the public domain" in the second half of the twentieth century seems prefigured in the antifas' own inner tensions between paramilitary revolutionary mass organizations and small, localized communities of antifascists serving as deputies to the Allies. The democratic "self-cleansing processes" that the KGF's *Aufbau* demanded, for example, took place not in mass rallies, but in the group's street cells, which organized weekly "discussion and reading nights" and "courses on general political, economic, and cultural topics."[39] These rudimentary "cells of public life" in the first postwar period had more in common with the exile antifascist cultural leagues than with the "totalitarian choreography of the masses" that characterized right-wing as well as left-wing politics during the interwar years.[40] Seemingly continuing antifascist activities of the war period, the KGF's publication *Aufbau* was

---

[37] See Kleßmann, *Die doppelte Staatsgründung*, 125. See also Arno Klönne, "Die gebrochene Tradition: Arbeitermilieu und gewerkschaftliche Organisation im Ruhrgebiet nach 1945," in Jan-Pieter Barbian and Ludger Heid, eds., *Zwischen Gestern und Morgen: Kriegsende und Wiederaufbau im Ruhrgebiet* (Essen: Klartext Verlag, 1995), 136–44.

[38] James M. Diehl, *Paramilitary Politics in Weimar Germany* (Bloomington: University of Indiana Press, 1977), 21, 4; see also Richard J. Evans, *The Coming of the Third Reich* (New York: Penguin, 2003), 73–4.

[39] Quoted in Brandt, *Antifaschismus und Arbeiterbewegung*, 113.

[40] See Peukert, *Die Weimarer Republik*, 164.

characterized more by "basic antifascist enlightenment" than by concrete discussion or analysis of national or international news. Rather, *Aufbau* printed articles that rejected a collective responsibility of Germans for the NS regime by explaining the historical trajectories of class and finance capitalism.[41]

Perhaps ironically, the tasks of reconstruction required the mobilization of a large part of the defeated German population – most notably German women, many of whom had only shortly before enjoyed the leisure activities of the BDM and other NS organizations. The much-analyzed absence of men in early postwar Germany through war and captivity might not have prevented the restoration of patriarchal gender norms in the 1950s, but it did seem to have had an enduring effect on the post-1945 public sphere. The often male-gendered rituals and the martial rhetoric of paramilitary politics did not return. As Elizabeth Heineman has shown, the foundational icon of West German collective identity became the "woman of the rubble," not the – predominantly male – antifa militia member.[42]

Rather than the slogans of revolutionary antifascism, West German politicians of the established parties used a language that emphasized national consensus, civic duty, and a restrained sense of patriotism instead of nationalist pathos. In the *Stuttgarter Zeitung* from September 26, 1945, SPD politician Carlo Schmid appealed to the Germans in the French Occupation Zone to participate in the reconstruction efforts under Allied direction. Schmid pointed out the necessity to "speak as little as possible in abstract terms [*Begrifflichkeiten*] but rather in concrete terms [*Dinglichkeiten*]." The article dismissed not only the disastrous "heroism of the downfall" that the Nazis promoted, but it also implicitly distanced itself from the Communist propaganda of a heroic antifascist struggle as basis for a new beginning. Schmid emphasized the concrete, but mundane chores of reconstruction under Allied direction and defended them against attacks of trading "the black flag of heroic uprising for the white flag of surrender." Employing Christian imagery,

---

[41] Brandt, *Antifaschismus und Arbeiterbewegung*, 119.
[42] See Elizabeth Heineman, "The Hour of the Woman: Memories of Germany's 'Crisis Years' and West German National Identity," *American Historical Review*, 101, 2 (April 1996): 354–95. For the limited and complex process of "remasculinazation" of returning German POWs in the FRG and the GDR, see Frank Biess, *Homecomings: Returning POWs and the Legacies of Defeat in Postwar Germany* (Princeton, NJ: Princeton University Press, 2006). For the "gendering" – and privileging – of the male antifascist fighter in the official culture of the GDR, see Catherine J. Plum, "Feminine Heroes, Masculine Superheroes? Antifascist Education and Children's Literature in the German Democratic Republic (GDR)," in *Témoigner entre histoire et mémoire. Revue pluridisciplinaire de la Fondation Auschwitz Bruxelles, No104 (July–September 2009) :L'Antifascisme revisité. Histoire – idéologie – mémoire* (Paris: Éditions Kimé, 2009): 161–74.

the southwest German politician called for a "work without pathos, a toiling for small, unglamorous things, a walk through a thousand humiliations, a daily moaning under blows to the neck."[43]

The Social Democrat Schmid was in many respects typical of the politicians who dominated the new and reestablished West German political parties in the immediate postwar period. During the war, Schmid had served as "legal advisor" to the German military command in occupied France, but he had been barred from any promotions or career advances because of "a lack of ideological reliability."[44] Like the Liberal Theodor Heuss and the Christian Democrat Konrad Adenauer, Schmid had suffered disadvantages through his noncompliance with the NS system without becoming what could be described as an all-out resistance fighter. The uncompromising revolutionary antifascism the antifas envisioned reflected the experience of far fewer Germans.

It was part of the new "structure of stability" in Europe after 1945 that most West Germans – after the demise of the antifas – did not regard antifascism as an appropriate base for mass politics. After the initial – and rather restrained – actions of popular retribution by the antifas, one aspect of antifascism – retribution against Nazi perpetrators – was first left to the Nuremberg Trials and other Allied tribunals, then allowed to peter out in the West German denazification courts. The other thrust of antifascist activism, the intense intellectual preoccupation with fascism and its relationship to German culture that had characterized exile periodicals and cultural leagues, but also reverberated in antifa leaflets and street cell discussions, found a new location in a public sphere of cultural-political journals and discussion circles.

The antifa movement in the second half of 1945 carried elements of the interwar paramilitary politics in the groups' organizational forms and rhetorical strategies, but the movement served as an intermediate form of mass politics that channeled the remaining potential for militant mobilization in Germany into early activities of denazification and reconstruction. The influence of the occupation powers and the lack of a mass basis led to very limited and restrained acts of popular retribution, but the antifas were also part of the critique of both the rehabilitative practices of the Allies and of sweeping conflations of Nazis and German antifascists. The demise of the antifa movement meant that these critiques were not to be continued in the realm of mass politics. After 1945, politics in West Germany became the business of the new *Volksparteien*

---

[43] Carlo Schmid, "Vaterländische Verantwortung," in Eberhard Rathgeb, ed., *Die engagierte Nation. Deutsche Debatten, 1945–2005* (Munich: Carl Hanser Verlag, 2005), 19–20.
[44] Ibid., 17.

rather than of quasi-revolutionary *Kampfgruppen* (militant groups) and grassroots democratic street cells.

A parallel development took place in the Soviet Occupation Zone. By Order No. 1 of June 9, 1945, the Russians established the Soviet Military Administration in Germany (Sowjetische Militäradministration in Deutschland [SMAD]). The order also dissolved many of the roughly 200 antifascist committees in the SBZ.[45] With the simultaneous demise of the antifa movement in the Western zones – through either Allied policies or lack of German support, or both – antifascism had ceased to be a revolutionary concept. By summer of 1945, SMAD Order No. 2 allowed the formation of political parties and mass organizations in the SBZ. As we will see, officially nonpartisan mass organizations aimed to combine interwar mass politics with the pluralist cultural discussion groups of the exile leagues. Antifascism survived the collapse of fascism not as a revolutionary force but as a project of *cultural* renewal.

---

[45] See Naimark, *The Russians in Germany*, 259. See also Vogt, *Denazification in Soviet-Occupied Germany*.

Part II

Contesting "Other Germanies"

4 Antifascism as Renewal and Restoration: The Cultural League for the Democratic Renewal of Germany, 1945–1946

One of the key organizations that carried the ideals and concepts of antifascism, especially the idea of a socialist humanism, into the postwar era was the Kulturbund zur demokratischen Erneuerung Deutschlands (Cultural League for the Democratic Renewal of Germany) in the Soviet Occupation Zone (SBZ). In many historical accounts, the establishment of the Kulturbund has served as an example of the Stalinist strategy during the early postwar years of binding intellectuals to the Communist Party under the guise of nonpartisan antifascism.[1] Other analyses stress the relative ideological openness of the early Kulturbund and its potential for a more democratic socialism than the one that eventually emerged in the form of the Socialist Unity Party (SED) dictatorship.[2] However, while many studies focus on the continuities between the communist objectives before and after 1945, this chapter places the Kulturbund in the context of wider intellectual trends in twentieth-century German history. It argues that in addition to serving communist front tactics, the Kulturbund and its brand of antifascism found broad appeal among communists *and* liberal intellectuals because it promised the fulfillment of prewar ideas of cultural renewal and the bridging of the deep rifts among German intellectuals since the interwar era and especially after 1933.

The transformation of antifascism into a cultural project continued within a unique public sphere that dominated the cultural scene of the first postwar years in all four German occupation zones. The decade-long

---

[1] See especially David Pike, *The Politics of Culture in Soviet-Occupied Germany, 1945–1949* (Stanford, CA: Stanford University Press, 1992) and Magdalena Heider, *Politik – Kultur – Kulturbund. Zur Gründungs- und Frühgeschichte des Kulturbundes zur demokratischen Erneuerung Deutschlands 1945–1954 in der SBZ/DDR* (Köln: Verlag Wissenschaft und Politik, 1993). Cf. Norman M. Naimark, *The Russians in Germany: A History of the Soviet Zone of Occupation, 1945–1949* (Cambridge, MA: The Belknap Press of Harvard University Press, 1995), 400–8.

[2] See, for example, Gerd Dietrich, *Politik und Kultur in der Sowjetischen Besatzungszone Deutschlands (SBZ), 1945–1949. Mit einem Dokumentenanhang* (Bern, Switzerland: Peter Lang, 1993).

"cultural civil war" between Nazi propaganda and antifascist intellectuals had given birth to a thriving landscape of literary-political journals among the rubble of German cities. In a development that ran parallel to the rich publishing activity, formal and informal discussion circles or cultural leagues were formed in many German cities.[3] It is not difficult to discern continuities with the exile cultural leagues, but also groups of the "inner emigration," such as the circle around the NS-approved, but in its own self-understanding oppositional paper *Das Innere Reich*.[4] As Jeffrey K. Olick argues, between 1945 and 1949, in the absence of an "official," i.e., state-orchestrated interpretation and memory of the recent past, these institutions – and intellectuals in general – became especially influential.[5] With the moral authority of the two major Christian churches compromised by their cooperation with the NS regime, intellectuals and their institutions assumed the quasi-religious responsibilities of mourning the past and expiating the nation's collective sins – however insufficiently they fulfilled these tasks in the eyes of contemporary and later observers.[6] The pages of the literary-political journals also provided the responses to the charges of collective guilt that were voiced from outside as well as inside defeated Germany.

The Kulturbund zur demokratischen Erneuerung Deutschlands in Berlin was one among the numerous "cultural leagues" that emerged in all four German occupation zones after May 1945. It exemplified the transition from the broad antifascist consensus of exile opposition movements and the grassroots antifas – and their vague ideas of non-party-bound political and social renewal – to the more rigid alignment of cultural-political movements, especially the Communist Party of Germany (KPD) in the SBZ.

---

[3] By 1946/47, under circumstances of limited paper supply, approximately 200 cultural journals had been founded, many reaching a higher circulation than the newly licensed daily newspapers. See Christoph Kleßmann, *Die doppelte Staatsgründung: Deutsche Geschichte 1945–1955* (Göttingen: Vandenhoek & Ruprecht, 1982), 161; the chapter on literary-political publications was written by Michael Streich.

[4] See Rhys Williams, "Das sichtbare und das unsichtbare deutsche Vaterland": Die Zeitschrift *Das Innere Reich*," in Hermann Haarmann, ed., *Heimat, liebe Heimat. Exil und Innere Emigration (1933–1945)* (Berlin: Bostelmann & Siebenhaar, 2004), 93–105.

[5] See Jeffrey K. Olick, *In the House of the Hangman: The Agonies of German Defeat, 1943–1949* (Chicago: University of Chicago Press, 2005).

[6] The most influential critique of the postwar period's failure to come to terms with the past is of course Alexander and Margarete Mitscherlich, *The Inability to Mourn: Principles of Collective Behavior*, trans. Beverley R. Placzek (New York: Grove Press, 1975). The German original edition was published under the title *Die Unfähigkeit zu trauern. Grundlagen kollektiven Verhaltens* (Munich: Piper, 1967). An influential diagnosis of postwar German literature's shortcomings is also W. G. Sebald, *Luftkrieg und Literatur. Mit einem Essay zu Alfred Andersch* (Munich: Hanser, 1999).

Debates of a cultural-democratic renewal in informal discussion circles and leagues also provided an alternative to political activism in parliamentary parties, which were seen as continuing the fragmentation of the Weimar public sphere. As Sean A. Forner argues, these interrelated concepts of cultural and democratic renewal contradict traditional stereotypes of the "unpolitical intellectual" in Germany; the Kulturbund was part of a wider network of intellectual circles that transcended the Allied occupation zones and their political demarcations and that sought alternatives to the wholesale adoption of political and socioeconomic models of East or West.[7] At the same time, periodicals from the Left-Catholic *Frankfurter Hefte*, edited by Walter Dirks and Eugen Kogon, to *Aufbau* in Berlin envisioned a reconstructed Germany infused with versions of "socialist humanism." The similarity in organizational structures and rhetorical tropes that writers and intellectuals used in all four occupation zones suggests that prewar cultural developments were carried forth independently of Allied policies. This includes organizational forms of the antifascist opposition, as well as ideas of cultural reform and renewal that had permeated Germany's intellectual scene long before 1933.

The Kulturbund, in particular, took up bourgeois reform ideas of the century's first half and carried the politicization of culture, which climaxed in the "culture wars" against the NS regime, into the postwar period and the context of the emerging Cold War. Note that not only German intellectuals, but the Soviet Union itself had an intense interest in the politics of culture. As Norman Naimark points out, for the Russian leadership, Soviet culture "combined the highest standards of the classics – Pushkin, Chekhov, Tchaikovsky – with the progressive accomplishments of Soviet society."[8] More recently, Anne Applebaum has drawn parallels between the officially sponsored "Goethe cult" in East Germany and the celebrations of Frederic Chopin in communist Poland.[9] By 1946, under the influence of Stalin's secretary for cultural policy, Andrei Zhdanov, campaigns all over Soviet-occupied Central and Eastern Europe would try to bridge the gap between agitprop and classical culture through a renewed enforcement of social realism and denunciations of so-called bourgeois (i.e., apolitical) influences in the arts.[10]

---

[7] See Sean A. Forner, *German Intellectuals and the Challenge of Democratic Renewal: Culture and Politics after 1945* (Cambridge: Cambridge University Press, 2014). See also "Für eine demokratische Erneuerung Deutschlands: Kommunikationsprozesse und Deutungsmuster engagierter Demokraten nach 1945," *Geschichte und Gesellschaft* 33 (2007): 228–57.

[8] Naimark, *The Russians in Germany*, 398.

[9] See Anne Applebaum, *Iron Curtain: The Crushing of Eastern Europe, 1944–1956* (New York: Doubleday, 2012), 323–5.

[10] See Kees Boterbloem, *The Life and Times of Andrei Zhdanov, 1896–1948* (Montreal & Kingston: McGill-Queen's University Press, 2004), 279–83.

The Kulturbund's antifascism was neither the expression of a seemingly timeless German obsession with culture that had survived the war unscathed and resurfaced in the communist East, nor was it merely an unambiguous result of communist tactics – the humanist face on a Stalinist smokescreen. Rather, the establishment of a mass organization for cultural renewal can be described as a blend of antifascist "front" politics, the politicized concept of German culture that emerged from the Weimar and NS periods, and earlier bourgeois and communist ideas of renewal. The result was a distinctive synthesis that attempted to take responsibility for the past (an early *Vergangenheitsbewältigung*) by drawing from a quasi-nationalist evocation of the Protestant Reformation. The early discussions in the Kulturbund highlight the organization's role in the interconnected themes of national unity, the idea of "two Germanys," and the mid-twentieth-century transformation of interwar-era mass politics. Far from serving only Stalinist positioning, the idea of a cultural renewal and a resurgence of the German humanist heritage linked communist and liberal activists in the early postwar period and reflected widespread discussions among intellectuals in East and West about German history and its interpretation. And rather than marking a cultural "zero hour," the organization also linked the intellectual preoccupations of the early twentieth century – with its bourgeois and leftist visions of spiritual and material restructuring – with the postwar myth of a rebirth from the war's rubble. Thus, the complex dynamics of bourgeois reform ideas, antifascist organizational patterns, and communist tactics propelled the remarkable emphasis on cultural policies in the SBZ. The Kulturbund's concept of socialist humanism was meant to be both a cultural foundation for a unified antifascist Germany – under Communist Party dominance – and the location of debates on German national identity and the catastrophe of Nazism. At the same time, the early Kulturbund's openness to antifascist unity and nonpartisanship, and its Marxist-influenced version of "coming to terms" with the past, did not withstand the process of German division and the pressure to conform to the demands of a centralized communist mass organization.

This chapter will briefly address the by now well-documented Communist instrumentalization of antifascism, but its emphasis will be on the early Kulturbund's combined agenda of cultural-political restructuring and attempts to restore prewar cultural movements and to heal pre-1945 divisions. For this purpose, this chapter links the early Kulturbund's rhetoric of cultural renewal to the pre-1933 ideas and writings of some of its prominent members. In a further step, the analysis focuses on the practical concepts and challenges of the project to refashion German culture. While this project constituted an early way of critically assessing Germany's past, the concept of the "other Germany" was ultimately transformed into a weapon of Cold War intellectual conflict. In the end, the Communist instrumentalization of the Eastern Zone's "humanist renewal" was aided by the inner contradictions and tensions that inhered in the concept of a national mass reeducation.

Cultural Renewal and Antifascist Bloc Politics

Unlike the cultural associations in the West, the Kulturbund in the SBZ was from the beginning under the influence of the KPD, although at the time of its foundation it could draw on the same broad pluralist alliance between working-class and liberal intellectuals as the exile organizations that provided a model for it. The establishment of a cultural-political organization that would continue the wartime Popular Front cooperation into the postwar era reflected the general KPD *Bündnispolitik* (politics of alliances) in 1945, which aimed at gaining support in wide circles, including the bourgeois parts of the *Intelligenz*. This renewed emphasis on an antifascist consensus had become necessary through the Soviets' decision to permit political parties and mass organizations in their zone by Soviet Military Administration in Germany (SMAD) decree No. 2 of June 1945. A few months later, the SMAD's dissolution of the last antifas in the Soviet Occupation Zone, such as the NKFD in Leipzig, was the signal that the open pursuit of postwar revolutionary change was replaced by calls for an "antifascist-democratic" regime. The euphemistic term was intended to assuage fears among Germans as well as Western Allies of a Sovietization of the Russian zone.[11]

The KPD's politics of antifascist "blocs" and mass organizations reflected "the need for creative tactics in pursuit ... of party dominance" in the face of "rival organizations ... whose existence was intended to foster the impression of a developing democracy."[12] The Communist bloc politics, with its emphasis on "antifascist unity," culminated politically in April 1946 with the merger of the KPD and the Soviet Occupation Zone SPD (Social Democratic Party of Germany) into the SED. In general, the KPD – more or less openly aided and prompted by the SMAD – aimed to foster Communist Party prominence by winning over the intelligentsia while at the same time employing the rhetoric of national unity against the Western occupation zones and anti-Communist Social Democrats in the West.

[11] See Pike, *The Politics of Culture in Soviet-Occupied Germany*, 3–4; 28.
[12] Ibid., 4.

To keep its options open for hegemony in a unified nation, the KPD paradoxically relied on the concept of "the other Germany" – the cornerstone of antifascism that gave the political use of culture heightened prominence. The evocation of "the other Germany" – classical German culture and its renewal under the term "socialist humanism" – appealed to the idealized consensus of the antifascist alliance instead of an ideological division along occupation zones. It helped the Communists that the antifascist project of representing "the other Germany," based on the heritage of humanist thought and culture, seemed to be supported by Stalin himself. The Soviet dictator's remark that "the Hitlers come and go, but the German people, the German nation, remains" was extensively used and quoted by German Communists as evidence for the Russians' conciliatory response to the crimes they had suffered due to the Germans' conduct during the war.[13] By 1945, however, the Russians, too, substituted the hope for an antifascist German uprising with accusations of collective guilt – e.g., in the articles of Soviet journalist Ilya Ehrenburg.[14] Consequently, the foundation of an intellectual-cultural mass organization with an agenda of reeducation and cultural renewal served simultaneously as an acknowledgment of collective responsibility and evidence for the existence of the other – i.e., antifascist – Germany among the "masses." Leading KPD functionaries, such as Wilhelm Pieck, linked the reeducating and reconciliatory goals of the democratic-antifascist bloc politics to the need for unity. Communist guidance in multiparty or nonpartisan alliances was to overcome both the prewar rifts between the working-class parties and the looming division of the country along the borders of the occupation zones. Thus, "the non-Marxian or even anti-Marxist expedient of collective guilt" was transformed "into a Marxist Leninist version of the will of the people" – while at the same time it avoided the rhetorical and political steps that looked like outright "Sovietization" of the Russian occupation zone.[15]

In the Western occupation zones, SPD chair and former concentration camp inmate Kurt Schumacher was perhaps the fiercest adversary of what he regarded as the Communist instrumentalization of collective responsibility. In his speeches, Schumacher asserted that "the complicity of large segments of the people for the bloody dominion of the Nazis lies in their belief in dictatorship and violence! This guilt cannot

---

[13] Quoted in Pike, *The Politics of Culture in Soviet-Occupied Germany*, 12; see also Naimark, *The Russians in Germany*, 76.
[14] See, e.g., Ilya Ehrenburg, *We Will Not Forget*. Information Bulletin, Embassy of the Union of Soviet Socialist Republics, Washington, DC, Special Supplement, June 1944. Shields Library, University of California, Davis, Special Collections P-005 72:2, especially p. 55.
[15] Pike, *The Politics of Culture in Soviet-Occupied Germany*, 29. See also pp. 12–30.

be expunged."[16] While Schumacher was unequivocal in his contention that the hardships the German people were experiencing were the result of their own political decisions and moral failures, he also saw "repentance and change" as a "prerequisite" for reconstruction.[17] However, the Social Democrat did not accept a confession of collective guilt from a party whose divisive politics before 1933 had led to "the failure of German parliamentary politics and to the opportunity for the Nazis to grab power." Therefore, Schumacher, himself a representative of the "other Germany," held that "the term 'collective guilt' [*Gesamtschuld*] is the beginning of a great historical lie, which cannot be the basis for Germany's reconstruction."[18] The Communists' rhetoric of collective guilt and redemption through reeducation, therefore, found its most ardent supporters not among Social Democrats, but among bourgeois intellectuals in Berlin.

From "Becher Circle" to Mass Organization

While the immediate political expediency in June 1945 and the political maneuvering of Communist functionaries such as Pieck and Walter Ulbricht provide an important backdrop, the appeal of a cultural-political organization to renew German culture would be hard to explain without noting the deep-seated desire among intellectuals and artists to overcome the divisions of the pre-1933 era, not only among the working class, but also among writers and intellectuals and their organizations. As Wolfgang Schivelbusch observes, both the Berlin chapter of the Schutzverband deutscher Schriftsteller (SDS) and the literature division of the Prussian Academy of the Arts had split in the early 1930s into rival leftist and conservative organizations.[19] After the *Gleichschaltung* in 1933, the cultural fissure continued and deepened between intellectuals who chose exile and opposition – most notably Heinrich and Thomas Mann – and those who quietly acquiesced to the Nazi regime or ceased all artistic production. An exclusive focus on the divisions that resulted

---

[16] Quoted in Olick, *The House of the Hangman*, 240.
[17] Ibid.
[18] Kurt Schumacher, "Konsequenzen deutscher Politik" (1945), in Eberhard Rathgeb, ed., *Die engagierte Nation. Deutsche Debatten 1945–1955*. On Schumacher's influence, see also Kleßmann, *Die doppelte Staatsgründung*, 135–42; on Schumacher's attitude toward Germany's Nazi past, see also Jeffrey Herf, *Divided Memory: The Nazi Past in the Two Germanys* (Cambridge, MA: Harvard University Press, 1997); and Olick, *In the House of the Hangman*, 237–43. Olick also discusses Karl Jasper's famous intellectual argument concerning the concept of collective guilt.
[19] See Wolfgang Schivelbusch, *In a Cold Crater: Cultural and Intellectual Life in Berlin, 1945–1948*, trans. Kelly Berry (Berkeley: University of California Press, 1998), 12–13.

from the emerging East–West confrontation often underestimates the intellectual conflicts that survived from the prewar period into the first few years after 1945.

The conceptualization of a cultural league based on a nonpartisan alliance of intellectuals and cultural activists indeed owed much to the organizational forms and activities of exile opposition groups during the war, especially the Freie Deutsche Kulturbund (FDKB) in Britain and the Heinrich-Heine Club in Mexico City. As Chapter 1 has shown, the exile cultural organizations in Great Britain and Mexico – considerably removed from Moscow's influence and flaunting broad ideological diversity – replaced concrete political or socioeconomic conceptions with a general identification with the tradition of German "humanism," especially the German Enlightenment thought of Kant and Lessing and the "Weimar classics," such as Goethe, Schiller, and Hölderlin. However, the theoretical foundations for the establishment of a cultural mass organization in postwar Germany was laid much earlier by KPD functionaries in Moscow, by Pieck and by writer and poet Johannes R. Becher, in exile in the Soviet Union since 1935. Like many antifascist activists, Becher diagnosed a deep-seated "dilapidation" [*Verwahrlosung*] of German culture under the influence of Nazi ideology and education. Becher, who considered the situation after the Nazii defeat the "continuation of the war against fascism by ... ideological means," emphasized the "cleansing" [*Säuberung*] of the educational and research system and of libraries, theaters, cinemas, and literary institutions.[20]

As we have seen, Becher was not the only one in Germany who tried to cure the contamination (*Verseuchung*) of German culture and society with a remedy of classical humanism. Anton Ackermann, who, along with Ulbricht and Pieck had been a member of the NKFD in Moscow, described how the Communist resistance had blended propaganda and humanist culture in its fight against Hitler. Ackermann portrayed the NKFD-operated German-language radio aimed at persuading Wehrmacht soldiers on the Russian front to defect as a weapon of "transformation [*Wandlung*]." The antifascist broadcasts sought a "surmounting of century-old traditions and deep-seated false ideas" by transmitting a mix of frontline news, ideological propaganda, classical and light music – because it was not useful to broadcast segments of fifty or eighty minutes of spoken words – and readings of the "cultural-literary heritage" of Germany, the works of Hölderlin, Goethe, and Lessing, as

[20] Heider, *Politik – Kultur – Kulturbund*, 28, 17.

well as those of Thomas and Heinrich Mann, and Communist authors such as Becher himself.[21]

Becher, still largely unknown to the broader public even though his first publications dated from before the First World War, nevertheless had the intellectual authority to link the artistic concepts of cultural renewal with the concrete political objectives of the KPD. The actual formation of a cultural mass-organization uniting antifascist artists and intellectuals seemed to have been initiated by Becher's return from Moscow in June 1945, in the company of Ulbricht and Ackermann.[22] Immediately upon his arrival, Becher became the center of an informal *Gesprächskreis* (discussion circle) of artists and intellectuals meeting in Becher's residence at the Cäcilienallee in Dahlem, the former villa of the director of the Deutsche Bank. Before the Russian occupation, the residence had been a meeting ground for representatives of the NSDAP leadership and German high finance; now the SMAD generously housed Becher with his wife and the families of fellow Communists Fritz Erpenbeck and Heinz Willmann in the villa.[23]

Although discussions about the formation of an organization to bind intellectuals to the Party had been held in Soviet exile – even Stalin was involved in these talks – it is unclear to what extent the Kulturbund foundation was initiated by Becher himself or if he acted on direct orders from Moscow.[24] There is no doubt, however, that Becher's ideas of a German cultural renewal found positive resonance among the non-party-affiliated and bourgeois artists and intellectuals who regularly attended the informal sessions at Becher's residence. As an informal discussion circle that partly took up or expanded contacts formed during exile or illegality and where intellectuals exchanged blueprints for cultural and political renewal, the circle in Dahlem was comparable to informal groups in Frankfurt, Heidelberg, and other places throughout occupied Germany.

---

[21] Anton Ackermann, "Das National Komitee 'Freies Deutschland – miterlebt und mitgestaltet," in Heinz Voßke, ed., *Im Kampf bewährt. Erinnerungen deutscher Genossen an den antifaschistischen Widerstand von 1933 bis 1945* (Berlin [East]: Dietz Verlag, 1977), 284, 315.

[22] For a firsthand account of the "Ulbricht Group's" return to Berlin from Moscow, see Wolfgang Leonhard, *Die Revolution entlässt ihre Kinder* (Cologne: Kiepenheuer & Witsch, 1955).

[23] See Schivelbusch, *In a Cold Crater*, 72.

[24] See Pike, *The Politics of Culture in Soviet-Occupied Germany*, 81–2. Cf. Magdalena Heider, "Kulturbund zur demokratischen Erneuerung Deutschlands," in *SBZ Handbuch. Staatliche Verwaltungen, Parteien, gesellschaftliche Organisationen und ihre Führungskräfte in der Sowjetischen Besatzungszone Deutschlands 1945–1949*, eds. Martin Broszat and Hermann Weber. Im Auftrag des Arbeitsbereiches Geschichte und Politik der DDR an der Universität Mannheim und des Instituts für Zeitgeschichte München (Munich: R. Oldenbourg, 1990), 715.

Eschewing conventional party politics as too divisive, the participants in the Dahlem circle supported Becher's plan to create a more formal organization that would not only align intellectuals of different political camps, but also reach out to "the masses."

The meeting on June 26, 1945, was later officially declared as the plenary session of the Kulturbund, although the license for which Becher and Heinz Willmann applied the next day seemed to have been granted by the SMAD in advance.[25] Willmann, who had witnessed the defeat of antifascist pluralist politics as a communist activist during the Saar struggle, and who had spent the war in Moscow as the editor of Becher's literary exile journal *Internationale Literatur/Deutsche Hefte*, emphasized in his memoirs the "ideological and political breadth" of the plenary session's participants, many of whom even were "committed to religious beliefs."[26] Willmann may have been alluding to Protestant pastor Otto Dilschneider, a former affiliate of Martin Niemöller's oppositional Bekennende Kirche (Confessing Church) during the Third Reich, and to Ferdinand Friedensburg, a founding member of the Christian Democratic Union (CDU) in the SBZ. Before 1933, Friedensburg had been a Prussian government official for the liberal Deutsche Demokratische Partei (DDP) until the Nazis dismissed him.[27] It is unlikely that men such as Friedensburg and other liberal representatives were unaware that they served the Communists as an alibi for the organization's pluralist makeup, but this did not prevent them from wielding significant influence in the early Kulturbund.

The participants in the plenary session issued an unsigned manifesto as the Kulturbund's official programmatic statement. The document was apparently drafted by Becher alone, and many of its key ideas echoed texts and speeches that the poet had written before 1945.[28] However, its rhetoric of reformatory zeal, its expression of shame over not-too-precisely-specified German misdeeds in the recent past, and its demand for a concerted effort to renew or "reawaken" a "contaminated" German culture by reviving the values of classical humanism, seemed to have struck a nerve with intellectuals in postwar Germany, with the diverse group of the Kulturbund founders as a representative sample.

---

[25] See Schivelbusch, *In a Cold Crater*, 74. In fact, the license seemed to have been granted two days *before* the plenary session, thus feeding into the assertions of a Communist ploy.

[26] Heinz Willmann, "Das sowjetische Volk war uns immer Freund und Helfer," in Voßke, ed., *Im Kampf bewährt*, 413; for Willmann's activities during the Saar struggle, see pages 380–1.

[27] Ibid., 413–14; Schivelbusch, *In a Cold Crater*, 73–4; Heider, "Kulturbund zur demokratischen Erneuerung Deutschlands," 715.

[28] See Pike, *The Politics of Culture in Soviet-Occupied Germany*, 84–5.

The "Appeal for the Foundation of the Cultural League for the Democratic Renewal of Germany" declared in its first sentence that the league "wants to revive the great German culture, the pride of our fatherland, and to erect a new German intellectual life." The manifesto then proceeded with a condemnation of the Nazi regime and its concomitant "want of principles, intellectual impoverishment, spiritual dullness and neglect." The document indicted the "intellectual class" in particular, for its historical failure "to ward off the destruction of Germany." As a result, "for Germany's renewal a fundamental resurrection" and the "rebirth of a new *Intelligenz* [intellectual class]" were necessary. The manifesto also recognized Germany's war guilt, reached out to the "cultural bodies of other countries," and promised to "make known to the German people the cultural achievements of all nations, especially also those of the Soviet Union." The appeal ended with another statement that employed a quasi-religious rhetoric of national redemption: "From ruins and exile a new German life and the fundamental, firm, spiritual foundation for the resurrection of our people must be created."[29]

The foundation of the Kulturbund and the manifesto received intensive coverage among the print media in Berlin. The SMAD-licensed *Berliner Zeitung* called the establishment of the Kulturbund "a significant occurrence in German intellectual life," but the event also received positive coverage among the Western-licensed newspapers.[30] The first public reading of the manifesto took place at the Kulturbund's inaugural rally on July 4, 1945, at the Großer Sendesaal of the Berliner Rundfunkhaus (Broadcast Center) in Berlin-Charlottenburg in front of more than 1,500 people, mostly from Berlin's western districts, where the cultural scene was concentrated. The inaugural event has been widely written on, and in the GDR literature it has acquired an almost mythological status as an event that seemingly prefigured the foundation of the "workers' and peasants' state" itself.[31] In his autobiographical account of the event, Heinz Willmann, for example, remembers wondering, "Who would want to come to a cultural event at a time when many lacked food and a roof over their heads?" But even with empty stomachs, people must have taken an interest in declarations of cultural renewal because the audience

---

[29] Deutscher Kulturbund, *Manifest und Ansprachen von Bernhard Kellermann [et al.] gehalten bei der Gründungskundgebung des Kulturbundes zur demokratischen Erneuerung Deutschlands am 4. Juli 1945 im Haus des Berliner Rundfunks* (Berlin: Aufbau Verlag, n. d.), 5. The citation is from the somewhat wooden contemporary translation in SAPMO – BArch DY 27/1395.

[30] *Berliner Zeitung*, June 29, 1945, page 4.

[31] See, e.g., Karl-Heinz Schulmeister, *Auf dem Wege zu einer neuen Kultur: Der Kulturbund in den Jahren 1945–1949* (Berlin [East]: Dietz Verlag, 1977), 48–50.

members "stood in dense packs, not only in the Großer Sendesaal, but also in the Kleine Sendesaal and in the corridors."[32]

Renditions of Beethoven and Tchaikovsky by the Berlin Philharmonic contributed to the festive atmosphere.[33] In their speeches and addresses at the inauguration, Becher and his collaborators reiterated the statements of the manifesto. Probably the most renowned Kulturbund founder and speaker at the event was seventy-one-year-old actor Paul Wegener. Because of his fame even among the Russians, Wegener had been made president of the Kammer der Kunstschaffenden (Kulturkammer, chamber of culture), an organization of artists that was soon to be overshadowed by the Kulturbund and that ceased to exist in April 1946.[34] In his speech at the inaugural event, Wegener's contribution underscored the Kulturbund's self-understanding as a movement of national revival: "The great era of humanism was destroyed by the second half of the nineteenth century and by Nazism. We have to bring back the spirit of Goethe. This is the task of the Kulturbund."[35]

Becher's address marked the culmination of the event.[36] His description of Germany's physical and spiritual landscape seemed to evoke the expressionist aesthetic of the early twentieth century. Becher declared that even his poetic craft could not give voice to "the dead silence of millions of graves, or the silence of the rubble. Because each of us feels that the silence of the ruins s c r e a m s – it demands retribution and judgment." However, if Germany in 1945 was a giant, silently screaming graveside, the German people could rise up again by acknowledging that their past "political and moral weakness makes all of us accomplices of Hitler's war crimes. Only with this insight, only with a sincere acknowledgement that we share guilt and responsibility, will we be able to rise up from the grave of our defeat and be resurrected as a new, freedom-minded German nation." Another precondition was the unconstrained investigation into the causes for Germany's lapse, which, for Becher, was a "vital question [*Lebensfrage*], a question of life or death for our nation."[37]

If Becher's vision of national redemption through an act of collective confession carried religious undertones, it was not surprising that his speech praised the contribution of the Christian churches, whose doctrines of human equality, he asserted, were fundamentally opposed

---

[32] Voßke, ed., *Im Kampf bewährt*, 414.
[33] Toby Thacker, *Music after Hitler, 1945–1955* (Aldershot: Ashgate, 2007), 35.
[34] See Schivelbusch, *In a Cold Crater*, 47–8, 55.
[35] Deutscher Kulturbund, *Manifest und Ansprachen*, 23.
[36] See Programm der Gründungsveranstaltung des Kulturbundes zur demokratischen Erneuerung, SAPMO – BArch DY 27/2751.
[37] Deutscher Kulturbund, *Manifest und Ansprachen*, 32, 34–5.

to Nazi racial ideology. Becher also seemed to echo Christian and conservative positions of his time when he branded National Socialism as "shallow, vulgar nihilism."[38] Similarly, Dilschneider had in his earlier speech at the event defined Nazi ideology as the "executor of a completely secularized and god-deprived [entgotteten] intellectual legacy of the last centuries."[39] As an alternative to the Nazi glorification of doom and barbarity, Becher conjured up a "philosophy of resurrection' [Auferstehungsphilosophie], a German doctrine of renewal, an ideology of reconstruction." This made the Kulturbund's task a *Reformationswerk* (act of reformation), building on the "rich heritage of humanism, classicism, and the workers' movement." The Protestant religious framework of Becher's speech was underscored by references to Johann Sebastian Bach's passion music and its refrain: "Resurrect! Yes, resurrect!"[40]

Journalist and Nazi resister Ruth Andreas-Friedrich was another contemporary observer who described the auditorium of the Sendesaal during the Kulturbund inauguration as "packed." Andreas-Friedrich asserted that "the people want democratic renewal. They are sincere in their willingness to work hard for reconstruction." But many of the people who were willing to join Andreas-Friedrich in a packed auditorium to contribute to the country's renewal may also have shared the diarist's sensitivity to the language of the manifesto and of the two and a half hours of speeches that followed it. For Andreas-Friedrich, the rhetoric and conviction of the fighters for renewal seemed to hearken back to earlier mass rallies: "Democratic renewal can't start with Nazi superlatives. Hardly anyone of the eight notables, who are talking here about coming to terms with the past and renewing our cultural life, seems to notice how little they've so far managed to renovate their own way of talking. It is still all about the greatest, the ultimate, the largest, and most magnificent [sic]. Without the least self-consciousness, they talk about reeducation, fighting morale, fulfillment of objectives and targets, and marching."[41] Andreas-Friedrich's reservations about the language of the Kulturbund's inaugural addresses were well founded, but perhaps it should be pointed out that "superlatives" and terms such as "reeducation," "fighting morale," and "marching" – in both its literal and metaphorical meanings – were not only parts of Nazi vocabulary, but had

---

[38] Stiftung Akademie der Künste Berlin (hereafter AdK Berlin), Nachlass (NL) Becher, 39/3, Bl. 7, Bl. 5.
[39] Deutscher Kulturbund, *Manifest und Ansprachen*, 25–6.
[40] AdK Berlin, NL Becher, 39/3, Blatt 7, Bl. 8.
[41] Ruth Andreas-Friedrich, *Battleground Berlin: Diaries 1945–1948*, trans. Anna Boerresen (New York: Paragon, 1990), 67.

characterized the political language of all parties in Germany during the first half of the twentieth century.

The rhetoric of cultural resurrection, especially – employed, as commonly argued, by Becher and the KPD for tactical reasons – seemed to express the sentiments of a large part of Berlin's bourgeois intellectuals. The tone of the Kulturbund's manifesto suggests that it did not only perpetuate the ideas and organizational structures of anti-Nazi exile groups; it also took up and continued debates and concepts of cultural reform that circulated in bourgeois literary-intellectual discussion circles – such as the George *Kreis* or the "Mittwochs-Gesellschaft" in Berlin – during the Wilhelmine and Weimar periods.[42] The moment of utter defeat and destruction was a chance not only to eradicate Nazism but also to rectify perceived cultural misdevelopments in Germany since the nineteenth century and to finally carry models of cultural reform to the masses. Whether or not they were conscious of this context, it arguably helped the Communists to find broad bourgeois support for their cultural policies at the same time that it laid the groundwork for a critical scrutiny of the German past.

Cultural Renewal and Rhetorical Continuity

The rhetoric of a "moral-intellectual rebirth" and wholesale reeducation of the German people obviously aided the Communists. It legitimized the leadership of the KPD and the pressure for unity among the working-class parties, since the failure to unite before 1933 was now seen as one of the gross historical errors that led up to the Nazi assumption of power. Moreover, long before June 1945, in speeches and articles written in Moscow, Becher had articulated concepts of cultural renewal and the need for a new *Nationalliteratur*, which would link the heritage of the German humanist classics to a Marxist-Leninist interpretation of history.[43] While the evidence for the KPD manipulation of antifascist ideals is conclusive and undisputed, the seemingly broad enthusiasm for the Communist project of cultural renewal among bourgeois intellectuals in the Kulturbund is not sufficiently explained by an exclusive focus on KPD tactics. And although statements such as the Kulturbund's manifesto and the speeches at its inauguration seem to support the notion of

---

[42] For the Mittwochs-Gesellschaft in pre-WWI Berlin, see Friedrich Meinecke, *Autobiographische Schriften*, ed. Eberhard Kessel. *Werke, Band VIII* (Stuttgart: K. F. Koehler Verlag, 1969), 238–40.

[43] See Johannes R. Becher, *Deutsches Bekenntnis. Fünf Reden zu Deutschlands Erneuerung.* Third, extended edition (Berlin: Aufbau Verlag, 1946), University of California, Davis, Shields Library – Special Collections, PAM 96:9.

a "zero hour" in 1945 by implying a rebirth of culture out of the rubble of the Nazi legacy, the Kulturbund's language and its theme of a cultural resurrection out of ruins echo ideas that the leading intellectuals in the organization had formulated many decades before.

Many of the Kulturbund officials of the late 1940s had viewed themselves as participants in projects of cultural reconstruction since the Wilhelmine period. As the designated head (*Rektor*) of Berlin University, philosopher Eduard Spranger was one of the first bourgeois intellectuals invited to participate in the Kulturbund formation. Born in 1882, Spranger was influenced by the neo-Kantian philosophy of the early twentieth century, and, like many nationalist-liberal intellectuals of his generation, he hoped for a revival of the humanist ideals of Wilhelm von Humboldt to fill the void left by the *Kaiserreich*'s breakdown during the Great War. For Spranger, humanism was most of all an ideal that enabled the individual to achieve his or her human potential, but he also saw in humanism "a political ideal" that "required the harmony between the individual and the moral spirit of an organization that transcends the individual."[44] Spranger was also a leading representative of the *Reformpädagogik* movement, a pedagogical concept aimed at combining neo-humanist ideas and practical education. In an essay on Goethe from 1924, Spranger emphasized the significance of catastrophic experiences for individual rebirths: "Many of the intellectual forces that have determined the destiny of mankind were achieved through the catastrophic upheavals within a lonely soul: as sudden breakthroughs and rebirths."[45]

An emphasis on metamorphosis, on transformations out of catastrophic experiences, also characterized Spranger's attitude toward German national history before and after 1945. Spranger was scheduled to speak, but prevented by illness from attending the Kulturbund inauguration. A brief address, read to the audience, emphasized the commemoration and celebration of the German national heritage, combined with the insight into collective mistakes as invaluable precondition for creation and rebirth:

> All re-creation is self-creation. Inner creation [*In-sich-schaffen*], therefore also new creation ... in the intellectual as well as aesthetic realm. We may only be proud of the great creators of our nation if we ourselves, inspired by them, fulfill our highest potential. Our fate has given us much to thrive on: tragic suffering,

---

[44] Eduard Spranger, *Das humanistische und das politische Bildungsideal im heutigen Deutschland* (Berlin: Ernst Siegfried Mittler und Sohn, 1916), 2.

[45] Eduard Spranger, "Goethe und die Metamorphose des Menschen" (1924), in Spranger, *Kultur und Erziehung. Gesammelte pädagogische Aufsätze*. Third edition (Leipzig: Quelle & Meyer, 1925), 69.

tragic guilt, the whole redeeming [*läuternde*] recognition of the inexpressible tragedy of human life."[46]

But long before 1945, Spranger had evoked the connection between spiritual processes and material creation, and the possibility of national redemption from suffering through a recourse to the national classical heritage: in 1923, in a speech at Berlin University celebrating Bismarck's *Reichsgründung* of 1871, Spranger claimed that Germany's unification had been "a spiritual process and a spiritual self-discovery in a much higher sense than other nations can appreciate, given the nature of their experiences." Speaking against the background of a lost world war, national humiliation through the Versailles Treaty, and hyperinflation, the philosopher went on: "A people in distress clings to the inalienable possessions of its history. And by holding on to the forces that made us strong we might also find entangled in them the circumstances that led to our temporary failure."[47]

There is an obvious continuity between Spranger's rhetoric of 1945 and 1923. Catastrophe is seen as the precondition for creation, and the memory of the national heritage is evoked as a source of redemption while political mistakes are interpreted as tragic flaws. Together with Becher's similar rhetoric, this suggests a striking continuity in intellectuals' reactions to the German defeats in World War I and World War II. The analysis of organizations such as the Kulturbund indicates that the same movements of cultural renewal that gave meaning to the earlier catastrophe – e.g., Spranger's *Reformpädagogik* but also artistic schools such as expressionism – provided the intellectual and conceptual tools that shaped the reactions to Hitler's war.[48]

Cultural movements and schools of thought such as Spranger's *Reformpädagogik* were especially suited to apply their prewar concepts of cultural rebirth and nonpartisan activism to the situation after 1945. During the First World War, Spranger was involved in the Deutsche Ausschuß für Erziehung und Unterricht (German Committee for Education and Instruction). According to the philosopher, the committee constituted an "education parliament" (*Erziehungsparlament*) that not

---

[46] Deutscher Kulturbund, *Manifest und Ansprachen*, 15–16.
[47] Eduard Spranger, "Der Anteil des Neuhumanismus an der Entehung des deutschen Nationalbewußtseins," Festrede gehalten bei der Reichsgründungsfeier der Friedrich-Wilhelms-Universität zu Berlin, January 18, 1923 (Berlin: Norddeutsche Buchdruckerei und Verlagsanstalt, 1923), 4.
[48] For the intellectual and artistic reactions to the First World War, cf. Anson Rabinbach, *In the Shadow of Catastrophe: German Intellectuals between Apocalypse and Enlightenment* (Weimar and Now: German Cultural Criticism, 14) (Berkeley: University of California Press, 1997); Jay Winter, *Sites of Memory, Sites of Mourning: The Great War in European Cultural History* (New York: University of Cambridge Press, 1995).

only aimed at "liberating the educational system from the alien pressures of politics and economic interests," but also strove "to go beyond mere academic and administrative matters and to shape the connection between education and life."[49] The *Reformpädagogik* agenda worked under the assumption that

> the cultural efflorescence that the people themselves create requires a spiritual culture for its conservation. The creation of associations for the preservation of folk art [*volkstümliche Kunstpflege*] was based on this insight. Special events for aesthetic education [*Kunsterziehungstage*] have made important contributions. The activities of the *Kunstwart* (administrative official for the arts), of the *Dürerbund* (Dürer Association), and the Deutscher Werkbund (German Craft Association) have played an invaluable part in keeping alive the creative and appreciative faculties of the nation.[50]

Spranger's idea of an "educational parliament" seems to have anticipated the formation of the Kulturbund – a pluralist association of cultural reeducation that ostensibly eschewed party politics and that had the ambition of connecting intellectuals of all political persuasions with the cultural activities of a broader and reeducated population. Arguably, therefore, the Soviet- and KPD-initiated formation of a Kulturbund to revive and reshape national culture on a broad scale was also the fulfillment of the reform-pedagogical ideals of the prewar period.

The Kulturbund also perpetuated early twentieth-century rhetorical tropes of cultural renewal among cultural producers and critics. The theater critic, playwright, and influential Kulturbund cofounder Herbert Ihering, for example, felt in 1926 that the contemporary generation of dramatic artists after World War I had "no choice but to start over because there isn't anything there [to continue]."[51] In an interwar period marked by paramilitary politics and the increasing politicization of aesthetic experience, it is not surprising that Ihering's most influential work of criticism carried the title *Der Kampf ums Theater* (*The Struggle for the Theater*). The function of a critic, Ihering wrote in 1928, was to arrive at a critique that "created values, a purposefully destructive [*zielhaft vernichtende*] as well as purposefully constructive [*zielhaft aufbauende*], systematic, intellectually discriminating [*geistig sondernde*], order-giving critique."[52] According to antifascist writer Carl Zuckmayer, as late as 1934, Ihering still believed in the Nazi movement's "potential to develop," and

---

[49] Eduard Spranger, "Die Bedeutung der wissenschaftlichen Pädagogik für das Volksleben" (1920) in *Kultur und Erziehung*, 140.
[50] Ibid., 142.
[51] Herbert Ihering, *Der Kampf ums Theater und andere Streitschriften 1918 bis 1933* (Berlin [East]: Henschelverlag Kunst und Gesellschaft, 1974), 14.
[52] Ibid., 22.

"he seriously wondered whether the [NS movement] was not essentially the very thing that [Ihering], Brecht, Piscator, and others had envisioned, only 'for the time being' with a militant-nationalist emphasis."[53] For his support of Brecht in the 1920s, the Nazis expelled Ihering from the Reich's press association; the regime did not, however, keep him from becoming a dramaturg at the Vienna Burgtheater in 1942.[54]

Already in 1926, Ihering – perhaps influenced by the ideas of Martin Heidegger – had demanded a language that employed "no academic jargon, no writing for the sake of artistic nuance, no feuilletonistic frills, no mere allusion and hints, but responsibility for every sentence. In addition, a self-made terminology that does not take anything for granted [vorraussetzungslose], refraining from any detour of formulation."[55] In an article in the Kulturbund journal *Aufbau* from October 1945, by now no longer attacking the pretensions of the bourgeois *Feuilleton* but the distortions of Nazi rhetoric, Ihering simply called for "the clarification of terms."[56] The situation of 1945 seemed to provide the ideal conditions for cultural reconstruction along the lines of Ihering's model of criticism. After all, as Ihering wrote in 1922, in a sentence that could serve as the guiding principle of the Kulturbund's project of democratic renewal, "in times devoid of ideas only ideas can help, in times devoid of intellect, only intellect can help."[57]

However, concepts of cultural rebirth had not only been the exclusive realm of bourgeois reform ideas and interwar literary criticism. They were also a key part of the appeal of communism, especially for bourgeois intellectuals. The circumstances of absolute moral and cultural breakdown in 1945, and the bourgeois–Communist alliance in the antifascist Kulturbund seemed to provide the conditions for the fulfillment of both bourgeois and Communist designs. And nobody exemplified the affinities between pre-1933 bourgeois and Communist aspirations of cultural renewal better than Johannes R. Becher. The first Kulturbund president and later GDR minister of culture seemed to embody the tropes of apocalyptic disaster and subsequent redemption not only in his early expressionist poetry, but in his very biography, which led him from bourgeois origins to participant in the expressionist bohéme, and from morphine addiction and suicide attempts to religious awakening and ultimately to the redemptive embrace of communist rebirth.

---

[53] Quoted in Ernst Klee, *Das Kulturlexikon zum Dritten Reich. Were war was vor und nach 1945* (Frankfurt a. M.: S. Fischer, 2007), 275.
[54] See ibid.
[55] Ihering, *Der Kampf ums Theater und andere Streitschriften*, 15.
[56] Herbert Ihering, "Lessing und Paul Wegener," *Aufbau* 2 (October 1945): 48.
[57] Herbert Ihering, *Der Kampf ums Theater* (Dresden: Sybillen Verlag, 1922), 109.

Becher was born in 1891 in Munich to a father who had worked his way up from rural backgrounds to serve as a civil servant and ultimately a high-ranking judge (*Gerichtspräsident*) in the Wilhelmine bureaucracy. Becoming a member of the Munich bohéme was the young Becher's expression of rebellion against his father's values and authority. His first major work of expressionist prose and poetry was published before the outbreak of war in 1914 under the title *Verfall und Triumph* (*Decay and Triumph*). Like many works of German expressionism, Becher's poetry reveled in apocalyptic images. Becher's biographer Alexander Behrens writes about *Verfall und Triumph*: Becher "played the chords of apocalyptic visions like nobody else, and he skillfully bundled the contemporary tendencies of the young literature of the Kaiserreich before the First World War."[58] But still in 1927, in the poem cycle *Die hungrige Stadt* (*The Hungry City*), Becher composed lines such as: "A cross from a grave crawls black-colored out of every window./The rag collectors poke around [*stochern*] in the trash./ A child is lying in the garbage. The mad wind is spooking/A hundred dogs find a thousand bones."[59]

Behrens places Becher's poetry squarely in the broader tradition of German expressionism as a style that emphasized destruction but lacked any constructive, redemptive vision. However, Becher's belief in destruction as a precondition for transformation and *Werden* (Becoming) seems to have gone beyond the conventions of expressionist aesthetics; as early as 1915, influenced by the teachings of Freud and by his own attendance at psychoanalysis sessions, Becher wrote a journal article under the title "On Destruction as Cause for Becoming [*Über die Destruktion als Ursache des Werdens*]." Becher inhabited Ihering's and Spranger's spiritual neighborhood of creative destruction decades before the three men became connected through a common project of cultural rebirth in 1945.

The "German catastrophe" thus was not only the climax of the wider crisis of the bourgeoisie in the first half of the twentieth century, but also the precondition for its solution. As another Becher biographer puts it, Becher's "provocative poeticizing of destruction as the birthplace of a mankind united in brotherhood and miraculously resurrected from orgies of violence, can be understood as the appropriate expression of a bourgeoisie that hoped for the fulfillment of its humanist ideals and its desire for a reintegrated world out of the heroic exaggeration ... of its own fragmentation."[60]

---

[58] Alexander Behrens, *Johannes R. Becher: Eine politische Biographie* (Köln: Böhlau Verlag, 2003), 33.
[59] Johannes R. Becher, "Die hungrige Stadt"(1927/28) in Johannes R. Becher,*Lyrik, Prosa, Dokumente: Eine Auswahl* (Wiesbaden: Limes Verlag, 1965), 73.
[60] Jens-Fietje Dwars, *Abgrund des Widerspruchs. Das Leben des Johannes R. Becher* (Berlin: Aufbau Verlag, 1998), 86.

Figure 3 Johannes R. Becher (1891–1958) in the 1920s. In his own biography, Becher seemed to embody the multiple cultural and political strands of German history in the first half of the twentieth century. Experimenting with a number of reform movements that both reflected and rebelled against his bourgeois upbringing, Becher's expressionist poetry displayed a preoccupation with decay and renewal even before World War II.
Photo by Frieda Riess / Ullstein bild via Getty Images.

In Becher's case, the themes of destruction and rebirth were reflected not only in his works, but in his biographical path from "avant-garde artist to the avant-garde of class struggle."[61] Becher seemed never truly at home in the Protestant bourgeois milieu into which he was born, and his personal conflicts expressed themselves in morphine addiction and repeated suicide attempts – one of which left a girlfriend dead and Becher himself unfit for military service in World War I. The suicide of his younger brother Ernst in 1918 caused Becher to search for more order and stability in his life. In early 1919, he joined a local chapter of the KPD for the first time; however, he left the Party, weakened and fractured after the assassinations of its leading figures, Rosa Luxemburg and Karl Liebknecht, after less than a year. According to Behrens, Becher "had envisioned something more glamourous and heroic than a party in which the tiniest ideological issue was debated with no end. Becher was a big-picture kind of man."[62]

Turning his back, for the time being, to radical politics, in the early 1920s Becher expressed interest in Christian mysticism and became friends with Karl and Elisabeth Raichle, whose farm in the Schwäbische Alb was characterized by an atmosphere that was full of "reformatory ideas, Christian, agrarian-revolutionary, and influenced by the Youth movement."[63] However, by 1922, Becher's mystical phase – which had inspired his poetry in the early 1920s – began to fizzle out, just like his relationship with painter Eva Herrmann. At the same time, Becher moved to Berlin, where he became part of a new circle of leftist artists and intellectuals. Becher seemed to have found the community of like-minded intellectuals that he had been looking for all his life – even though in his own memoirs, he credited his reading of Soviet author Maxim Gorki for his renewed turn toward communism. In 1923, convinced that "the truly great creations … have always been communal acts," Becher joined the KPD for a second time.[64] Thus, after a series of self-destructive personal crises and experiments in bourgeois reform circles, Becher finally completed his own transformation from bourgeois artist to KPD intellectual. For Becher and others of his generation, the self-destruction of Germany in 1945 held out a similar promise for the nation as a whole.

Becher's central ideas on Germany's national reawakening are perhaps conveyed in his lengthy essay "Deutsches Bekenntnis [German Confession]," which introduced the first issue of the Kulturbund journal *Aufbau*. The essay presented Becher's Marxist interpretation of German history, his general ideas on transformation, and the emphasis

---

[61] Behrens, *Johannes R. Becher*, xi.
[62] Ibid, 62.
[63] Ibid.
[64] Ibid., 73–5.

on political and cultural unity to overcome the mistakes of the past. Reiterating the need for a renewal and transformation of German society, Becher painted a brief sketch of Germany's fateful historical development from the Reformation to Hitler. Nazi barbarism and Germany's current "self-inflicted loneliness" were the results of a long-term historical development. Similarly to Alexander Abusch's *Irrweg einer Nation*, Becher evoked the Protestant Reformation as the birthplace of a culturally unified but politically fragmented Germany. The period from 1914 to 1945 had been "a second Thirty-Years' War" in which "imperialists and monopoly capitalists" had prevented German unity just like the territorial princes during the Reformation era.[65]

However, "just as in religious life, the concept of 'transformation' [*Wandlung*] also applies to the life of a people. A whole people can transform itself, can change. We Germans are called upon to undergo such a transformation, such a change." Becher's concept of a national transformation seemed influenced as much by Protestant religious sentiment as by Marxist analysis: "A transformation, however, requires that one goes inward, that one examines from top to bottom how much guilt oneself carries for the catastrophe."[66] The result of this process of inward examination and admission of guilt would be the "ideological and moral rebirth of our people," the "greatest work of reformation [*Reformationswerk*] in our history." Eventually, "the work of reformation that we call for is to be the intellectual-moral foundation, on which the durable structure of a new freedom-minded realm [*Reich*] can rise."[67] It is only fitting that this mixture of vague cultural nationalism and Protestant redemption rhetoric corresponded to Becher's musical taste; as GDR minister of culture he reportedly preferred Bach and folk music to opera.[68]

While the continuity of hopes for cultural renewal seems to corroborate the long-standing historical interpretation of the German middle-classes' elevation of culture over politics, it is important to remember that both bourgeois and Communist intellectuals found an environment in 1945 – after the antifascist culture wars and amidst the emerging Cold War – in which the discussion of humanist culture could no longer be divorced from party politics. Before Communists appropriated Germany's humanist tradition for their postwar bloc politics, the exile opposition notion of a "militant humanism" (see Chapter 1) had blurred the lines between politics and culture for decades.

---

[65] Johannes R. Becher, "Deutsches Bekenntnis," *Aufbau* 1 (September 1945): 3–7.
[66] Ibid., 7–8.
[67] Ibid., 11–12.
[68] See Thacker, *Music after Hitler*, 35.

Not all the Communist and bourgeois representatives in the Kulturbund shared a decades-long fascination with destruction and recreation. However, it can be argued that the situation in 1945 did not confront Communist and liberal intellectuals with an unprecedented situation, but with a scenario of cultural rebirth that had been broadly painted for some time. "Zero hour," the conditions for rebirth out of the utter spiritual and material devastation of a ruined landscape, had been conceived of long before Allied fire storms and NS orgies of destruction. The question is thus not whether the idea of a nonpartisan Kulturbund was predominantly a Communist ploy; there can be little doubt that it was. What is important to note is that the Communist strategy was successful because it tapped into a preexisting discourse that since 1933 had already been increasingly politicized.

Renewal and Restoration

The opening of the GDR and Soviet archives since 1989 has given scholars the opportunity to trace the internal communications within the KPD and SED and to show the extent to which the Party used the tactics of antifascist coalition-building for its political purposes in the early postwar period. Viewed against this background, the election of Johannes Becher as the president of the Kulturbund was paradoxically a defeat for the KPD, because the Party's strategy at the time was to leave the formal leadership in nonpartisan organizations to bourgeois representatives while only key positions would be held by Communists.[69]

The affinity between Becher's aesthetic outlook and the concepts of the bourgeois representatives in the Kulturbund might explain the unquestioned moral authority the Communist poet wielded in the organization. Even with Becher as president, the newly elected twenty-four-member board (*Präsidialrat*) of the Kulturbund still had the pluralist makeup of Popular Front organizations. Becher's vice presidents were all non-communists: novelist Bernhard Kellermann, painter Carl Hofer, and classicist Johannes Stroux, the president of the former Prussian and future German Academy of the Sciences. Communist Heinz Willmann was elected general secretary. The board and the extended group of influential members was essentially the same as the circle at Cäcilienallee.

Just as at the plenary session at the Dahlem villa, the board spanned early postwar Berlin's range of artistic-intellectual activities and political doctrines. KPD functionaries like Willmann, Ackermann, and Klaus Gysi

---

[69] See Pike, *The Politics of Culture in Soviet-Occupied Germany*, 83; Schivelbusch, *In a Cold Crater*, 75.

were complemented by the artists Kellermann, Wegener, and Ihering. Members of the board also included Christian Democrats Friedensburg and Ernst Lemmer, as well as Gustav Dahrendorf from the SPD executive committee. The Christian churches were represented by the Protestant pastor Dilschneider and the Catholic Melchior Grossek. Besides Stroux and Spranger, Shakespeare scholar Walter Schirmer, musicologist Bernhard Bennedik, and historian Robert Holtzmann, among others, represented Berlin's academic scene.[70] While the Communist novelist Theodor Plivier had spent the war in Moscow exile, painter Karl Hofer and sculptor and professor Renée Sintenis represented prominent artists whose works the Nazis had ostracized even though they had spent the NS period in "inner emigration," relatively undisturbed by the regime.[71] In the 1920s, Hofer had ranted against Weimar parliamentarianism, describing it as a "hollow-chested and feeble-minded pseudorepublic."[72] Yet, in 1933, he had also attacked Nazi conceptions of folk art in an article whose title – "Kampf um die Kunst [Struggle for Art]" – is reminiscent of Ihering's rhetoric. The makeup of the Kulturbund leadership promised to reconcile the experiences of inner émigrés, such as Hofer and Ihering, and exiles, such as Becher and Plivier. On the other hand, there seemed to be little interest in a more balanced representation of the genders; until the return of Anna Seghers from Mexico in 1947, Renée Sintenis was the only female board member, and if the board meeting's minutes are an indication, never very vocal in its discussions.

The youngest member of the Kulturbund's leadership circle and signatory of the inaugural manifesto was twenty-two-year-old Wolfgang Harich, Wegener's personal assistant. If artists such as Wegener and Kellermann connected the Kulturbund with the cultural scene of the pre-1933 era, Harich stood for the organization's attempt to reach out to the younger generation. Among the eight speakers at the inaugural rally at the Masurenallee, Harich was the self-declared "speaker of German youth." Pointing out the broad support for the NS regime especially among the young, Harich, a former Wehrmacht deserter, had reminded the audience that "we, the o t h e r s, were vilified by our peers; suffered humiliations at the hand of our teachers, youth leaders, and, later, our military superiors; were persecuted by the authorities and had to justify

---

[70] See "Biographien leitender Kulturbund Mitarbeiter," SAPMO – Barch DY 27/2751; Heider, "Kulturbund zur demokratischen Erneuerung," in *SBZ Handbuch*, 716.
[71] For Sintenis, see Klee, *Das Kulturlexikon zum Dritten Reich*, 572; for Hofer, see Jost Hermand, *Culture in Dark Times: Nazi Fascism, Inner Emigration, and Exile*, trans. Victoria W. Hill (New York: Berghahn, 2013), 158.
[72] Quoted in ibid., 158.

ourselves before the courts; languished in prisons and concentration camps; and many of us paid with [our] lives in the fight for truth and justice." The experiences of "marginalization and illegality," however, made these representatives of the "other Germany" "fit to be the core of the new German youth." A transformed educational system would hearken back to the German and European classics, Marx and Engels included: "We demand for us a new education in the richness of religion, of philosophy, and the arts. We want to mature with Shakespeare's spiritual wealth, Goethe's wisdom, Jean Paul's baroque depth, Kant's unbending morals, and Hegel's dialectics. We want to grow up with the characters in Balzac and Dickens, Dostojewski and Tolstoi. We want to rediscover the blue flower of romanticism. We want to grasp the scientific laws of historical development, as Marx and Engels discovered them."[73] Unlike the other speakers' contributions at the inauguration, Harich's speech was never published, yet more than anybody else, the philosophy student seemed to express the Kulturbund's attempted synthesis of the German *Bildungsbürgertum* and the Marxist youth movement.[74] Harich's speech also reflected the sense of martyrdom and national mission inherent in the "other Germany's" self-definition and hinted at the ongoing rift between oppositional intellectuals and the representatives of the "inner emigration."

This rift would still dominate early discussions and decisions of the Kulturbund board. At the Kulturbund's *Gründungskonferenz* (charter committee meeting) on August 8, 1945, Becher had initially nominated Kellermann for president, a writer who had spent the NS years publishing trivial literature in inner emigration while the Nazis had prohibited his anti-militaristic novel *Der neunte November*.[75] However, Becher was the unanimous preference of the meeting's attendees, with Pastor Dilschneider even expressing his preference for considering Becher the "Führer" (Dilschneider's infelicitous word choice – which confirms Andreas-Friedrich's assertion that the Kulturbund founders often failed

---

[73] Wolfgang Harich, "Die Forderungen der deutschen Jugend an den Kulturbund zur demokratischen Erneuerung Deutschlands," unpublished speech at the inaugural event on July 3, 1945, at the Großer Sendesaal des Berliner Rundfunkhauses, SAPMO – BArch DY 27/1395 Bl. 2, 4.

[74] Harich's association with Walter Janka, who became the victim of an SED purge in 1956, may account for the official GDR historiography's silence on Harich's contribution to the Kulturbund's establishment. For a sketch of Harich's biography, see Beate Ihme-Tuchel, "Wolfgang Harich," in Karl Wilhelm Fricke, Peter Steinbach, and Johannes Tuchel, eds., *Opposition und Widerstand in der DDR. Politische Lebensbilder* (Munich: C. H. Beck, 2002), 216–23.

[75] See "Biographien leitender Kulturbund Mitarbeiter," SAPMO – Barch DY 27/2751.

to renovate their language – was in all official transcripts of the minutes changed to *Präsident*).[76]

At the end of the session, Becher accepted the unanimous vote – including the KPD members' Ackermann, Gysi, and Willmann – for his election. Pike and Schivelbusch, among others, emphasize how, after an "almost comical" exchange, the election was "forced" on Becher by the liberal Kulturbund members.[77] But little attention is usually paid to the actual arguments made at the session. Becher's initial decline of the presidency emphasized the still existing rift between former exile intellectuals and representatives of the inner emigration: "Kellermann has an advantage over me that should not be slighted. He has stayed in Germany in these twelve years and behaved himself very decently. That's a big plus." The discussion then moved to the fact that Kellermann's novels were more widely published abroad while Becher had an integrative effect within Germany.

It is unlikely that the non-Communist board members were completely unaware of the KPD's agenda, and just as improbable that they elected Becher to consciously thwart the Communists' tactics of antifascist bloc building. What emerges out of the discussion at the charter meeting is the question of who represented German culture in 1945, the exiled proponents of the "other Germany," or the ones who stayed behind and whose achievements rested, like Kellermann's, on their works of the period before 1933? Or would the catastrophe of 1945 create the opportunity to finally unite bourgeois and working-class intellectuals in the century-long project of cultural reform? In any case, first on the Kulturbund's agenda was not the creation of new culture, but the healing of the wounds and divisions that National Socialism had inflicted on German intellectuals and artists during its twelve-year reign. The questions that the charter committee pondered in 1945 were still the debates of the culture wars before 1945 rather than the politics of the Cold War that were beginning to replace them.

The election of Becher as president and the Kulturbund's agenda in general thus need to be placed in the wider context of a revised definition of antifascism after 1945. To what extent could the writers and intellectuals who had opted to stay in Germany after 1933 be part of a project of antifascist cultural renewal? Exile intellectuals during the Nazi era saw themselves as representatives of the humanist "other Germany," a concept that had demarcated sharp boundaries between antifascists

---

[76] Sitzungsprotokoll des Kulturbundes zur demokratischen Erneuerung Deutschlands am 8. August, 1945 (Gründungskonferenz), SAPMO – BArch DY 27/907.
[77] Schivelbusch, *In a Cold Crater*, 75.

and those intellectuals whose public stance – or public silence – enabled them to stay and often even publish in Germany after 1933. Now the Kulturbund – in line with official SMAD and KPD policies – played a crucial role in the rehabilitation and reintegration of right-conservative or apolitical intellectuals – such as conductor Wilhelm Furtwängler or author Hans Fallada – whose status under the NS system had made them controversial figures.[78] Again, despite its rhetoric, the Kulturbund neither envisioned a radical new beginning nor aimed at splitting intellectuals along lines of East and West; rather, the Kulturbund strove to reconnect the strands of cultural renewal that had been severed in the early 1930s.

As Harich's speech at the Kulturbund inauguration indicates, the rehabilitation of the "inner émigrés" and their cultural productions under the NS regime was at odds with many intellectuals who had suffered concrete persecutions under the Nazis. It was also still at odds with the views of many former exile intellectuals, among them the artist whom Becher would have favored to be the figurehead of the Kulturbund. Like no other public figure, Thomas Mann would have had the stature that could integrate the bourgeois and leftist German intellectual traditions, and bridge the gap between exiles and inner émigrés. Ever since his radio addresses from exile, Mann had espoused the idea of a socialist humanism on which to build a post-Nazi Germany. However, in September 1945, in response to pleas for him to return to Germany, Mann had published an open letter in which he listed the reasons "why I won't go back to Germany." The letter contained a sharp attack on everything that had received the Nazis' approval for publication: "It may be superstitious, but in my view books that were allowed to be printed in Germany between 1933 and 1945 are less than worthless and shouldn't be touched. They exude a stench of blood and ignominy; they should all be made into pulp."[79]

Thomas Mann's well-documented refusal to return to Germany – a seminal event in German postwar cultural history – thwarted any possibilities of linking the world-famous novelist to the organization in Berlin. But as Kulturbund president, Becher still insisted on an informal figurehead. His choice of eighty-three-year-old Gerhart Hauptmann as

---

[78] Even though some of Fallads books could be read as a veiled criticism of Nazi policies, they kept selling well in the Third Reich and were popular with, among others, Joseph Goebbels; see Hermand, *Culture in Dark Times*, 151. See Dwars, *Abgrund des Widerspruchs*, 514–17. Furtwängler, although protesting NS cultural policies in 1934, publicly endorsed the Nazi regime and became one of its major cultural representatives; see Klee, *Das Kulturlexikon zum Dritten Reich*, 171.

[79] Thomas Mann, "Warum ich nicht nach Deutschland zurückgehe" (1945), in Rathgeb, ed., *Deutsche Debatten*, 23.

the Kulturbund's honorary president, which Becher proposed to the Kulturbund board at its session on October 17, 1945, is difficult to understand at first glance.[80] Hauptmann had not published in the Third Reich, but he had accepted lavish honors from the Nazis, who saw affinities between his naturalism and official NS concepts of *völkische* art.[81] During the board session of October 1945, Becher argued that the Nazis had tried to instrumentalize Hauptmann and defended the naturalist playwright's lack of protest: "And I must say, he has kept very eloquently silent (*er hat doch sehr beredt geschwiegen*)." The much-publicized meeting between Becher and Hauptmann – who was too infirm to travel to Berlin – at the older writer's domicile in Polish-occupied Silesia symbolized the reconciliation between the "other Germany" and the inner emigration.[82] At the same time, the unanimously positive reaction of the board members to Becher's proposal and to a declaration by Hauptmann in which he identified with the Kulturbund's agenda, demonstrates the extent to which the early Kulturbund members' sensibilities – and their concept of cultural renewal – were geared toward restoration rather than innovation. The history professor and Kulturbund board member Holtzmann responded to Bechers suggestion by exclaiming that with Hauptmann, the Kulturbund was honoring "a truly great poet and human being ... who surpasses Thomas Mann in his intellectual potential as well."[83]

The Kulturbund's emphasis on reintegration and reconciliation was not limited to prominent members and intellectuals. Consistent with its doctrine of pluralist, nonpartisan antifascism, membership in the new organization was open to everybody but former NSDAP members, except for those who were born after 1920 and those who were automatically transferred from the NS youth organizations into the party.[84] From 1947 on, however, exclusion from the organization was limited to "NS activists" and individuals who had been directly involved in NS crimes.[85]

---

[80] For more detailed accounts of Becher's futile attempt to win Thomas Mann as the Kulturbund's honorary president and his attitude toward Hauptmann and Fallada, see Schivelbusch, *In a Cold Crater*, 84–8. Cf. Dwars, *Abgrund des Widerspruchs*, 514–17, 527–8.
[81] See Klee, *Das Kulturlexikon zum Dritten Reich*, 223.
[82] See, e.g., *Berliner Illustrierte*, November 1945.
[83] Sitzungsprotokoll des Kulturbundes zur demokratischen Erneuerung Deutschlands am 17. Oktober 1945, SAPMO – BArch DY 27/907, Bl. 75 and Bl. 76.
[84] Hinweise und Richtlinien für die Wirkungsgruppen des Kulturbundes, 1945, SAPMO – BArch DY 27/2751, Blatt 2.
[85] See *SBZ Handbuch*, 717.

Cultural Renewal in Practice

According to the provisions of the Potsdam Conference and the creation of the Allied Control Council (ACC), the Western Allies moved into Berlin on July 4 and took over the administrations of their sectors on July 11. The rushed pace of the Kulturbund's licensing and inauguration – on the very day before the Western Allies' arrival – shows the priority that the Communist leadership, supported and prompted by the SMAD, gave to the creation of a cultural organization. In an act that symbolized antifascism's victory in the culture wars against the NS regime, the Kulturbund established its headquarters in the building of Goebbels's former *Reichskulturkammer* in Charlottenburg's Schlüterstraße.[86] The building was now in the British sector, but, according to the ACC's directives, licenses granted by the Russians before July 4 stayed in force, at least until further notice.[87] The Kulturbund, many of whose prominent members still resided in the western part of the city, could thus claim that it represented all of Berlin, not only the Soviet-occupied part.

But the Kulturbund, supported by the SMAD's information officer, Colonel Sergei Tjulpanov, and the chief cultural officer, Alexander Dymshits, aimed at being a national movement, not a club of Berlin artists.[88] A week after Becher's election, the *Deutsche Volkszeitung* summed up the Kulturbund's agenda by stating: "The German intellectuals who came together in the Kulturbund believe in the necessity of an examination of our nation's historical development and the detection of the positive and negative forces as they affected all realms of our intellectual life. At stake is the rediscovery and resurrection of the freedom-minded, humanist, genuinely national traditions of our people."[89] But how was the project of "examining a people's historical development" and "resurrecting its humanist traditions" to be put into practice?

The actual program activities and organizational structures of the Kulturbund were formulated in a series of agenda documents and directives. On the most general level, the organization's purpose was to "unite all cultural producers and friends of the arts and sciences who want to contribute to the reconstruction of a democratic Germany."[90] The

---

[86] See Schivelbusch, *In a Cold Crater*, 40ff.
[87] Abschrift aus dem Verordnungsblatt der Stadt Berlin, Jahrgang 1, Nr. 5, August 20, 1945, SAPMO – BArch DY 27/1395.
[88] See Gerhard Wettig, ed., *Der Tjul'panov Bericht. Sowjetische Besatzungspolitik in Deutschland nach dem Zweiten Weltkrieg* (Göttingen: V&R unipress, 2012), 308–14.
[89] "Um Deutschlands geistige Neugeburt. Beschlüsse des Kulturbundes," *Deutsche Volkszeitung*, July 8, 1945.
[90] Satzung des Kulturbundes, 1946, SAPMO – BArch DY 27/441, Blatt 4.

Kulturbund's activities were to be guided by seven guiding principles (*Leitsätze*) that spelled out the organization's agenda in more concrete terms. The first point was the "annihilation of the Nazi ideology in all realms of everyday and intellectual life." The new organization was to fight against "the intellectual initiators of Nazi and war crimes and purge all reactionary and militaristic ideas from public life."

The second *Leitsatz* contained the "formation of a national united front of the German intellectuals [*Geistesarbeiter*]." This united front was to cement the "indestructible unity of the intelligentsia [*Intelligenz*] and the people" and lead to the "rebirth of the German mind [*Geist*] representing a militant democratic disposition."

Other demands included the "examination of our nation's general historical development"; the "rediscovery and sustenance of freedom-oriented, humanistic, and genuinely national traditions of our people"; and the "initialization of an understanding with the cultural agents of other peoples." Finally, the last point proclaimed the "fight for the moral regeneration of our nation" by exerting influence on the education of the young, e.g., by the granting of awards and prizes for outstanding efforts by young people.[91]

The Kulturbund's concrete activities were to encompass the publishing of educational literature of all genres, the planning and coordination of cultural events that would serve the "exchange of ideas," the development of school curricula and textbooks – especially in German history – and "the exertion of influence on the country's cultural life."[92] Before the foundation of a German state or the establishment of other nationwide political authorities, therefore, the officially non-party-based Kulturbund had evolved from an informal circle of Nazi-oppositional intellectuals to an organization that in many respects assumed the functions of a ministry of culture.

Since July 31, 1945, the SMAD allowed Kulturbund activity in the whole Soviet Occupation Zone.[93] Intellectuals, artists, and educators in the SBZ now received letters that invited them to form local sections of the Kulturbund. The text of the invitations read: "At our request, the institution of higher learning of which you are a member has identified you as an intellectual force that may contribute to the Kulturbund's

---

[91] "Leitsätze des Kulturbundes zur demokratischen Erneuerung Deutschlands," SAPMO – BArch DY 27/1395.
[92] Organisationsschema des Kulturbundes, SAPMO – BArch DY 27/2751.
[93] Memorandum der sowjetischen Militärverwaltung in Deutschland – Propagandaabteilung, July 31, 1945, SAPMO – BArch DY 27/1395. For the important role that Tjulpanov played in shaping German cultural activity in the SBZ, see Naimark, *The Russians in Germany*, 318–52.

work of reconstruction and who might be willing to participate in this effort." Some of the invitations also contained a list of "themes that we recommend the local chapters of the Kulturbund to address."[94] The list of topics – and the order in which they are recommended – give a conclusive picture of the thematic priorities of German antifascist intellectuals directly after the war. Number one on the Kulturbund's list was a "Revised Interpretation of German History [*Revision des deutschen Geschichtsbildes*]." Second on the list of recommended topics was "The German Protest and the figure of Martin Luther." This was followed by 3) "Friedrich II and Goethe"; 4) "The Wars of Liberation and Freedom in Anguish"; and 5) "The Failure of the Bourgeoisie (1848)." Bismarck, Nietzsche, and Heine were other historical figures on the Kulturbund's list of priorities.

Observers who were wary of the Kulturbund's role in Germany's Sovietization might have noted that the Communist-conceived organization's list did not recommend any Russian-themed items; instead the list had room for "English Socialism" and "Intellectual Life in Modern France." Only as its fourteenth and fifteenth points – "Contemporary Problems in Education" and "School Reforms" – did the Kulturbund letter list topics that pertained to contemporary issues and actual policies. The "War Crimes Trials" was also at the bottom of the list, which was dominated by themes of eighteenth- and nineteenth-century history and high culture. However, the high priority given to a revised historiography indicates that the Kulturbund saw itself less as a contributor to everyday politics and more as an organ to shape a new Germany's understanding of itself and its history.

The emphasis on the Reformation and the 1848 revolutions is especially noteworthy and was not just an anticipation of upcoming anniversaries (Luther died in 1546). The celebration of Luther suggests the underlying influence of Protestantism on the Kulturbund's early approaches of "coming to terms with the past" through inward retrospection and repentance. As Becher's speech at the inauguration made clear, the Kulturbund founders saw themselves as part of a new German reformation that would also fulfill the thwarted aspirations of the 1848 revolutions, an event that centered on the problem of German national unity and failed through the disunity of revolutionary and democratic forces.

In addition to the formation of local intellectual associations, the second important tool for the renewal of German culture was the establishment of the Aufbau Verlag publishing house, which was decided on

---

[94] SAPMO – BArch DY 27/2751.

Figure 4 Kulturbund Poster, Oktober 1945. The caption reads Nation – Arts – Science unified in the Cultural League for the Democratic Renewal of Germany. In combination with the portrait of Goethe, this poster perfectly captures the spirit of the early Kulturbund's blend of political mobilization by appealing to the iconic figure of classical German bourgeois humanism.
©Bundesarchiv.

at the Kulturbund's second board meeting on August 24, 1945.[95] The Aufbau Verlag's task was the republication of German and foreign literature that the Nazis had prohibited, as well as the discovery of new talent. In October, the board agreed on the initial publications of the publishing house: Georg Lukács' new history of German literature, a volume of Becher's poetry, re-editions of Heine, Goethe, Schiller, Lessing, and Hauptmann, as well as Heinrich Mann's novel *Der Untertan*.[96] Pastor Dilschneider also reminded the board members of the 400th anniversary of Luther's death in 1946 and suggested a republication of Luther's *Von der Freiheit eines Christenmenschen* (*The Freedom of a Christian*).[97] Dilschneider's suggestion testifies to the ideological breadth of the early Kulturbund as well as to the attempt of many of its members to cast the organization in the tradition of Germany's national and religious reawakening in the sixteenth century.

While the Aufbau Verlag's catalog of publications in 1945 can only be called *bildungsbürgerlich*, the journal *Aufbau* was a site of concrete cultural-political debates. The first issue of the "literary monthly journal for literature, criticism, and philosophy" was to have about forty pages and a circulation of 20,000 copies that were to be sold for two Reichsmark each.[98] In fact, the first issue had to be printed in 50,000 copies, which sold out after a few days.[99] Although circulation of the *Aufbau* in the Western zones faced great logistical difficulties, the Kulturbund board rejected suggestions for a second publication in the West. Becher emphasized that "the *Aufbau*'s focus is neither on the East, nor West, South, North, or on anything else but Germany.... With our journal we want to represent" German unity under all circumstances as intellectual unity."[100]

The centerpiece of the first *Aufbau* issue was the *Leitsätze* of the Kulturbund and Becher's "Deutsches Bekenntnis." Early issues of the journal also gave Becher a forum for his more recent poems on the German situation, heavy-handed invocations of postwar German rubble that sounded like parodies of the Kulturbund president's earlier expressionist works: "*O Deutschland, schwer geprüft wie nie zuvor! / Ich seh dein Bild durch einen Trauerflor* [O Germany, put harder to the test than

---

[95] For a history of the Aufbau Verlag publishing house, see Carsten Wurm, *Der frühe Aufbau-Verlag 1945–1961. Konzepte und Kontroversen* (Wiesbaden: Verlag O. Harrassowitz, 1996). See also Nicholas Jacobs, "Trials and Triumphs of East German Publishing," *New Left Review* I/231 (September–October 1998): 146–51.

[96] Sitzungsprotokoll des Kulturbundes zur demokratischen Erneuerung Deutschlands am 17. Oktober 1945, SAPMO – BArch DY 27/907, Blatt 65.

[97] Sitzungsprotokoll, 24. August 1945, SAPMO – BArch DY 27/907, Bl. 36.

[98] Ibid., Blatt 35.

[99] Heinz Willmann, report to the Kulturbund board, October 17, 1945, SAPMO – BArch DY 27/907, Blatt 65.

[100] Ibid., Blatt 72.

ever before / I see your image through a funeral wreath]."[101] Outdoing Becher in cliché images of desolation, poet Horst Lommer contributed lines such as "*Deutschland, blutende Erde, / Mutter in Schmerzen und Pein* [Germany, bleeding earth, / Mother in pain and agony]."[102]

But the central theme of the *Aufbau* was the discussion of German history and the explanation for the Nazi catastrophe. Most contributions agreed that the NS dictatorship had long roots in German history and thus adopted versions of what later would be called the German "special path" (*Sonderweg*). In the first issue of September 1945, for example, Marxist literary critic Georg Lukács critiqued the German tendency for inwardness and the disparity between thinking and acting in the German intellectual tradition.[103] In the following issue, Lukács upheld the humanism of the late eighteenth and early nineteenth centuries – e.g., Hegel's definition of freedom and Goethe's concept of world literature – as a tradition that stood in marked contrast to the "insane ideas of race [*Rassenwahn*]" that superseded it.[104]

But the *Aufbau*'s investigations into the dynamics of NS coercion and ideology tended to focus on the heroic role of NS resisters – e.g., in the poems and plays of writer and Kulturbund board official Günther Weisenborn – rather than on the details of NS race policies and their victims. In a January 1946 article, Arnold Bauer thematized the roots of German antisemitism since the nineteenth century, without, however, any direct mentioning of its conclusion in the Nazi genocide that had just ended.[105] Only an article by Victor Klemperer in the March 1947 issue placed antisemitism and racial thinking at the center of NS ideology. Klemperer not only provided a differentiated analysis of German romanticism and Nazi racial thought, but also differentiated National Socialism, with its emphasis on race, from Italian Fascism.[106] Shortly before the polarization of inter-zonal relations, therefore, the *Aufbau* article offered an early modification of antifascism's lopsided focus on socioeconomic factors, though without influencing the tenets of the later GDR's official antifascist ideology.

If the pages of the *Aufbau* occasionally exposed the often reductionist assumptions of antifascist core beliefs, they also revealed the limits and

[101] Johannes R. Becher, "Heimkehr," *Aufbau* 2 (Oktober 1945): 172.
[102] Horst Lommer, "Deutschland, blutende Erde," *Aufbau* 1 (January 1946), 93.
[103] Georg Lukács, "'Das innere Licht ist die trübste Beleuchtungskraft,'" *Aufbau* 1 (September 1945): 52–6.
[104] Georg Lukács, "Der Rassenwahn als Feind des menschlichen Fortschritts," *Aufbau* 2 (Oktober 1945): 100–14.
[105] Arnold Bauer, "Der Einbruch des Antisemitismus im Deutschen Denken," *Aufbau* 1 (January 1946): 152–64.
[106] Victor Klemperer, "Die deutsche Wurzel," *Aufbau* 3/1947: 201–8.

inherent contradictions of a project that aimed to renew a culture and reeducate a whole nation. The very first issue of September 1945 emphasized the need to get rid of Nazi educational material and its influence on children. Under the title: "Disinfection of Our Children's Bedrooms" the article described a mother's struggle to resist the influence of Nazi education on her children. Nobody on the *Aufbau* editorial board, however, seemed to have noticed that the article employed the very same vocabulary of hygiene and eradication that characterized Nazi terminology: "Whether the children were at school or at daycare, whether they were doing sports or youth activities: everywhere the air was contaminated.... Countless numbers of people have out of ignorance or indifference advanced the infection by the Nazi germs! Not to mention those who, consciously or subconsciously, were themselves carriers of the germs." As a remedy for this contamination, the article demanded, "the new educational policy of school and state must be accompanied with an intellectual-political disinfection of the children's rooms by the family, by the mother in Germany."[107]

Inadvertently the well-intentioned project of cultural renewal and national reeducation echoed the tropes of earlier campaigns of national hygiene, eradication, and cleansing. The project of a democratic renewal of German culture still had ways to go.

The aftermath of the catastrophic German defeat in the summer of 1945 provided the fertile ground for projects of cultural renewal. In many cases, this meant the resumption of concepts and rhetorical tropes that had permeated discussions in Germany in the first half of the twentieth century. Not only did cities like Berlin, and Germany as a whole, resemble the apocalyptic images conjured up in earlier aesthetic movements, Soviet policies and strategies in their occupation zone now encouraged and enabled intellectuals of all convictions to realize their prewar ideals of cultural reform and transform them into a national mass movement. Sprung out of the unique postwar public sphere of cultural-political journals and discussion circles that continued the activities of exile and anti-Nazi groups, the Kulturbund zur demokratischen Erneuerung Deutschlands redefined antifascism by combining the rhetoric of early twentieth-century cultural movements with interwar Communist front tactics.

The result was an organization that carried an ideal of collective introspection – with deliberate allusions to the Protestant Reformation – into the postwar political realm. The actual activities of the Kulturbund

---

[107] Majabert Foerstner, "Desinfektion unserer Kinderzimmer," *Aufbau* 1 (September 1945): 83–4.

centered on the analysis of Germany's long-term development toward Nazism and on the achievement of antifascist unity. The emphasis on unity and reconciliation promised to overcome the still existing rifts between German intellectuals at the same time that it legitimized the Communists' call for an end of the political fragmentation that had brought about the German catastrophe of 1933.

The quasi-religious rhetoric of collective transformation and national reawakening through the expiation of political sins and the revival of suppressed traditions suggests that organizations such as the Kulturbund assumed some of the functions of "collective mourning."[108] But the early discussions in the Kulturbund and its publications also hinted at potential contradictions within the project of cultural renewal. How can a movement of collective reeducation avoid the coercion and the subsuming of culture into politics that characterized earlier mass movements? And how could an organization that depended on the KPD and the Soviet occupation authority retain its nonpartisan, pluralist character? Contrary to the Kulturbund founders' intentions, the notion of an antifascist "other Germany" not only created unity, but spurred further division.

---

[108] For cultural rituals of "collective mourning" after World War I, see Winter, *Sites of Memory, Sites of Mourning.*

5 Humanism with a Socialist Face: Sovietization and "Ideological Coordination" of the Kulturbund, 1946–1947

With the initially very pluralist, nonpartisan makeup of its membership and leadership, and its programmatic goal of antifascist democratic renewal, the Kulturbund's history from 1945 to 1948 is part of the wider historical narrative of the increasing Stalinization and suppression of noncommunist elements in the Soviet Occupation Zone (Sowjetische Besatzungszone [SBZ]).[1] The development of the Kulturbund from 1945 to 1948 displays the classical pattern of "Sovietization," the takeover of Eastern and Central European regimes by Communists. Like other antifascist movements, the Kulturbund underwent a first stage of "genuine coalition" between Communist and non-Communists, followed by a "bogus coalition" during which non-Communists were increasingly pushed into the opposition, and finally a third stage of centralized Communist hierarchy, discipline, and organization.[2] The Kulturbund undoubtedly had many parallels with other cultural organizations in Soviet-occupied Central and Eastern Europe, for example, the Central Section of Political Education in Romania, which by 1948 was transformed into the Stalinist "Propaganda and Agitation Department."[3] In this sense, the Kulturbund was, as Anne Applebaum contends, "an archetypical postwar Eastern European institution."[4]

---

[1] For the "Stalinization" of the Kulturbund, see especially David Pike, *The Politics of Culture in Soviet-Occupied Germany, 1945–1949* (Stanford, CA: Stanford University Press, 1992); Magdalena Heider, *Politik – Kultur – Kulturbund. Zur Gründungs- und Frühgeschichte des Kulturbundes zur demokratischen Erneuerung Deutschlands 1945–1954 in der SBZ/DDR* (Köln: Verlag Wissenschaft und Politik, 1993); Gerd Dietrich, *Politik und Kultur in der Sowjetischen Besatzungszone Deutschlands (SBZ), 1945–1949. Mit einem Dokumentenanhang* (Bern, Switzerland: Peter Lang, 1993).

[2] The "classical" model of the "Sovietization" of Eastern Europe is Hugh Seton-Watson, *The East European Revolution*, third ed. (New York: Frederick A. Praeger, 1956). Cf. George Schöpflin, *Politics in Eastern Europe, 1945–1992* (Oxford: Blackwell, 1993). See also the essays in Vladimir Tismaneanu, ed., *Stalinism Revisited: The Establishment of Communist Regimes in East-Central Europe* (Budapest: Central European University Press, 2009).

[3] See Christian Vasile, "Propaganda and Culture in Romania at the Beginning of the Communist Regime," in ibid., 367–99.

[4] Anne Applebaum, *Iron Curtain: The Crushing of Eastern Europe, 1944–1956* (New York: Doubleday, 2012), 334.

However, as much as the process that led to the Kulturbund's transformation may have resembled developments throughout the Eastern Bloc and was directed by the Soviets and the Socialist Unity Party (SED), this chapter redirects its emphasis on the dynamics between non-Communist and Communist intellectuals. Especially since 1989, historical studies have, in John Connelly's words, "helped chip away at the monolith of East European stalinism," but much of the scholarship still focuses on the uniformity of Communist tactics in the various societies that became part of the Soviet sphere.[5] The analysis of the concrete goals and failures of the intellectuals in the Kulturbund does not aim to revise the traditional historiographical models of Communization, but it links it to the debates of antifascist intellectuals and their vision of cultural renewal before 1945. This chapter aims to show how specific German continuities, the intellectual legacy of antifascist humanism, and debates of cultural renewal accompanied the move from antifascism to Communist one-party rule in East Germany.

The following pages will analyze the Kulturbund's self-imposed mission of reeducating a nation through antifascist cultural renewal. The different approaches to censorship within the Kulturbund and other cultural institutions in the SBZ reveal not only the well-documented end of antifascist nonpartisanship, but also the frictions inherent in the concept of an antifascist mass reeducation. This tension became even more evident in the attempt by Communists as well as non-Communist Kulturbund activists to re-politicize the concept of cultural renewal and create a true mass movement for it in the SBZ. Ultimately, due to liberal and bourgeois ambitions to centralize the Kulturbund's leadership and to "re-politicize" the population, the Kulturbund supported the gradual expansion of Communist influence. The bipartisan, ambitious vision of creating a rejuvenated antifascist German culture nurtured the SED's tactics even as the conceptual differences between socialist humanism and liberal interpretations of the German past made the antifascist consensus increasingly difficult to maintain.

At its foundation in the immediate aftermath of World War II, the Kulturbund zur demokratischen Erneuerung constituted an attempt at overcoming Germany's cultural divisions and at appealing to long-standing ideals of cultural reform, under Communist organizational guidance but with widespread nonpartisan support. Germany's *political* unity had from the beginning been an underlying but not exclusive subtext. When, at the Kulturbund's second board meeting in August 1945,

---

[5] John Connelly, *Captive University: The Sovietization of East German, Czech, and Polish Higher Education, 1945–1956* (Chapel Hill: University of North Carolina Press, 2000), 7.

painter Carl Hofer asked, seemingly casually, "when will the iron curtain be lifted that isolates us from the rest of the world?" Johannes R. Becher's response was: "The better and quicker we'll do our work, the sooner [it will be lifted]." The Kulturbund president was ready to "almost guarantee" that if the Kulturbund kept working for another two or three months, "then Russian, American, and English writers will come here, and there will be the beginning of an exchange."[6]

Becher's optimism hints at how much the Kulturbund overestimated the influence of its cultural programs on the global political dynamics of the Cold War. This overestimation calls to mind the attempts of exile literary clubs to stem the National Socialist (NS) onslaught on Europe by organizing reading circles of humanist literature. History obviously proved Becher wrong. Two or three months of Kulturbund cultural renewal did not lift the Iron Curtain. Rather, as this chapter argues, the Kulturbund's attempt at making cultural reform a mass project sped up the demise of its multi-partisan leverage and therefore contributed to the dynamic that would ultimately end in two German states. Furthermore, the breakdown of antifascist consensus had consequences for the concept of the "other Germany," which for one and a half decades had rallied working-class and liberal forces under the banner of classical humanist tradition. The idea of an alternative German cultural tradition of emancipation and antifascism was well suited for the continuing intellectual division of Germany, now no longer between antifascist and Nazi camps, but between a Communist East and a capitalist West.

Cultural Reform vs. Cultural Cleansing

The Kulturbund's main priority in 1945 was the restoration and preservation of German intellectual unity. For this reason, the majority of the board rejected Pastor Dilschneider's suggestion in August 1945 to establish a separate Kulturbund in the Western occupation zones, or publish a "West Edition" of the journal *Aufbau*. Becher, as well as CDU member Ernst Lemmer, identified the Kulturbund's priority as cultural and intellectual unity. Lemmer underscored the need for the Kulturbund's publications to be distributed in the American and Western zones. However, he had grave concerns that a "dualism" could develop: "We need to assume a unified concept of Germany, and because the initiative was taken here, we have to make the strongest efforts at spreading our

---

[6] Sitzungsprotokoll des Kulturbundes zur demokratischen Erneuerung Deutschlands am 24. August 1945, SAPMO – BArch DY 27/907, Bl. 38 and Bl. 39. Hofer's use of the term *eiserner Vorhang* shows that the term was already in use before Churchill's famous speech in March 1946.

intellectual productions from here to all other occupation zones. This seems to me an unconditional necessity. We must strive most of all for unity in the intellectual realm [*im Geistigen*]."⁷

However, even if the Kulturbund was in theory a nonpartisan, nationwide organization whose concept of culture was not meant to be the expression of one particular ideology other than antifascism, the board had to take account of the differences in cultural policies between the occupation zones. Also during the August session, during the discussion of the Aufbau Press's future publishing program, philosophy professor Paul Hofmann brought up what he described as a "sensitive issue [*heiklen Punkt*]": "We are obviously not Russian, ... but we, Aufbau publishing house and the rest of the press here, we are under a very strict censorship. I believe these circumstances are the reason why the English and American occupation zones regard Aufbau Press with a certain degree of suspicion."⁸

Becher was quick to respond: "I'd like to say something about that.... Undoubtedly, these things are part of a development, and not a negative one. We need to put ourselves into a censor's position.... The fact is, we need to work loyally, honestly, and convincingly with these gentlemen, so that they gradually gain political trust and so that the difficulties will become smaller. They won't become smaller if we overemphasize unpleasant matters." If Becher's sympathetic understanding for the Soviet censor's position seemed to betray his role as Communist Party of Germany (KPD) functionary and his exile years in Moscow, it needs to be added that CDU cofounder Ferdinand Friedensburg agreed with Becher: "I notice that with every passing day I'm leaning more towards the views that Herr Becher has presented. It's important that we, who are Western-leaning [*westlich orientiert*], understand this foreign world and this foreign world understands us; these days I'm more partial towards working with the Russians than with the Western powers. In regard to Germany, the Western powers are still in the experimental stage and even more unpredictable than the Russians."⁹

The exchange between Hofmann, Becher, and Friedensburg over Soviet censorship exposed an early potential conflict between the Kulturbund's pluralism and the realities of Communist cultural politics. However, the discussion also showed that the issue of Russian politics did not jeopardize the consensus between Communists and liberal representatives, such as Friedensburg and Lemmer, in the Kulturbund. After

---

⁷ Ibid., Bl. 69.
⁸ Ibid, Bl. 72.
⁹ Ibid.

all, the press in the Western zones was also subject to military censorship. But the question of censorship went beyond attitudes toward the occupation authorities. It touched on what an *Aufbau* article from September 1945 called the "disinfection" of German thought of its Nazi pollution.

By late summer of 1945, the SMAD had created KPD-dominated "central administrations [*Zentralverwaltungen*]," which basically prefigured the ministries of the later GDR. While most central administrations dealt primarily with economic matters, the Deutsche Zentralverwaltung für Volksbildung (German Central Administration for the People's Education, later Deutsche Verwaltung für Volksbildung [DVV]), with the KPD's Paul Wandel in charge, was originally responsible for schools and educational institutions. Later its responsibilities were expanded "to include, apart from schools, the supervision of artistic activities, museums, theaters, movie theaters, and scientific institutions engaged in 'enlightenment.'"[10] The DVV's official duties seemingly overlapped with the Kulturbund's agenda; however, further SMAD orders in fall 1945 mentioned "confirmation procedures" and "approvals" of cultural institutions among the DVV's tasks. Stated in more concrete terms, the DVV, was designed as the SMAD's and the KPD's arm in the enforcement of censorship.[11]

The Kulturbund board got an early taste of this approach to cultural renewal when the board's approaches to censorship clashed with that of more Party-aligned institutions. At the board session of August 24, Becher brought up the topic of an index of fascist literature that had been compiled by the Zentralverwaltung für Volksbildung and the Chamber of Cultural Producers (Kammer der Kulturschaffenden), another cultural institution that seemed to overlap with the Kulturbund's self-assigned mission to bring together artists and intellectuals. Becher suggested a commission to examine the index and delineate a Kulturbund position on the subject. Actor Paul Wegener, whom the Russians had made the Chamber's president, was most vehemently against the idea of an index: "I am very skeptical about this index affair. Those are Nazi methods. We should start becoming more free, not building that many barriers.... We should educate the youth to *see* [emphasis in original] instead of prohibiting things." On the other hand, a defense of the index came from CDU representative Lemmer: "We mustn't forget the extent of the intellectual

---

[10] For the functions of the DVV, see also *SBZ Handbuch. Staatliche Verwaltungen, Parteien, gesellschaftliche Organisationen und ihre Führungskräfte in der Sowjetischen Besatzungszone Deutschlands 1945–1949*, eds. Martin Broszat and Hermann Weber. Im Auftrag des Arbeitsbereiches Geschichte und Politik der DDR an der Universität Mannheim und des Instituts für Zeitgeschichte München (Munich: R. Oldenbourg, 1990), 229–38.
[11] Pike, *The Politics of Culture in Soviet-Occupied Germany*, 93.

susceptibility [*geistige Anfälligkeit*]; therefore I have some understanding for the position of a state authority that a certain cleansing should occur bureaucratically [*dass eine gewisse Reinigung behördlich geschieht*]."[12] At the end of the session, the board appointed a commission consisting of Lemmer, Friedensburg, Herbert Ihering, and literary scholar Paul Wiegler.

The Kulturbund representatives drafted a statement that rejected the idea of an index. The official Kulturbund position read:

> The decisive question for the evaluation of a literary work is the artistic worth and the sincere creative attitude. If both exist, we will pay our respect even to those who do not share our views.... The Kulturbund does not consider its objective to be the creation of an index. Rather, those who are practically involved in these matters should learn, with the highest sense of responsibility, to protect real freedom and at the same time safeguard our people from any dishonest abuse.

The statement was signed by Friedensburg, Ihering, and Wiegler, but not by Lemmer.[13]

The protocol of a meeting in November 1945 by the Central Cleansing Committee for the Eradication of Fascist Literature (Zentraler Säuberungsausschuß zur Ausmerzung der faschistischen Literatur) – entrusted by the SMAD with the task of cleansing libraries of Nazi publications – sheds light on the reactions to the Kulturbund declaration by the more openly Communist-dominated institutions.[14] The Cleansing Committee objected that the Kulturbund representatives had distanced themselves from the censorship plans developed by the Chamber of Cultural Producers and the Central Administration for the People's Education. The Kulturbund, particularly Dr. Friedensburg, was accused of sympathizing with a Senate declaration of the Academy for Musical Arts of Berlin, which "unequivocally protested 'in the name of an imperiled democracy' against restrictive measures in the field of literature."[15] Kulturbund cofounder Bernhard Bennedik was the head of the Academy and therefore carried responsibility for the Senate declaration.

In a rendering of the committee's meeting with Friedensburg, the Cleansing Committee's criticism of the Kulturbund and its Christian Democrat board member went further: "To the astonishment of all attendants, and as if he pulled it out of his sleeve, Dr. Friedensburg suddenly presented a 'preliminary' list of people whom he and the Kulturbund

---

[12] Sitzungsprotokoll des Kulturbundes, 24. August 1945, SAPMO – BArch DY 27/907, Bl. 78.
[13] Sitzung des zentralen Säuberungsausschusses zur Ausmerzung der faschistischen Literatur, November 2, 1945, SAPMO – BArch DY 27/520.
[14] See *SBZ Handbuch*, 236.
[15] Sitzung des zentralen Säuberungsausschusses, SAPMO – BArch DY 27/520.

Figure 5 Vice Mayor of Berlin Ferdinand Friedensburg addresses the delegates at the First Federal Congress of the Kulturbund, Berlin, May 20, 1947. Johannes R. Becher is seated next to him in the middle. The relationship – based on a mutual interest in cultural renewal – between the liberal Christian Democrat Friedensburg and the Communist Becher was characteristic for the early Kulturbund's blend of political activism and "bourgeois" cultural sensibilities. As it turned out, the relationship would not withstand the corrosive influence of the Cold War and the SED's assertion of power.
©Bundesarchiv.

were going to protect." Friedensburg's list of Kulturbund protégées, as reproduced in the Cleansing Committee's report, named mainly conservative and ultra-nationalist writers. The most prominent included (with the Cleansing Committee's biting comments in parenthesis): "Felix

Dahn (*Teutonenbarde*),¹⁶ E. Jünger (NS writer), v. Simpson (Junker poet), Winnig (vile renegade, guardian angel of the Baltic Free Corps, anti-Bolshevik), and D'Annunzio (friend of Mussolini's, glorifier of fascism)." The Cleansing Committee added "that if this list's underlying viewpoint prevails, then the work that has been accomplished so far, will be squandered, and the goal that it set out to fulfill will be harder than ever to attain."¹⁷

There is no indication that Friedensburg, or any of the other Kulturbund representatives, agreed with the worldviews of the people on the list. Rather, it reflected the Kulturbund statement's assertion of recognizing artistic merit even of opposing viewpoints. The debate between the Cleansing Committee and the Kulturbund reveals the limits and challenges of the Kulturbund's nonpartisan, pluralist approach to cultural renewal, but also its objective of (re)integrating compromised artists and intellectuals into a regenerated society. Was there room – based on the artistic merit of their works alone – in a renewed antifascist and humanist German culture for publishing openly fascist artists, such as D'Annunzio, or writers, such as Ernst Jünger, whose militarist and nationalist tendencies seemed to have much in common with NS ideology? Or was the idea of an index compatible with the reformation of a society that had until recently been told what to read and think? Friedensburg's list never seemed to have been discussed in any of the Kulturbund board meetings. But even though this suggests that Friedensburg's action was not coordinated with the Communist board members, the different approaches of Friedensburg and Lemmer – both of them CDU members who eventually resettled in the West – indicates that the conflict between cultural renewal and cultural cleansing was not necessarily one that neatly divided Communists from non-Communists in the Kulturbund. Rather, both the liberal and the Communist Kulturbund intellectuals saw eye to eye in their goal of a broad national mobilization that would disseminate the vision of humanist renewal among the masses.

The "Other Germany" in the South

At the beginning of 1946, the Kulturbund had about 15,000 members in the SBZ, and it had established contacts with cultural associations in the West, such as the Freie Deutsche Kulturgesellschaft (Free German

---

¹⁶ Dahn was the author of the popular historical novel *Ein Kampf um Rom* (*A Struggle for Rome*); his description of Germanic sacrificial deaths in battle had greatly impressed Hitler; see Ernst Klee, *Das Kulturlexikon zum Dritten Reich. Wer war was vor und nach 1945* (Frankfurt a. M.: S. Fischer, 2007), 106.
¹⁷ Sitzung des zentralen Säuberungsausschusses, SAPMO – BArch DY 27/520.

Cultural Association), which emerged in Frankfurt under the influence of the left-Catholic Walter Dirks.[18] In the relatively fluid political climate before 1947, many prominent Kulturbund board members – Stroux, Dilschneider, and Bennedik, among others – still lived in the Western sectors of Berlin, and their activities transcended occupation zones. Under these conditions, the historical geographical dividing line in Germany between north and south was initially at least as pronounced as the more recent East–West rift that the Iron Curtain was creating. For example, when the *Ministerpräsident* (governor) of the newly established state *(land)* Württemberg, Theodor Heuss, was invited to speak at a Kulturbund rally in Berlin on March 18, 1946, Friedensburg referred to the liberal politician not as a representative from the Western zones, but as a "proponent of ... German unity from the South."[19]

By April 1946, the Kulturbund had grown to 28,000 members in 248 local chapters in the SBZ. Generally distrustful of organizations that originated under the Soviets, the Western Allies never licensed the Kulturbund as a trans-zonal organization, although locally groups sprang up that adopted the Kulturbund name and appeared to stand in loose contact with the Berlin association.[20] The British Occupation Zone, which included the industrialized northwest, had forty-two such groups. The number of Kulturbund groups and of total members was smallest in the U.S.-occupied south, which might be an indication that the organization's Protestant rhetoric of national reformation had less appeal in Catholic regions.[21]

Kulturbund president Becher and *Aufbau* editor Klaus Gysi experienced firsthand the different conditions for cultural renewal in the other occupation zones. In a report of their visit to Heidelberg in the summer of 1946, the two Communist Kulturbund functionaries reiterated Friedensburg's criticism of the U.S. attitude toward German reconstruction. Unlike the Russians, the Americans in their zone mistrusted any indigenous German effort at cultural renewal, relying on their own denazification program instead.[22] Becher and Gysi also pointed out the fundamental differences in experience between the war-ravaged, industrialized German north and the landscapes and cities in the south, which had experienced relatively few of the war's damages. Consequently, the two Berlin delegates claimed that the calls for a radical democratic

---

[18] See "Bericht über die Arbeit des Kulturbundes seit seiner Gründung," SAPMO – BArch DY 27/908, Bl. 24.
[19] *Tägliche Rundschau*, March 16, 1946.
[20] See *SBZ-Handbuch*, 719.
[21] Präsidialratssitzung vom 29. April 1946, SAPMO – BArch DY 27/908, Bl. 90.
[22] Ibid, Bl. 135.

renewal of German culture found less appeal in southern Germany than in northwest Germany and the SBZ. In their encounter with the representatives of the Heidelberg Kulturbund, Becher and Gysi also claimed that despite their organizations' common names, misconceptions about the possibilities of democratic renewal in the SBZ abounded in the west and south. Bragging to Becher and Gysi about their tolerance for sometimes letting a priest speak at their events, the southern Germans were surprised to learn that a church representative (Pastor Dilschneider) not only regularly spoke at the Berlin Kulturbund, but was a member of the organization's board.[23]

On the other hand, the speech that Heuss gave at the Berlin rally demonstrated that the Kulturbund's emphasis on the role of culture for German postwar unity was shared by leading West German politicians. Under the title "Germany – Destiny and Obligation," the future president of the Federal Republic affirmed, "The great economic questions, whether we will be able to survive, are today decided by other powers; we can present arguments, but we can't make decisions in this realm. A different matter entirely is the *spiritual-moral realm* (emphasis in original), in which we have been inwardly soiled [*innerlich beschmutzt*] during the past twelve years."[24] It could have been a speech given at the Kulturbund inauguration, although Heuss's contention that Germans were free to make decisions in the cultural-moral realm might have been premature. Even if Becher and Gysi on their trip to the West were able to educate their hosts in Heidelberg about the Kulturbund's pluralism and openness to non-Communist voices, the organization's emphasis on culture and its general antifascist outlook left its concrete politics and its concept of democracy undefined.

Once more it was up to Friedensburg – next to Becher probably the most vocal board member of the early Kulturbund years – to force the Kulturbund to take a position on the *political* conditions for German unity. In February 1946, a month before Heuss's visit, Friedensburg presented a paper and declaration to the Kulturbund board that attacked centrifugal ideas of federalism – which at the time were being voiced especially loudly in Bavaria – and also defended the continuing use of the term *Reich*.[25] Paul Wegener demanded a more precise definition of "democracy":

I think [the prospects] for unity would look much better if we had a clearer position on the question of democracy. Reading the newspapers, I'm led to

---

[23] Ibid.
[24] *Tägliche Rundschau*, March 19, 1946.
[25] See Präsidialratssitzung vom 12. February 1946, SAPMO – BArch DY 27/908, Bl. 51, 54.

believe that people understand democracy very differently. It makes a big difference whether one refers to Stalin-like, Truman-like, or Churchill-like democracy. It's my understanding of the Kulturbund that [it] ought to create a spiritual preparation and foundation in Germany, and Germany will then create its own democracy, through elections, etc., and it won't just adopt one of the other democracies. I'd like to know how the Kulturbund envisions democratic renewal, if it just wants to prepare the path or acquire one of the ready-made democracies.

Friedensburg answered, "I think we all agree that the Kulturbund's mission has to be the realization of the specifically German form of democracy."[26]

The exchange took place against the background of the looming, controversial union of the KPD and the SPD into the SED. Yet, this concrete political context was never explicitly mentioned. Instead, KPD functionary Klaus Gysi took issue with another formulation in Friedensburg's declaration. It read: "In an inexperienced people such as ours, a healthy democracy can best be realized through a systematic reconstruction from bottom to top and therefore requires a strong autonomy of the state's various parts." Gysi suggested striking the formulation "from bottom to top," because "that's exactly what the federalist and more or less openly separatist propaganda is exploiting to the extremes." Becher seconded this opinion: "The federalists would tell you, 'from the bottom to the top' contradicts the idea of a central leadership. [But] the Kulturbund was founded in Dahlem at the top and found appeal from below. In a next development step, forces would grow from below, so that the 'the top' was to be differently constituted. A mechanical separation seems to be a rather demagogic matter."[27]

As it had so many times before, Becher's eloquence swayed the board members and Gysi's modification of Friedensburg's resolution was accepted. It also needs to be remembered that many non-communists were still under the impression of the failure of Weimar democracy, with its proliferation of splinter parties. In an *Aufbau* article of January 1946, the CDU's Lemmer wrote: "The trend to anchor the developing democracy in only a few parties is becoming evident. The memory of the fragility of Weimar Democracy, with its myriad parties, is still alive; therefore, among all segments of the politically educated population we can discern the aversion towards a renewed paralysis of political decision-making."[28] Portrayed in this light, the KPD–SPD merger could be sold as a strengthening, rather than a threat to democracy. Still, the

[26] Ibid, Bl. 53.
[27] Ibid., Bl. 63.
[28] Ernst Lemmer, "Demokratischer Block," *Aufbau* 2, Heft 1 (January 1946): 118.

question of the Kulturbund's specific alternative to the Soviet politics in the SBZ remained unanswered. And Gysi's and Becher's insistence on top-down organizational structures began to cast an ominous shadow on the Kulturbund's independence from the dominant political force in the SBZ, a Communist Party that since April 1946 invoked the idea of socialist unity in its name.

Mass Movement without Mobilization

Becher's and Gysi's preference for top-down procedures was reflected in the Kulturbund's more or less centralized organizational structure: its organizations on the *Landes* and *Bezirk* levels were subordinated to the directives of the board in Berlin.[29] However, the success of the Kulturbund among intellectuals of all political persuasions in Berlin was not always matched by a similar response in the provinces, where interest in the Soviet-licensed organization appeared to be much smaller. Norman Naimark points out, for example, that of the fifty "leading members of the intelligentsia" who in 1945 were invited to establish a Kulturbund chapter in the town of Brandenburg, twenty-three heeded the call. The commitment of the provincial intellectuals and educators to cultural renewal seemed to have been less than overwhelming, though, as "all of those who were elected to the presidium ... tried to resign the next day."[30] Other regional organizations ended up being dominated by the bourgeois CDU and Liberal-Democratic Party of Germany (LPD). In Saxony, CDU writer Wolfram von Hanstein was elected regional director (*Landesleiter*). Hanstein's lack of coordination with the Berlin leadership led to his resignation in December 1945, apparently after the intervention of Becher and Kulturbund general secretary Heinz Willmann.[31] Not surprisingly, the Soviets started to become disenchanted with the ideological openness and "bourgeois tendencies" of the organization whose establishment they had encouraged.[32]

But besides the influence of non-Communists in the organization, the Kulturbund faced a more fundamental dilemma, one that had already surfaced in the conflict surrounding censorship. How does an organization mobilize a population and reeducate it from fascism without resorting to the often coercive mass politics of the pre-1945 period? The Kulturbund in the SBZ had gradually grown by

---

[29] See *SBZ Handbuch*, 716.
[30] Naimark, *The Russians in Germany*, 403.
[31] *SBZ Handbuch*, 718.
[32] Naimark, *The Russians in Germany*, 401.

mid-1947 to almost 100,000 members and 633 local chapters. From July to December 1947 alone, the Kulturbund would sponsor more than 8,300 events throughout the zone.[33] However, most of these were readings, lectures, and exhibitions in the tradition of the exile cultural leagues during the Third Reich. If the preoccupation with humanist German culture had a political function in the "culture wars" against the NS regime, in 1946–7, the Kulturbund was on its way to become an umbrella for local clubs of poetry readers and stamp and butterfly collectors.

Pastor Bruno Theek, a founding member of the Kulturbund chapter of Ludwigslust in Mecklenburg-Vorpommern, fondly remembered how the local board, upon request by the population, held presentations on trout fishing. Among the Kulturbund's activities in the northeastern province town was a working group for *plattdeutsch* (the north German coastal dialect) and a club for hobby magicians. "The Magic Club with its roughly ten members had especial appeal," according to Theek. "We even went on tours of the nearby villages."[34] This was hardly the redemptive antifascist cultural reformation that Becher and his cohort had conjured up during the Kulturbund inauguration at the Große Sendesaal.

Not the KPD functionaries on the Kulturbund board, but liberal representatives were the first to voice discontent with this development. At the board session of January 9, 1946, the non-party-affiliated music professor Bennedik reminded the board of the original mission of the Kulturbund: "In my view, it is not enough for us to give intellectual lectures, organize exhibitions, and support artists, as valuable as those things may be; the emphasis of our work must be on the 'democratic renewal of Germany,' and so far there hasn't been much done in this respect." Bennedik disapproved of the language of the *Aufbau* as too elitist, and he warned against a rift between intellectuals and the common people as it had developed after 1918.[35] He also criticized the Kulturbund's lack of engagement in contemporary issues and questions of the recent past: "Telling people the truth about the past is especially important, and this is not happening enough. News on the Nuremberg Trials [is] only broadcast at 11:30 PM. These days, nobody has enough fuel or power to listen to the radio that late." Bennedik then proposed a public reading of

---

[33] *SBZ Handbuch*, 731–2.
[34] *... einer neuen Zeit Beginn. Erinnerungen an die Anfänge unserer Kulturrevolution 1945– 1949* (Berlin [East]: Aufbau-Verlag, 1981), 483. See also Jan Palmowski, *Inventing a Socialist Nation: Heimat and the Politics of Everyday Life in the GDR, 1945–90* (Cambridge: Cambridge University Press, 2009), 23–64.
[35] Präsidialratssitzung vom 9. January 1946, SAPMO – BArch DY 27/908, Bl. 2 and Bl. 3.

Roosevelt's 1939 speech to Hitler. Following this speech, he suggested allowing an American journalist "speak about democratic conditions in America."³⁶

But while the Nuremberg Trials were at least acknowledged – and approved of – in the pages of *Aufbau*, and the Kulturbund had organized a rally affirming the trials in November 1945, Bennedik wanted the movement to go further: "A large part of the German people also knows nothing about the Yalta Conference ... we could have the opportunity to organize a number of public rallies to expose many things that would enlighten the German people about all the things that it hasn't been told. The German people would thereby assume the role of an additional plaintiff."³⁷ Friedensburg seconded Bennedik's suggestions, emphasizing the need to reignite the ambitions that had led to the Kulturbund's foundation: "We need an inner renewal, a real revolution.... In our publications, though, this burning desire for reform can only be felt in the works of Herr Becher." It is remarkable, but not uncharacteristic for the atmosphere in the early Kulturbund, that the Christian Democrat Friedensburg held up the Communist Becher as a model for his ideas of reform. Friedensburg went on: "There is something else missing in our work, and that's intellectual confrontation and struggle [*geistige Auseinandersetzung und Kampf*]. People will not become engaged when they're constantly offered something, it goes over their heads. They attend events to relax, not to be transformed [*umgestaltet*]. People will only get involved if we can get them to speak out ... on the great problems that the new Germany faces."³⁸

There seemed to be a remarkable impatience among the liberal members of the board about the Kulturbund's lack of political mobilization, even though the CDU member and writer Theodor Bohner remarked that while the need for a political dimension to the Kulturbund's work was unquestionable, the movement should not forget its task to "humanize" the people. The Social Democrat Gustav Dahrendorf joined in the bourgeois-liberal complaints by criticizing the Kulturbund's lack of progress in the education of the youth: "To a large degree, this cannot be done by issuing manifestos but it [youth education] needs the confrontation [with issues].... We need to develop structures that allow for such confrontations. In regard to democratic renewal, we can only make progress with constructive criticism and confrontation."³⁹

---

³⁶ Ibid.
³⁷ Ibid., Bl. 4. For the Kulturbund's declaration on the Nuremberg Trials, see SAPMO – Barch, DY 27/65.
³⁸ Präsidialratssitzung vom 9. January 1946, SAPMO – BArch DY 27/908, Bl. 5.
³⁹ Ibid., Bl. 8.

The demands for a stronger "confrontation" with topical issues constituted a challenge for the Communists on the board because it meant that ideological differences among the Kulturbund members might resurface. Dahrendorf, for example, was an outspoken opponent of the impending merger of his party with the KPD.[40] Becher did not comment on these political questions – or on Bennedik's equally sensitive reference to the Yalta Treaty and Soviet democracy – but he admitted the lack of political engagement and confrontational arguments in the *Aufbau*. He pointed at the lack of qualified personnel that staffed the journal. His fellow KPD member Willmann joined him in moving the discussion to staffing problems: "Democratic renewal ... cannot be done by individuals but there must be a staff of people who know the direction and who have arrived at an understanding about their goals and responsibilities.... We should start by summoning the representatives of the Berlin subchapters here every two weeks and present them our positions on individual problems."[41] The desire to rekindle the Kulturbund's reformist fervor had led to a first step toward the increasing centralization of its leadership.

The anxiety over the Kulturbund's development toward becoming an expression of the apolitical *Bildungsbürgertum* lingered on in the board sessions of 1946. On April 29, it was Becher who diagnosed the tendency of the Kulturbund, especially in the provinces, "to degenerate into cultural clubs [*zu Kulturvereinen zu entarten*]." The expressionist poet was especially perturbed by a performance in Rostock of Lessing's play *Nathan der Weise* that did not make any political references to the present. Lessing's Enlightenment defense of religious tolerance had had symbolic relevance for the exile cultural leagues during their struggle against the NS regime. Now, without fascism to combat, antifascism was in danger of losing its political relevance. Becher reminded the board that the Kulturbund was meant to be "a German movement of purification [*deutsche Reinigungsbewegung*]" and again targeted *Aufbau*. The movement's main organ was supposed be modeled after Luther's theses, accessible to the masses but resonant of the political discussions of its time.[42] But the Kulturbund's dilemma remained. How was it possible to mobilize the masses in the name of antifascism when fascism was gone,

---

[40] Because of his opposition to the foundation of the SED, Dahrendorf left the Kulturbund and the SBZ in February 1946. In 1947, he became vice president of the bi-zone economic council. The ranking Social Democrat on the Kulturbund board gave up on the antifascist coalition much sooner than the Christian Democratic representatives. See *SBZ Handbuch*, 884.

[41] Präsidialratssitzung vom 9. January 1946, SAPMO – BArch DY 27/908, Bl. 9 and 10.

[42] Präsidialratssitzung vom 29. April 1946, SAPMO – BArch DY 27/908, Bl. 87 and Bl. 88.

and how could a mass organization be politicized without continuing the totalitarian mass politics of the pre-1945 period?

The decline in reformist fervor and popular enthusiasm for the Kulturbund's project became evident at the organization's first anniversary, which was celebrated with a rally in Berlin on July 7, 1946. At the event, organizational gaffes and especially speeches that went on too long had led to an exodus among the audience members long before the rally was over. The Kulturbund board members agreed that the rally was a disaster. At the board meeting of July 15, 1946, Becher announced that the Kulturbund had become a "real mass organization ... To some extent it could be seen as a society of the arts [*Kunstverein*], in other words an organization that could already have existed under the Nazis, or before 1933. But how can the Kulturbund differentiate itself from such an association?" Once again, Friedensburg was of the same mind as the Communist Kulturbund president: "The rally [on July 7] showed that we run the risk of either descending into predictable postures or becoming a general art club. But it is our responsibility to be a real movement of renewal, one that touches people's minds and hearts, and that stirs them up and forces them to reflect."[43]

Friedensburg not only concurred with Becher on the Kulturbund's degeneration into an arts club; he also demanded personal changes in the organization's administrative leadership:

> I believe that the Kulturbund leadership lacked the energy to execute and implement everything that would have been useful.... Perhaps it will be necessary to recruit additional people. We need somebody who is better qualified for this missionary work [*missionarische Aufgabe*] than Herr Willmann [the Kulturbund's general secretary].... Maybe someone who is able to support him with the intellectual responsibilities and who has the ruthlessness [*Rücksichtslosigkeit*] to implement the decisions we make.[44]

If CDU member Friedensburg called for more ruthlessness in the Kulturbund's leadership, his fellow-liberal representative Bennedik demanded more centralization: "The risk of becoming a cultural club has been there from the beginning; ... we need to place more emphasis on directing the [local] groups centrally. We must demand better discipline."[45]

Other noncommunist voices joined in the discussion. The Catholic priest Melchior Grossek remarked that "people are overwhelmed with

---

[43] Präsidialratssitzung vom 15. July 1946, SAPMO – BArch DY 27/908, Bl. 148 and Bl. 149.
[44] Ibid., Bl. 151.
[45] Ibid., Bl. 152.

their daily worries. For the time being, people don't have the inner capacity to reflect on these problems very deeply. It seems to me we should first strive for the democratic renewal of Germany through culture." Klaus Gysi reminded him that the Kulturbund's cultural mission could be fulfilled without fixing its organizational deficits: "We need people who combine two things: An intellectual mind [*Geist*] and organizational talent.... Nothing about the Kulturbund's work is purely organizational, everything has an intellectual context.... What matters is the ideological guidance."[46]

As a preliminary step, the board – on Dilschneider's initiative – created a tighter leadership circle, referred to as the board committee [*Präsidialausschuß*] or working committee [*Arbeitsausschuß*]. Nominated by Becher and elected to this inner circle were Friedensburg, Dilschneider, Bennedik, scientist Robert Havemann, writer and CDU member Theodor Bohner, Becher, and Gysi.[47] Except for Becher and Gysi, all the members of the working committee were non-Communists. But perhaps paradoxically the dissatisfaction with the Kulturbund's perceived failure to mobilize the masses for its project of cultural renewal – a criticism expressed not only by Becher but at least as vocally by the bourgeois-liberal representatives – had paved the way for a more centralized organization. Even more importantly it had legitimized the demand for someone on the board who combined what Friedensburg had called "ruthlessness" and Gysi defined as "ideological guidance."

Cultural Renewal and Ideological Coordination

On July 16, 1946, a day after the board session, Alexander Abusch arrived in Berlin after having stopped in Moscow on his return from Mexico.[48] By then, his book *Der Irrweg einer Nation*, written during his antifascist exile in Mexico, had already been published by the Kulturbund's Aufbau Press. The former editor of *Alemania Libre* had apparently prepared himself to shore up the struggling Communist Party in the Western zones, but on Walter Ulbricht's request, he stayed in Berlin.[49] With the antifascist project in crisis after the defeat of fascism, the former link between KPD bureaucracy and exile artists was seen as the right person to take the movement for cultural renewal in a new direction.

---

[46] Ibid., Bl. 155.
[47] Ibid., Bl. 156.
[48] See Wolfgang Kießling, *Alemania Libre in Mexico. Band 1. Ein Beitrag zur Geschichte des antifaschistischen Exils (1941–1946)* (Berlin [East]: Akademie Verlag, 1974), 261.
[49] See Alexander Abusch, "Aus meinen Erinnerungen an die ersten Jahre unserer Kulturrevolution," manuscript, SAPMO – BArch, SgY 30/1084/1, Bl. 38 and Bl. 47.

The very next day after his return to Berlin, Abusch received a visit from Becher. The two men's friendship went back to Abusch's days as editor of the *Rote Fahne*, the KPD paper in the Weimar Republic, and in his memoirs, Abusch referred to the meeting as a *Kadergespräch* (cadre meeting). Becher greeted Abusch with the words: "You know already that we are going to work closely together now. You are to become my deputy and secretary for ideological issues in our Cultural League for the Democratic Renewal of Germany." Abusch was hesitant, but Becher stayed firm: "Have you forgotten the time in Berlin, the years in Paris with the writers, have you forgotten Mexico? You are definitely the right man.... Who other than you would be able to provide the ideological direction in such a complicated organization, with many older bourgeois intellectuals, members of the new democratic bloc parties and non-party affiliates, and soon with a lot of young people?"[50]

Abusch claimed that Becher's announcement took him by surprise. But if Becher's suggestion really came as a shock, it is startling that the Kulturbund president would treat as a *fait accompli* the appointment of a new secretary only two days after a board session at which specific candidates were not even mentioned and the position itself was discussed only in vague terms. It supports the suspicion that Becher had given in to SMAD pressure for more ideological streamlining of the Kulturbund, and that the decision for Abusch's involvement had been made unilaterally by the SED leadership. However, it was the discussion at the board session of July 14, with its calls for more political fervor and discipline, that prepared the ground for Abusch's ascension. In a sense, the attempt to revive the antifascist sense of purpose as it had existed in the Mexican exile community resulted in the end of nonpartisanship by according a central role to that community's architect.

In the end, Abusch agreed to play a role in the Kulturbund. Whether due to personal modesty or because of the exigencies of Communist bloc politics, Abusch asked Becher during their cadre meeting that he not be officially nominated for vice president.[51] Nevertheless, the minutes of the next board session, on July 30, 1946, list Abusch as deputy to the president, but the change was evidently not discussed during the session. Instead, the board members declared in a statement on the organizational modifications: "A new ideological-cultural department is to be created, with control of the newspapers and journals, the publishing house, and the intellectual-cultural advisory office, with all its working groups. The new department will be administered by Mr. Gysi.... The

---

[50] Ibid., Bl. 47 to Bl. 49.
[51] Ibid., Bl. 57.

ideological, cultural-political activities ... are overseen directly by the president and his deputy."[52] Apparently without any dissenting voice a decisive step toward the Sovietization of the Kulturbund was made.

Even if non-Communists still made up the majority of the board and its working committee, one of the few SED members on the board was given responsibility for an ideological department with control over publications and cultural activities. Moreover, the head of this department did not report to the full board, but to "the president and his deputy," i.e., Becher and Abusch. In practical terms, though, it seemed to have been Abusch who took charge of the ideological department. While Gysi focused on his responsibilities as chief editor of the *Aufbau*, a Kulturbund memo from August 3, 1946, states that Abusch was to "strengthen the ideological leadership in the Kulturbund's central administration and will be in control of all publications."[53]

The first test of the Kulturbund's new understanding of political activism was the district and communal elections in all four zones, including the SBZ, in October 1946. As an officially licensed, nonpartisan mass organization, the Kulturbund was eligible to participate at the elections and nominate its own candidates for the Berlin city council. Becher was generally partial to Kulturbund participation. At the board session of July 30, 1946, though, Friedensburg made a passionate argument against the Kulturbund's involvement in party politics. Friedensburg remarked that "the mere thought of the Kulturbund ... someday making use of this permission [to participate in elections]" would be very dangerous for the movement. "We are proud of the fact that we don't care about our party affiliation. We might get caught in a conflict between our loyalty to our party and the Kulturbund."[54] Friedensburg's balancing act of more Kulturbund politicization without political partisanship seemed to have been successful. The board decided against a Kulturbund participation at the October elections, which ushered in a resounding triumph of Kurt Schumacher's SPD over the KPD in the Western zones.

The differences between Friedensburg, who would become one of the Kulturbund vice presidents in May 1947, and Abusch, the head of its ideological department, were increasingly hard to bridge. In the manuscript of his memoirs, Abusch explained: "In our work in the Kulturbund we took as a fact that the board's presidential board, with its great diversity in ideology and social origins, required much understanding and

---

[52] Präsidialratssitzung vom 30. July 1946, SAPMO – BArch DY 27/908, Bl. 182 and Bl. 183.
[53] Angaben über die leitenden Mitarbeiter des Kulturbundes zur demokratischen Erneuerung, 3. August, 1946, SAPMO – BArch DY/2751.
[54] Präsidialratssitzung vom 30. Juli 1946, SAPMO – BArch DY 27/908, 173.

flexibility in the dealings with its members." Abusch praised "outstanding bourgeois men, such as Bernhard Kellerman, Herbert Ihering, and Johannes Stroux," but he also acknowledged: "Despite our striving for unity, dealing with some members of the CDU was more ideologically difficult, especially with Dr. Ferdinand Friedensburg and a pastor from West Berlin, Dilschneider; eventually also with Ernst Lemmer; all of these turned out to be guided by the Western powers' politics of division."[55]

While the tone between the Communist Becher and the CDU politician Friedensburg was characterized by mutual respect and often striking similarities in rhetoric and opinion, Abusch clashed openly with the liberal Kulturbund cofounder. One of the disagreements erupted during an Abusch presentation on "Mexico Today" in winter 1946. According to Abusch's memoirs, Friedensburg, who was also head of the Institute for Market Research, tried to demonstrate "with colonialist arguments" that the Mexican policies of expropriation had harmed the country economically. Abusch put Friedensburg's self-definition as "German democrat" in quotation marks.[56]

While the shared experiences of men of Becher's and Friedensburg's generation during the first half of the century produced wide-ranging agreements among the Kulturbund's ideologically diverse founders, the movement's self-declared mission to reeducate and shape the young generation brought more divisions to the surface. In July 1947, the Kulturbund held an "academy" for young members. For Abusch, this event was significant not because of its themes and their presentations, but because it gathered a

> large number of talented, active young people with good character fighting for the unwavering democratic renewal of our culture. Their intellectual attitudes, their behavior, their actions in the decades that followed were for me personally the historical answer to many of the arguments that we had had in exile with those antifascists who despaired of the German 'character,' who thought of Hitlerism as a sort of 'hereditary sin,' and who had no hopes for the future for German youth influenced by fascism.[57]

Friedensburg's contribution to the academy, again, disrupted the idyllic congregation of stalwart young democrats: "One day Dr. Ferdinand Friedensburg of the CDU came along with a speech on his old-fashioned notions of bourgeois democracy; however, his attempt at an indiscriminate defense of Weimar 'democracy' provoked counterarguments of

---

[55] Abusch, "Aus meinen Erinnerungen an die ersten Jahre unserer Kulturrevolution," manuscript, SAPMO – BArch, SgY 30/1084/1, Bl. 56/57.
[56] Ibid., Bl. 67.
[57] Ibid., Bl. 82.

the younger members who demanded that the fundamental historical lessons of this 'democracy' of big capitalism be articulated."[58]

In the summer of 1947, it became evident that Friedensburg's understanding of democratic renewal did not have a future in Abusch's ideological planning. The currency reform and the foundation of a separate East CDU in 1948 finally caused Friedensburg and Lemmer to break with the Kulturbund and resettle in the West.[59] In the same year, Abusch and Becher were voted into the SED party leadership. As Abusch put it, with this step, "the double leadership of the Kulturbund was now formally represented in the uppermost management organ of the Party."[60] By the time the Kulturbund held its second national congress in 1949, elections to the Kulturbund board "were no longer in question." Rather, the "inner-organizational complications [of the Kulturbund's leadership] had been gradually settled by the very loyal cooperation with important personalities and in the appropriate ways of intellectual confrontation."[61] No Soviet pressure had seemed necessary to bring Abusch into a position of power in the Kulturbund. SMAD officer Sergei Tjulpanov, in charge of the development of the political parties in the SBZ, was in any case pleased with the new direction that Abusch gave the organization. In his report to his superiors in Moscow, Tjulpanov wrote about the developments of 1948: "It was discernible that the Kulturbund began to engage in activities among the masses [*Massenarbeit*], and that it strove to transcend the narrow limits of a club and to overcome the local chapters' distant attitudes towards urgent social and political problems. The Kulturbund's leadership has been working extraordinarily successfully toward this goal." As a result, "the authority of the organization has been strengthened."[62] What Tjulpanov, who was in charge of the development of the SBZ's political parties, really said, was that the originally nonpartisan project of cultural renewal had ended up as a subordinate organization within a centralized one-party system.

The loss of antifascist unity in the Kulturbund demonstrates the difficulty of keeping up antifascist alliances without fascism as a political opponent, not only in Germany, but in all postwar European societies. However, unlike in liberated countries, the insight into German historical responsibility led to heightened demands for cultural renewal and

---

[58] Ibid., Bl. 80.
[59] See Pike, *The Politics of Culture in Soviet-Occupied Germany*, 520.
[60] Abusch, "Aus meinen Erinnerungen an die ersten Jahre unserer Kulturrevolution," manuscript, SAPMO – BArch, SgY 30/1084/1, Bl. 60.
[61] Ibid., Bl. 57.
[62] Gerhard Wettig, ed., *Der Tjul'panov Bericht. Sowjetische Besatzungspolitik in Deutschland nach dem Zweiten Weltkrieg* (Göttingen: V&R unipress, 2012), 311.

thoroughgoing national reeducation. This attempt to revive and energize a mass base for an antifascist cultural renewal opened the door for a more centralized and politicized leadership structure in the Kulturbund and a closer allegiance to the newly created SED. Therefore, although the development of the Kulturbund in some ways follows the pattern of Sovietization of antifascist coalitions in other Eastern Bloc countries, the intrinsic dynamics and assumptions of cultural renewal in Germany played a role in its transformation into a Stalinized organization.

The practical implications of antifascist cultural renewal – the cleansing of German literature and education from influences of fascism – opened up questions about the Kulturbund's attitude – and especially that of its non-Communist members – toward censorship and coercion. The Kulturbund, under the influence of representatives such as Friedensburg and Ihering – tolerated by Becher but contrary to the beliefs of CDU men such as Lemmer – steered the Kulturbund on a more liberal course that differentiated the organization from more directly Communist/Soviet-controlled institutions such as the Deutsche Verwaltung für Volksbildung (DVV). The early Kulturbund's atmosphere of antifascist, Popular Front cultural activism under guiding influence of the KPD was reminiscent of the dynamics within the exile communities during the war. Thus, it is no coincidence that the ideological "coordination" of the Kulturbund was to a large extent shaped by Alexander Abusch, who had presided over the relatively open and tolerant Popular Front community in Mexican exile without losing sight of the KPD's interests. Under the conditions of Soviet occupation, the establishment of an "ideological division" – an extension of Abusch's role in Mexico as mediator between communist and liberal intellectuals – was a key factor in the development toward a less pluralist and politically independent movement after 1945. However, as the discussions on the Kulturbund board showed, Abusch and the SED were propped up not only by the Russians, but by the unique context and history of twentieth-century German cultural reform projects, which influenced the political development of the movement. The Kulturbund's insistence on a national reawakening provided a necessary – if rudimentary – discussion of the recent German past, but it might have also opened the door wider for the forces of renewed authoritarianism.

6   The Limits of Humanism: Cultural Renewal and the Outbreak of the Cold War, 1947–1948

Paradoxically, the 1946 merger of the Communist Party of Germany (KPD) and the Social Democratic Party (SPD) in the Soviet Occupation Zone (SBZ) accelerated the deterioration of a unified political left under the banner of Popular Front antifascism. After the West SPD's victory in the Greater Berlin communal elections of October 1946, Hans Leonhard, the publisher of the SMAD-licensed literary-political journal *Weltbühne*, wrote that all "self-declared socialist formations, whether their attitudes are social-reformatory, Christian, or estate-oriented, have almost always led to fascism."[1] Leonhard's sharp attack read like the Stalinist KPD declarations that had vilified Social Democracy as "social fascism" before 1933. A year later, at the Kulturbund's first *Bundeskongreß* (federal congress), Becher's speech did not include the detailed references to the resistance movement's ideological breadth that had been part of every official Kulturbund address during the preceding two years.[2]

However, until the end of 1947, the vision of antifascist German intellectual unity that transcended political parties and occupation zones was still alive. It found its most vocal – and arguably last – manifestation in the First German Writers' Congress, which the Kulturbund organized and held in Berlin in October 1947. The congress exhorted writers and intellectuals to demonstrate unity and to lend their voices to the struggle against the looming political division of Germany. Instead, the First German Writers' Congress became a symbol for the emerging cultural Cold War. It also invites us to rethink many of our assumptions about the origins of the German division – especially as it concerns the relationship between culture and politics and between international and domestic German tensions. Did the gradually intensifying political division in Germany in the years from 1946 to 1948 correspond to a beginning split of German "national culture" that culminated in the construction

---

[1] Hans Leonhard, "Quo vadis, SPD?" *Die Weltbühne*, 9 (November 9, 1946): 269.
[2] Dieter Schiller, *Johannes R. Becher und die Krise des Kulturbunds 1949–1951. Drei Studien* (Hefte zur DDR Geschichte, 63 (Berlin: Helle Panke, 2000), 12.

of a distinct GDR culture? Was this cultural division brought about by the increasing antagonism of the occupation powers, or was it inherent in positions and unresolved tensions among German intellectuals that played out independently of the Cold War?

While there is no doubt that the congress took place in a climate of escalating Cold War tensions, the dominant interpretations tend to separate the intellectual concerns of the congress's participants from the political objectives of the Cold War rivals.[3] By placing the congress of 1947 in a wider thematic and chronological context, this chapter argues that cultural debates among German intellectuals preceded and fed into the Cold War split that occurred during the congress. Even before the eruption of open tensions between East and West on the third day of the event, the congress exposed rifts and unresolved conflicts within Germany's cultural scene that reached back to at least 1933. Specifically, three interrelated debates had already divided German postwar intellectuals before the outbreak of the East–West confrontation: the contrast between German antifascists in exile and "inner émigrés"; the discussion of the wider meaning of the German catastrophe; and the role of a renewed German culture in postwar Europe. Taken together, these conflicts weakened the vision of an all-German cultural nationalism espoused by the antifascist writers and enabled it to be transformed into the divisive rhetoric of the Cold War and into a supporting pillar of the GDR's foundation.

Socialist Humanism and the "Other Germany"

Even before the culmination of political tensions in the course of 1947, discussions of antifascism's central cultural concept, "socialist humanism," had taken a turn that revealed the different sociopolitical trajectories

---

[3] See Waltraud Wende-Hohenberger, ed., *Der erste gesamtdeutsche Schriftstellerkongreß nach dem Zweiten Weltkrieg: im Ostsektor Berlins vom 4. bis 8. Oktober 1947* (Frankfurt am Main: Verlag Peter Lang, 1988); Wolfgang Schivelbusch, *In a Cold Crater: Cultural and Intellectual Life in Berlin, 1945–1948*, trans. Kelly Berry (Berkeley: University of California Press, 1998), 72–106; Gert Dietrich, *Politik und Kultur in der Sowjetischen Besatzungszone Deutschlands (SBZ) 1945–1949. Mit einem Dokumentenanhang* (Berlin: Peter Lang, 1993), 96–101; cf. Carsten Gansel, *Parlament des Geistes: Literatur zwischen Hoffnung und Repression, 1945–1961* (Berlin: BasisDruck, 1996), 41–92. Seminal accounts published in the GDR include Karl-Heinz Schulmeister, *Auf dem Wege zu einer neuen Kultur: Der Kulturbund in den Jahren 1945–1949* (Berlin [East]: Dietz Verlag, 1977); and Gerhard Schmidt, *Der Kulturbund zu Frieden und Demokratie in den Jahren 1948/49: Ein Beitrag zur Vorgeschichte der Gründung der Deutschen Demokratischen Republik. Teil 1 and Teil 2* (Berlin [East]: Kulturbund der DDR, 1984). The complete speeches and discussion protocols of the congress were published in *Erster Deutscher Schriftstellerkongreß. 4. – 8. Oktober 1947*, eds. Ursula Reinhold, Dieter Schlenstedt, and Horst Tanneberger (Berlin: Aufbau, n.d.)

of the Eastern and Western occupation zones. At the board meeting of December 6, 1946, Alexander Abusch introduced himself – and the Kulturbund's new ideological position – by giving a presentation on "Die geistige Haltung unseres Volkes [The Intellectual Attitude of Our Nation]," which was also published as an article in *Aufbau*. At the previous board session in October, Becher had expressed his conviction that the Kulturbund was "very weak" in the realm of ideology and announced that "perhaps at our next session we will need to give not only an organizational report, but also to speak about the political-ideological situation that we have in Germany today."[4] The result was Abusch's paper at the December board meeting.

The presentation reiterated and defended the Kulturbund's rehabilitation of the compromised "inner émigrés" Hans Fallada, Wilhelm Furtwängler, and Gerhart Hauptmann. At the same time Abusch critically observed that the intellectuals as a whole had still not made their decision for "the democratic path." "Personal confusion and misjudgment [*persönliche Verwirrung und Irrung*]" were just indicative of the "general misery of the German intelligentsia," presumably its lack of insight into the historical-materialist implications of culture.[5] Only unswerving adherence to Abusch's concept of socialist humanism, as he had outlined in *Irrweg einer Nation* could offer a solution to the intellectual crisis. Commenting on the presentation, Pfarrer Otto Dilschneider asked Abusch to define the term "humanism" more precisely:

If we ... come back to humanism again and again, we might want to think about how we understand [the term] humanism, and what we mean by 'humanist renewal.' We need to keep in mind that this is not a clear-cut concept. There is one [humanism] in the mold of Goethe and Herder, and another one that Marx and Engels developed.... If we claim to create a new beginning based on this concept, then we need to consider which of these two directions we want to follow.

Abusch's answer seemed noncommittal:

"The humanism of Goethe or the humanism of Engels? The answer is: The humanism of Goethe, and the one of Engels, and also the one that the Church represents; the Kulturbund is the framework in which these three currents can come together to support the democratic renewal of our people.[6]

---

[4] Präsidialratsitzung vom 4. Oktober 1946, SAPMO – BArch DY 27/908, Bl 184.
[5] Präsidialratsitzung vom 6. Dezember 1946, SAPMO – BArch DY 27/908, Bl. 212, Bl. 216.
[6] Ibid., Bl. 238.

The exchange between Abusch and Dilschneider seemed to signal a continuing consensus, but in reality the discussion of humanism had already become an indirect and veiled means of addressing the very real differences between communism and liberal democracy, differences that the project of antifascist cultural renewal had been evading since the 1930s. Abusch's assertion of antifascist unity under the umbrella of humanist culture might have sounded familiar to the exile Nazi opponents in the Mexico City of 1942, but in the Berlin winter of 1946, humanism had ceased to be a unifying force. Rather, it became a tool to redefine – once more – the "other Germany."

In the pages of *Aufbau*, the widening gap between Abusch and his liberal counterparts on the Kulturbund board looked initially also non-confrontational. In the spring of 1947, the journal published the transcripts of a debate on Abusch's paper under the title "Is There a Special German Intellectual Crisis?" Participants in the discussion were, among others, Abusch, Bernhard Bennedik, Ferdinand Friedensburg, and Dilschneider. Friedensburg introduced the discussion by asserting the general agreement that "the serious spiritual disease that our people went through – and perhaps they are still going through it – is not merely a German matter, but this disease, this shock wave is part of a general intellectual and cultural crisis that afflicts humankind at large."[7] Abusch for his part emphasized that the common traits of "the Christian, the bourgeois-democratic, and the socialist types of humanism ... were crucial in the struggle for the democratic renewal in the realm of culture." But he also contended that "we cannot simply declare the intellectual crisis in Germany as identical with the ... symptoms of crisis in the rest of the world." German intellectuals had the responsibility "to comprehend the causes for the German catastrophe and to understand the particular German guilt for it as a precondition for democratic renewal."[8]

The difference between Abusch's socialist humanism and the interpretation of Nazism as symptom of a wider crisis of the West forms an important intellectual backdrop to the political conflicts that merged in the nonpartisan Kulturbund. Abusch had defined his concept of a socialist humanism in his book *Irrweg einer Nation*, written during the war. In his work, one of the showpieces of the early Aufbau publishing program, Abusch had criticized the classical humanism of Goethe and Schiller for its alleged preference for the "inner life." The concept of socialist humanism was essentially a fusion of classical German Weimar culture with the Marxism-derived insight into the historical-materialist contexts of

---

[7] "Gibt es eine besondere Deutsche Geistige Krise?" *Aufbau* 3, Heft 4 (1947): 305.
[8] Ibid., 309, 307.

its production. Without materialist-dialectical analysis, humanism would turn into Nietzschean cultural criticism, lose its connection to the working class, and ultimately become the anti-humanism that bolstered the rule of German Junkers, "monopoly capitalists," and ultimately fascists.[9]

An attentive reader of Abusch's account may have observed indications of this slip into anti-humanist cultural criticism in the "bourgeois tendencies" of the Kulturbund. It could also be perceived in wider discussions that dominated the Western zones. The cultural-political journal *Merkur* – a Western counterpart to *Aufbau* – launched its first issue in 1947 with an article by Denis de Rougemont that summed up nationalism, antisemitism, and other doctrines as "the diseases of Europe."[10] A year earlier, Friedrich Meinecke's influential interpretation of modern history, *The German Catastrophe*, had been published in the West. Meinecke had spent the Nazi years in inner emigration after his statements critical of National Socialism (NS) forced him to resign as chair of the Historische Reichskommission (Imperial Commission for History) and as editor of the *Historische Zeitschrift*.[11] *The German Catastrophe* was meant to provide intellectual guidance and leadership to a traumatized nation. Meinecke interpreted National Socialism as the catastrophic culmination of the modern era's two converging "waves," the national and the socialist mass movements. This "universal process of transformation in the West" made the German catastrophe a question that went beyond Germany and affected the fate of the occident: "The *Hitlermenschentum* (Hitler-humanity) ... was made possible by a shifting of the inner forces in man, which had been occurring since the age of Goethe, and which can also be understood as a disruption of the inner balance between rational and irrational forces."[12]

Despite the anti-liberal conditions that a militaristic aristocracy and a materialist bourgeoisie had created in nineteenth-century Germany, Meinecke argued, the Nazi dictatorship was not predetermined, but "could have been successfully prevented," a circumstance that for Meinecke complicated the German people's guilt for having brought Hitler to power: "A unique personality and a unique constellation succeeded in rising to power and in forcing the German people for a limited time on an errant path.... For the German people this provides the

---

[9] See Alexander Abusch, *Der Irrweg einer Nation* (Berlin: Aufbau, 1946), 139, 161, and passim.
[10] See Denis de Rougemont, "Die Krankheiten Europas," *Merkur* 1, 1 (1947): 17–26.
[11] See Mark W. Clark, *Beyond Catastrophe: German Intellectuals and Cultural Renewal after World War II, 1945–1955* (Lanham, MD: Lexington Books, 2006), 15; for Meinecke's career and thought before and after 1945, see also pages 15–43.
[12] Friedrich Meinecke, *Autobiographische Schriften*, ed. Eberhard Kessel. *Werke, Band VIII* (Stuttgart, K. F. Koehler, 1969), 325–31, 376.

reassuring opportunity and responsibility to purify themselves from the horrors they experienced." For the purification of the German mind, Meinecke envisioned the foundation of *Goethegemeinden* (Goethe communities) in all major cities and towns, which would carry the "living testimonies of the great German mind" through public readings "into the audience's hearts."[13]

In an *Aufbau* article of January 1947, Abusch launched a sharp refutation of Meinecke's liberal interpretation. His article condemned the discussions of a "collective guilt of the West" and "a general European spiritual crisis" as evading questions of the specific German guilt for Nazism and neglecting the investigation of Nazism's causes. Abusch criticized especially Meinecke's disregard for the "economic structures of Wilhelmine-Hitlerite Germany." For Abusch, these evasions were a consequence of Western liberalism and capitalism "where democratic renewal applies cheap dime-store methods, where it is confined to the scheduling of elections, but where the democratization of the state and the economy is stalled, there the intellectual cleansing is sabotaged as well."[14]

Abusch also disagreed with Meinecke's apparent belief that Germany could "just like that" become a part of Western civilization again, and he scoffed at the West German historian's "very humanistic conclusion" – the dream of reviving the intellectual climate of the Goethe era. Instead of Meinecke's liberal humanism, Abusch demanded the "explanation of the objective economic-political driving forces that established Hitler's rule." And unlike Meinecke's general reflection on the disruption in modern Man's inner forces, Abusch reminded his readers that "in the middle of the twentieth century, German hands, on Hitler's orders, conducted the industrialized gassing and burning of millions of innocent human beings."[15]

Abusch's response to Meinecke's theses is a reminder that the crackdown on liberal political voices in the SBZ after 1946 was not only the result of Stalinist front tactics, but also the belief by many intellectuals that liberal approaches to democratic renewal, as Abusch evidently perceived them in the Kulturbund, did not go far enough in their assessment of the German past. The official postwar Communist antifascism, with its reductionist focus on socioeconomic determinants of Nazism, was part of East Germany's legitimizing foundation myth, but for many intellectuals, it was also a necessary corrective to the overly general diagnosis

[13] Ibid., 388, 420, 443.
[14] Alexander Abusch, "Die deutsche Katastrophe," *Aufbau* 3, Heft 1 (January 1947): 8, 2.
[15] Ibid., 8.

of the "crisis of the West," which diluted concrete German actions and responsibilities.

There were other indications that the humanist concept of culture, which had held the "other Germany" together during the NS period, was coming apart at the seams. In an *Aufbau* article of 1946, Wolfgang Harich, the representative of the young generation in the Kulturbund, pounced on writer Ernst Jünger's attempt to cast himself as a Nazi resister in inner emigration. Harich vehemently objected to the impression that men such as Jünger were the spokespersons of a new Germany.[16] On one level, therefore, Harich's criticism was an expression of the still ongoing conflict between the "other Germany" of exiles and resisters and the conformists and inner émigrés.

But the same *Aufbau* issue also contained an attack on philosopher Martin Heidegger, not only because of his questionable moral conduct under the NS regime, but also for his commanding role in the development of modern existentialism.[17] Subsequent *Aufbau* articles assailed the existentialism not only of Heidegger, but also of the French resistance icons Jean-Paul Sartre and Albert Camus.[18] The critiques were variations of Abusch's view of existentialism as a "philosophical fad [*Modephilosophie*]" and a "philosophy of exaggerated subjectivism." In 1947, Abusch wrote: "This philosophy abandons the humanist content of classical bourgeois philosophy, denies [classical philosophy's] relevance for human, i.e., social practice, and instead of realizing the historical necessity of surmounting ... bourgeois existence through the overcoming [*Aufhebung*] of capitalist class society, it engages in philosophizing about the 'general doubtfulness' of human existence."[19] Even before the "anti-formalism campaign" in the late 1940s once and for all condemned "bourgeois" thought and artistic expressions, existentialism and humanism, the ideological pillars of the "intellectual resistance" in Europe, were no longer sufficient to keep the antifascist consensus alive.[20] These

---

[16] See Wolfgang Harich, "Ernst Jünger und der Frieden," *Aufbau* 2, Heft 6 (1946): 556–70.

[17] See Henri Mougin, "Wie Gott in Frankreich: Heidegger unter uns," *Aufbau* 2, Heft 6 (1946): 579–84.

[18] See J Alvarez de Vayo, "Die Existenzialphilosophie und ihre politischen Folgen. Bemerkungen über Jean-Paul Sartre," *Aufbau* 2, Heft 11 (1946): 1158–61.

[19] Alexander Abusch, "Gibt es eine besondere deutsche Krise?" (1947) in *Kulturelle Probleme des sozialistischen Humanismus. Beiträge zur deutschen Kulturpolitik, 1946–1961 (Schriften, Band III)* (Berlin [East]: Aufbau-Verlag, 1962), 41.

[20] For the Europe-wide significance of humanism and existentialism for postwar concepts of intellectual renewal, see James D. Wilkinson, *The Intellectual Resistance in Europe* (Cambridge, MA: Harvard University Press, 1981). For the Soviet condemnation of "formalism and the propagation of socialist realism, see David Pike, *The Politics of Culture in Soviet-Occupied Germany, 1945–1949* (Stanford, CA: Stanford University Press, 1992), especially 170–284. See also Kees Boterbloem, *The Life and Times of Andrei*

ongoing aesthetic debates – and their political undertones – are important to understand the tensions at the First German Writers' Congress, which was to be held later in the year.

The First German Writers' Congress

Scholarship in East and West has described the First German Writers' Congress as the last attempt at intellectual unity among German writers at the beginning of the Cold War. In West Germany, for example, literary historian Waltraud Wende-Hohenberger cited the official GDR literature by maintaining that "there was unity and unanimity among the numerous participants, ... the 'congress centered fully on a clear and unambiguous avowal of the democratic unity of Germany.'"[21] In a similar vein, literary scholar Manfred Jäger, who left the GDR in 1955 to publish in West Germany, calls the congress a "symbol" that demonstrated how "the Germans' willingness to engage in dialogue [*Begegnungsbereitschaft*] was gradually subverted by the confrontation between the Western powers and the Soviet Union."[22] These interpretations paint a picture of well-meaning German intellectuals and writers engaged in the maybe naïve, but certainly futile attempt to stem the political current by espousing their own model of cultural unity, an attempt that ultimately broke down in the face of the more powerful, divisive forces of the Cold War political order. Moreover, this assumption seems to confirm the idea of the century-old bifurcation of culture and politics in Germany and runs the risk of reiterating the myth of the German intellectual who places aesthetic over political concerns.

Standard historical interpretations also imply that the Cold War was carried to the intellectuals in occupied Germany by forces from "without," embodied by the opposing non-German participants at the congress, American journalist Melvin J. Lasky and Soviet writers Vsevolod Vishnevski and Valentin Kataïev. While the East German historiography condemned a perceived American attempt to use the event as a staging ground for anti-Soviet propaganda, U.S. historian David Pike notes the "belligerence" of the Soviet representatives, who "descended upon the congress." Pike emphasizes that "the tenor of remarks made there both by the Russians and the German Communists certainly suited the

---

Zhdanov 1896–1948 (Montreal & Kingston: McGill-Queen's University Press, 2004), 279–83.

[21] Wende-Hohenberger, ed., *Der erste gesamtdeutsche Schriftstellerkongreß*, v, quoting from Schulmeister, *Auf dem Wege zu einer neuen Kultur*.

[22] Manfred Jäger, *Kultur und Politik in der DDR, 1945–1990* (Köln: Edition Deutschland Archiv, 1995), 18–19.

hardline policies developing in connection with the SED conference in late September," a step toward the further Stalinization of the SBZ.[23]

Since 1946, there had been discussion in the Kulturbund about staging a congress in Berlin to reaffirm the unity of German writers across the increasingly diverging occupation zones. The idea was initiated by author Günther Weisenborn, the secretary of the Kulturbund's literary commission and board member of the Schutzverband deutscher Autoren (SDA), the successor organization to the Nazi-suppressed Schutzverband deutscher Schriftsteller (SDS). In a note from October 1946, Abusch confirmed his and Becher's agreement to the congress and put Weisenborn in charge of the event's coordination and organization.[24] Weisenborn was able to draw on the generous support by the SMAD's cultural officer, Alexander Dymshits. The Western Allied occupation authorities also supported the congress, but the Americans, who at this point increasingly questioned the Kulturbund's nonpartisanship, insisted that the Kulturbund did not serve as the congress's official organizer.[25]

Originally planned for July, the First German Writers' Congress took place October 4–8, 1947, in the eastern sector of occupied Berlin and drew more than 280 participants from Germany and abroad. The event came on the heels of the Truman Doctrine, the consolidation of the Bizone and the introduction of the Marshall Plan, and the formation of the Communist Information Bureau (Cominform) in September 1947.[26] Because the SED was not officially a Communist party, it did not take part in the formation of the Cominform. Moreover, Soviet Central Committee member Andrei Zhdanov's "Two Camps" thesis, which opened a "cultural front" in the early Cold War, was not released by Stalin until October 22.[27] However, the congress was staged during a time when Communist parties all over Eastern Europe tried to woo Western intellectuals and at the same time consolidate the claim to leadership of the Soviet Union and its Communist Party. As SED party member Wolfgang Leonhard observed at the second SED Party Conference of September 1947: "The thesis of a separate road to Socialism was not officially set aside, but ... [i]n contrast with the period of 1945–46, our

---

[23] Pike, *The Politics of Culture in Soviet-Occupied Germany*, 376.
[24] Note from Alexander Abusch to Günther Weisenborn, October 10, 1946, SAPMO – BArch DY27/55.
[25] See *Erster Deutscher Schriftstellerkongreß*, 18.
[26] See Christoph Kleßmann, *Die doppelte Staatsgründung: Deutsche Geschichte, 1945–1955* (Göttingen: Vandenhoek & Ruprecht, 1982), 182–4.
[27] See Wilfried Loth, *Stalin's Unwanted Child: The Soviet Union, the German Question and the Founding of the GDR*, trans. Robert F. Hagg (New York: St. Martin's Press, 1998), 75, 82.

Figure 6 Participants at the First German Writers' Congress approach the Kammerspiele building, Berlin, October 1947. The Congress failed spectacularly in its attempt to present a vision of German cultural unity to counter the forces of political division. Its failure demonstrated that the unacknowledged cultural nationalism of the "other Germany" had no place in the post-1947 reality of a divided Cold War Europe.
©SLUB Dresden / Deutsche Fotothek.

The Limits of Humanism

links with the Soviet Union were now openly proclaimed."[28] The prospect of a united Germany seemed more and more tenuous.

Despite – or because of – these hardening divisions, the congress was meant to be a signal of unity among German intellectuals in East and West. Officially sponsored by the SED and the Soviet Military Administration in Germany (SMAD), the congress was designed as a continuation of the pre-1945 German antifascist coalitions, even though by 1947 this ideal was already in the process of being replaced with official Soviet attacks on Western modernism, combined with the Zhdanov-inspired defense of bourgeois humanist culture against Western "formalism" all over Soviet-occupied Eastern Europe.[29]

Joint commissions of the Kulturbund and the SDA spent almost a year planning the event and discussing its program. The event's main organizers were Weisenborn and Günther Birkenfeld, as representative of the SDA. Birkenfeld was also the editor of the literary journal *Horizonte* and one of the more outspoken liberal Kulturbund board members. While the SDA had planned on a meeting of authors to discuss mainly technical and professional questions, the Kulturbund envisioned a congress of writers whose statements of unity would provide an alternative to the increasingly divisive political discussions at the time. The result would be a "renewal" of German culture within Europe after the Nazi catastrophe. Weisenborn had conceived the basic themes of the congress. The first day was to honor the victims of fascism and to discuss the contributions of exile writers, the second day was dedicated to the debate of ideological issues, and the third day was to conclude the event with a public declaration and an "appeal to the world."[30] It was Abusch who gave this basic scheme a more concrete shape. Abusch understood the congress as a continuation and revival of the politicized meetings of exile writers during the NS period, especially the congress in Paris in 1938. Like the Paris conference of 1938, the Berlin congress was to represent the antifascist, humanist "other Germany" to the wider world by declaring responsibility for the Nazi past – e.g., the Nazis' persecution and murder of numerous European intellectuals – and to demonstrate the attempt by antifascist-humanist intellectuals to renew German culture.

---

[28] Wolfgang Leonhard, *Child of the Revolution*, trans. C. M. Woodhouse (London: Ink Links, 1979), 363.
[29] See Günter Erbe, *Die Verfemte Moderne: Die Auseinandersetzung mit dem "Modernismus" in der Kulturpolitik, Literaturwissenschaft und Literatur der DDR* (Opladen: Westdeutscher Verlag, 1993), 59; see also Pike, *The Politics of Culture in Soviet-Occupied Germany*, 376; Anne Applebaum, *Iron Curtain: The Crushing of Eastern Europe, 1944–1956* (New York: Doubleday, 2012), 331–60.
[30] See *Erster Deutscher Schriftstellerkongreß*, 20.

The letters of invitation that the SDA sent out to writers in East and West expressed the hope "that this gathering will demonstrate to Germany and the world that we are actively working for the renewal of German literature in a spirit of cosmopolitanism."[31] By May 1946, the SDA and the Kulturbund had agreed on a duration of four days and the following broad program points: "SDA Welcome Address," "Honoring the Dead," "German Writers at Home and Abroad," "The Writer's Responsibilities Today," "Economical Issues of the Profession," "Final Declaration." However, the response to the congress's invitations was mixed. Prominent German writers and intellectuals declined their invitations, among them Thomas Mann, Alfred Döblin, and Karl Jaspers. Attempts at recruiting prominent internationals such as John Steinbeck and Louis Aragon failed. However, a number of writers from the Soviet Union, the CSSR, Yugoslavia, and also from Great Britain attended.[32] To ensure the participation of all four occupation powers, the SDA, which was seen as more interested in technical matters and which was well represented in the Western zones, was declared the congress's main organizer. In contrast, the Western Allies already had well-founded reservations about the Communist influence on the Kulturbund.[33]

After further organizational complications, the congress was opened on the evening of October 4, 1947, with addresses of the representatives of the four occupation powers as well as by Friedensburg, who had become the Christian Democratic vice mayor of Berlin in October 1946. The list of speakers and discussion leaders was carefully balanced to represent all four occupation zones and all political persuasions. However, the broadest dividing line was still the one that separated the exile writers from their colleagues in inner emigration, from resisters and former Nazi prisoners to writers who had accommodated themselves under fascism. Symptomatic of the congress's agenda of finally reconciling these two groups of intellectuals was the choice of Ricarda Huch as the congress's president and speaker of the congress's welcoming address. The eighty-three-year-old poet and "grand old dame of German literature" had resigned from the Academy of the Arts in March 1933 to avoid an oath of loyalty to the new regime. A month later she wrote to the Academy's president, Max von Schillings: "The national attitude that this government sets down is not my idea of Germany [*Deutschtum*]. The centralization, the use of compulsive force, the brutal methods, the defamation of dissenters, the conceited boasting, I find all this un-German

---

[31] Letter of Invitation for Heinrich Berl, July 14, 1947, in *Erster Deutscher Schriftstellerkongreß*, 487.
[32] Ibid., 49.
[33] Ibid., 24–5.

and perilous."³⁴ This courageous act made her a respected representative of the "inner emigration," even though a film version of one of her novels was released in 1939 and she even received a gift of 30,000 Reichsmark from the regime for her eightieth birthday.³⁵

On the morning of October 5, Huch introduced a memorial event for the victims of fascism at the Hebbel theater in the Soviet sector of Berlin. Huch's speech showed how the diagnosis of German history as an "errant path" had by now become a standard trope among postwar intellectuals. Like Abusch in his *Irrweg*, Huch traced the Hitler period back to Germany's political and social "backwardness" in the early modern period and the formation of a unified nation-state tainted by chauvinism. Huch declared herself "free of one-sided nationalism" even though she "felt real national sentiment [*Aber national fühle ich mich durchaus*]." This seemingly contradictory statement tied in to the Kulturbund's project of reviving the nation by cleansing its nationalist past. And as during the Kulturbund inauguration, Martin Luther served as a reference. Huch praised the Protestant reformer for being very "close to the times and to the people [*sehr zeit- und volksnah*]"; by quoting Luther's statement "*Für meine Deutschen bin ich geboren, und ihnen diene ich auch* [I was born for my Germans, and I serve them]," Huch's opening speech drew, as the Kulturbund did, a connection from resistance against fascism to a revived, modernized version of the Protestant Reformation.³⁶

After the public reading of poems commemorating the victims and resisters of political oppression in Germany, Weisenborn delivered the second major address of the opening day. His speech was titled "On the Death and the Hope of Poets," and he started out by comparing the experiences of his generation, the experience of total war and mass slaughter, with the generation of Gryphius and Grimmelshausen, the poets of the Thirty Years' War. Asserting that "being a poet in Germany is a dangerous profession," Weisenborn explicitly compared the activity of writing to the act of political resistance.³⁷ Arguably, the writers' congress was as much about retaining an aesthetic self-understanding in which artistic production and antifascist politics were inextricably linked as it was about German unity.

---

[34] Quoted in Ernst Klee, *Das Kulturlexikon zum Dritten Reich. Wer war was vor und nach 1945* (Frankfurt am Main: S. Fischer, 2007), 270–1.
[35] Ibid, 271. See also Jost Hermand, *Culture in Dark Times: Nazi Fascism, Inner Emigration, and Exile*, trans. Victoria W. Hill (New York: Berghahn, 2013), 155.
[36] *Erster Deutscher Schriftstellerkongreß*, 102–3.
[37] "'Von Tod und Hoffnung der Dichter.' Rede Auszüge von Günther Weisenborn," *Berlin am Mittag*, October 6, 1947.

Figure 7 Ricarda Huch (1864–1947) giving the opening speech at the First German Writers' Congress, Berlin, October 1947. The eighty-three-year-old poet and "grand old dame of German literature" had spent the Nazi years in "inner emigration" in Germany. Tensions and open clashes between returning exile intellectuals and "inner émigrés" contributed to the Congress's failure, even though Huch's speech showed that both groups employed similar tropes of cultural renewal. Photo by Ullstein bild via Getty Images.

The honoring and remembrance of antifascist literature and resistance was tied to the congress's other main objective: Germany's "readmission" into the international cultural scene after more than a decade of either forced or self-imposed exclusion. Weisenborn's speech put this in emphatic terms: "We turn to the great powers of this earth and solemnly appeal to them for the end of [our] intellectual isolation. We plead as decent men who are engaged in a struggle of life and death.... We reach out to the world and appeal to the men of thought and intellect. We will fight and keep the voice of conscience alive so that future generations will be able to say, a call went out from Germany, and we heard it and heeded it."[38] Weisenborn's mixture of antifascist ideology, internationalism, and the sense of a German universal mission – along with his and other speakers' references to the Protestant Reformation – reflected an implicit but seemingly unacknowledged cultural nationalism inherent in the concept of a humanist cultural renewal in Germany. This belief – which also characterized much of the early Kulturbund rhetoric – in a regenerated "other" German culture that had survived twelve years of Nazi rule and war untainted underestimated the differences in perspective between German antifascists and writers in other countries and ran the risk of conflating a sense of German martyrdom at the hands of the Nazi regime with the barbarism that Germany had inflicted on other countries during the war. In 1947, the rest of the world showed little inclination to heed calls that went out from Germany, whether by antifascists or otherwise. The British general secretary of the International PEN Club, Hermon Ould, commented on Weisenborn's speech: "I'm not sure if the Germans are aware of how strong the sentiments against them still are, especially in those countries that have suffered from German occupation, e.g., France and Czechoslovakia."[39] Clearly the project of German cultural renewal made little impression on non-German intellectuals, who did not usually list German culture among Nazism's prime victims. On the other hand, Jovan Popovič, the Yugoslavian representative, earned the applause of the congress when he exclaimed that

Goethe, Heine, and other great German poets were not to be found in the knapsacks of Hitler's soldiers – we found ham and silk stockings in them. But Goethe was carried in the knapsacks of the Yugoslav freedom fighters, and he was read just as much, or almost as much, as Tolstoy's *War and Peace*.... Therefore nobody

---

[38] Ibid.
[39] "Gespräch mit Hermon Ould," *Berlin am Mittag*, October 6, 1947. The reference to Czechoslovakia seems a strategic choice given the still open-ended political situation in the Central European country.

should hold German culture in contempt, because German culture was not on the side of the fascists, it was on the side of those who fought against fascism.[40]

"The Home of the Poet"

In trying to heal the deep rift that Nazism's legacy had opened up between Germany and the rest of the world, the congress might have bitten off more than it could chew. As it turned out, not even the divisions within the German intellectual community, between exiles and inner émigrés, were healed. The afternoon of October 5, after Huch's and Weisenborn's opening speeches in the morning, had the theme: "Literature and Violence: Reports on the Frame of Mind [*geistige Haltung*] of Writers on the Inside and on the Outside." The speeches were given by novelist Elisabeth Langgässer, a representative of the inner emigration, and by veteran of illegality and exile Alfred Kantorowicz. Like her Jewish-born father, Langgässer was a baptized and committed Catholic. In 1936, she was prohibited from publishing, but she was able to stay in Germany. In "inner exile" between 1936 and 1945 she wrote her novel *Das unauslöschliche Siegel* (*The Indelible Seal*), which "despite its inner contradictions, can be read as offering hope for a religious transformation and thus as a work of resistance against satanic Nazi fascism."[41] During the war, she was forced to work in a munition factory while her daughter – as a "three-quarter Jew" – survived deportation to Theresienstadt and Auschwitz.[42] At the congress in 1947, her continued espousal of a Catholic-Christian concept of art stood in marked contrast to Kantorowicz's "politically concrete definition of art and literature."[43] Despite these differences, Kantorowicz's speech was conciliatory, acknowledging that the writers who had stayed in Germany possessed an intimate knowledge of daily life under the NS dictatorship that the emigrants did not share. At the same time, he emphasized the success of the more than 250 exile writers of all political persuasions in reminding the wider world of the "other Germany."

Langgässer's and Kantorowicz's speeches revealed that by 1947, after the experiences of dictatorship and exile, two distinct aesthetic positions had developed among German intellectuals. Langgässer declared that "the home of the poet is language." Since Nazi propaganda had appropriated the German language to an unprecedented extent, this implied

---

[40] *Erster Deutscher Schriftstellerkongreß*, 134.
[41] Hermand, *Culture in Dark Times*, 155.
[42] See Klee, *Das Kulturlexikon zum Dritten Reich*, 353.
[43] Wende-Hohenberger, ed., *Der erste gesamtdeutsche Schriftstellerkongreß nach dem Zweiten Weltkrieg*, xvii.

that the writers who had stayed in Germany had been as much in exile as their colleagues in foreign countries. For now, Langgässer demanded for language to be granted "a period of peace and silence."[44] In contrast to this emphasis on reflection and language – which Langgässer maintained was not be confused with a retreat to an inner life – Kantorowicz, the Spanish Civil War participant, reminded his audience of the times when writers exchanged "the typewriter for the machine gun" – without ceasing to be writers.[45] While novelists such as Langgässer could still distinguish between their political and artistic identities, for Kantorowicz, as for Weisenborn and other representatives of the "other Germany," the identities of writer and antifascist resistance activist were not only compatible, but closely intertwined.

The two speeches triggered an intense discussion among the congress participants about the moral equivalence of inner and outer emigration and about the merit of literature published between 1933 and 1945 in Germany. Writer Karl Schnog, who had spent five years in Dachau and Buchenwald, was the first to express his resentment of the inner émigrés: "I find it inappropriate that we almost put the clever and tolerably decent ones, who kept working under the Hitler regime with little or no blemish, on the same level with the ones who were real fighters."[46] Greta Kuckhoff, the widow of executed poet Adam Kuckhoff, chimed in by attacking Langgässer's "dangerous idea" to give language a "grace period" in response to National Socialism: "Our authors and poets must not be silent at this time, they need to say the right thing."[47] On the third day of the congress, poet Eva Richter-Schoch responded in defense of the inner émigrés: "During the first two days of this congress, I have gotten the terrible feeling that a new *Übermensch* writer is being envisioned here. He is supposed to be politically immaculate, he's supposed to be a militant. You know, when I closed my eyes, I sometimes thought I was back in Hitler's days, because that's what Hitler demanded from his writers."[48]

Not for the first time – and not for the last – it was Wolfgang Harich who made the most provocative points, laying bare not only the gap between inner émigrés and exiles, but also the generational differences

---

[44] *Erster Deutscher Schriftstellerkongreß*, 137, 141.
[45] Ibid., 144, 145.
[46] Ibid., 153.
[47] Ibid., 156. On Greta Kuckhoff, see Joanne Sayner, "Communicating History: The Archived Letters of Greta Kuckhoff and Memories of 'Red Orchestra,'" in Mary Fulbrook and Andrew I. Port, eds., *Becoming East German: Socialist Structures and Sensibilities after Hitler* (New York: Berghahn, 2013), 79–98.
[48] *Erster Deutscher Schriftstellerkongreß*, 324.

that marked a congress that was meant to be a display of unity. Harich, who as editor of *Weltbühne* had already fiercely attacked writers such as Ernst Jünger, entered the discussion not as an inner or outer émigré, but "from the perspective of someone who had come of age in Germany in those twelve years [of NS dictatorship]. Today, I sometimes ask myself, why did I not become a Nazi?" Harich ascribed his antifascist and pacifist convictions to the reading of books published before 1933 or of exile publications that had been illegally distributed in Nazi Germany. The writings of inner émigrés did not have the same effect: "If I had had to depend on this literature, I might as well have turned into a staunch SS trooper." The audience responded with laughter and uproar to Harich's remarks.[49]

Harich singled out philosopher Karl Jaspers, and his use of terms such as "mass existence, mass order, mass organization, and bureaucratic rule." Jasper's critique of mass society in his work *Die geistige Situation der Zeit* (*The Intellectual Condition of the Times*) of 1930 had prepared the way for the retreat into the inner life (*Innerlichkeit*) that had been so conducive to Nazi rule. Harich did not seem to realize that, as we saw in Chapter 4, many of the proponents of post-1945 cultural renewal had employed the same critiques of mass society as Jaspers before 1933. In allusion to Jasper's influential postwar tract on the concept of collective guilt, Harich lashed out:

> And the same Herr Jaspers has now written a brochure on the question of guilt, in which he tries to deflect the real moral question of general responsibility for fascism by talking about a general guilt of human existence. In the name of the young antifascist intellectuals, who resisted the poisonous influences of fascism, I answer: We don't need a philosophy that in 1933 advocated the retreat into the private life and which now tries to dismiss the question of guilt as hypocrisy.[50]

The debate of the existentialist diagnosis of the "diseases of Europe," which had already been the subject of discussions in the Kulturbund and in *Aufbau*, had reached the congress and merged with the older conflict between inner emigration and activist resistance or exile. At the same time as the antifascist consensus was falling apart under political pressures, young intellectuals such as Harich dismantled the ideological and philosophical foundations of humanist cultural renewal, a project that, as we have seen, was at least partly grounded in pre-1933 cultural critiques of mass society.

---

[49] Ibid., 158–9. For the reactions to Harich's speech, see also "Erster deutscher Schriftsteller Kongreß," *Tagesspiegel*, October 8, 1947.
[50] *Erster Deutscher Schriftstellerkongreß*, 160–1.

The first day of the congress, which had centered on the conduct of writers during the rule of violence, ushered in a debate between exile writers and inner émigrés and ended with a discussion of German intellectuals' attitude towards the "masses." The controversial debate on *Vermassung* (development toward a mass society) continued on the second day of the congress, which had the official theme "Literature and Society." During the morning sessions, writer and Kulturbund cofounder Ernst Niekisch launched an attack on the "bourgeois idea of freedom," a freedom ostensibly denied to those who provided the material underpinnings of liberal society. For Niekisch, this had traditionally led to fear of and contempt of the masses in Germany, an attitude that had not only contributed to Nazi ideas of the "superman," but continued today with the admiration of José Ortega y Gasset among intellectuals. Niekisch extended this critique to the philosophy of existentialism, a form of freedom that led to "general nihilism and general chaos."[51] Existentialism, a philosophy still associated with some leading representatives European of antifascism, had become the idea that had enabled Nazism. Niekisch's attack on Ortega y Gasset led to passionate disagreement by some congress participants, but it could not hide the fundamental divisions among the proponents of cultural renewal.[52]

The Cold War at the Congress

In the afternoon of the second day, a member of the Russian delegation, writer and dramatist Vsevolod Vishnevski, focused on a larger division confronting the world: "Today the world is divided. Keep in mind ... that the first part is represented by the black reaction, by barbarism, by ideologies of militarism and a hate of humanity, and the second part by millions of plain people who live and fight for peace, millions of regular people who fight for democracy." Vishnevski also reminded his audience that during the Nazi siege of Leningrad, Russian citizens sheltered the works of German writers and the triumphs of German humanism from the Wehrmacht's bombardment of the city's libraries. However, the ideologies of barbarism, militarism, and inhumanity that Vishnevski had mentioned did not refer to fascism; it was the "American and British reaction" that tried to divide democratic mankind and create an iron curtain.[53] The Cold War had finally reached a congress that was still

---

[51] Ibid., 228–9.
[52] For Niekisch's speech, see also "Das Parlament der Einzelgänger. Zwischenbericht vom Autoren-kongreß," *Die Neue Zeitung*, October 7, 1947.
[53] *Erster Deutscher Schriftstellerkongreß*, 245–7.

trying to heal the wounds of the period before 1945. The struggle against fascism and the debate between exile intellectuals and the inner emigration had been overshadowed by the Cold War, but German humanist culture was still enlisted as a combatant.

Just as German politicians in the occupation zones were repeatedly reminded of their limited influence in the conflict between the global powers, the attempts of German writers to display East–West unity were thwarted by the international participants of the event. The theme of the third day of the congress, Tuesday, October 7, was the "development of German literature today." In his opening remarks, before the first presentation, Weisenborn, as organizer, felt the need to declare that

> underneath the surface of this congress everybody can feel a certain tension. There are sharp differences present in this room.... This is the case wherever thinking people come together. We have the same differences among the organizers here in Berlin but we still work together in a spirit of solidarity.... We don't know what today will offer but the one thing we know is that the organizing board is absolutely non-partisan.... We urge everybody to settle our differences with solidarity and dignity, deserving of the international format of this congress.

Weisenborn's statement was greeted with applause.[54]

However, Weisenborn's appeal could not prevent the morning of the third day from developing into a major confrontation that brought the tensions and political conflicts between East and West finally out into the open. The occasion for the disagreement was the speech, directly following Weisenborn's declaration, of the American representative, Melvin J. Lasky. According to Ursula Reinhold, the journalist Lasky – the congress organizers and the SMAD had hoped that the much more famous John Steinbeck would represent the United States – was "sneaked" into the program by Birkenfeld as a response to Vishnevski's polemic.[55] The fact that Lasky, a fluent German speaker, was the Berlin correspondent for two U.S. journals – *The New Leader* and *Partisan Review* – which "normally could have never afforded a foreign correspondent" gave rise to the never confirmed suspicion that Lasky was paid by the American CIA.[56] In fact, the U.S. Office of the Military Government in Germany (OMGUS), unlike the Soviet authorities, considered the congress a "German-only" event that did not warrant any heightened initiative.[57]

---

[54] Ibid., 293.
[55] Ibid., 49.
[56] Interview with Melvin J. Lasky, quoted in *Erster Deutscher Schriftstellerkongreß*, 49. Lasky's later activities as editor of the journal *Der Monat* and as initiator of the anticommunist "Congress for Cultural Freedom" were partly financed by the CIA.
[57] Giles Scott-Smith, "'A Radical Democratic Political Offensive': Melvin J. Lasky, *Der Monat*, and the Congress for Cultural Freedom," *Journal of Contemporary History* 35, 2 (April 2000): 265.

Lasky's speech on cultural freedom found initially undivided applause and approval, for example, when he described the damage that the Hitler period had inflicted on German culture and emphatically declared, "I am convinced that [German] writers and artists – even if not the people as a whole – have nothing but fear and disgust for a totalitarian society." Lasky then went on to praise American society for being founded on the principle of cultural freedom and the "contest of ideas." The U.S. journalist also mentioned violations of this principle in America in the past, e.g., the censorship of works by James Joyce before and of Leon Trotsky during the war.[58] Lasky did not mention the investigation of Bertold Brecht, which was launched in 1947.[59]

The speech ended, however, in tumultuous disturbances when Lasky not only expressed his solidarity with the writers and artists in the Soviet Union, but assailed the practices of censorship in the Communist country: "They are engaged in the struggle for cultural freedom, too.... We know how discouraging it is to work in the awareness that the political censor is standing behind you, and the police behind the censor. Consider how it affects the Russian writers to be in constant vigilance as to whether the new party doctrine, the revised state policy of social realism or formalism or objectivism or whatever it may be, might already be outdated; from one day to the next they may be branded as 'decadent counterrevolutionary tools of the reaction.'" Lasky's remarks were met with applause, but also with exclamations of disapproval and outrage. When Lasky mentioned the concrete cases of Sergei Eisenstein and G. F. Alexandrow, the atmosphere in the audience became so turbulent that Günther Birkenfeld interrupted the speech and reminded the audience of Weisenborn's appeal from earlier in the morning. It took a while for the turbulence to calm down and Lasky to resume his speech, all the while interrupted by exclamations such as "Bravo," "fewer lies," and "violation of guest privilege."[60]

Lasky's speech, more than the controversies about inner emigration or mass society, divided the congress once and for all. Despite the ongoing turmoil, the American journalist was able to finish his address with the words: "In all countries on earth the great writer has always been to some extent a revolutionary fighter.... He carried the seed of rebellion and revolt into people's minds and hearts. Respectable citizens, official powers, the authorities, and tradition, if they had been farsighted enough, would have immediately recognized him as their enemy."[61] This ending

---

[58] *Erster Deutscher Schriftstellerkongreß*, 296–8.
[59] See Wende-Hohenberger, ed., *Der erste gesamtdeutsche Schriftstellerkongreß nach dem zweiten Weltkrieg*, xxiv.
[60] *Erster Deutscher Schriftstellerkongreß*, 300–1.
[61] Ibid., 301.

of Lasky's speech was greeted by enthusiastic applause – including by Ricarda Huch, the congress's honorary president.

At this point, the Soviet delegation, led by the SMAD's cultural officer, Lieutenant Colonel Alexander Dymshits, had already shown its protest by conspicuously leaving the room during the speech.[62] Ironically, Lasky and Dymshits, who had invested a great deal of personal effort in the congress's success, could have found much common ground in different circumstances. Both men were intellectuals of Jewish descent with an affinity for German culture and proficiency in the German language. As a former Trotskyist and member of the New York left, Lasky also deeply believed in the political function of the arts.[63] While Lasky had critically commented on censorship in the United States, Dymshits had used his influence to restrain the censorship of German writers in the SBZ.[64] In Berlin in the fall of 1947, all of this counted for little, however. During the afternoon sessions of October 7, Soviet writer and editor Valentin Kataïev was among the speakers; his address was a direct reply to the Lasky speech: "I'm glad that I have finally seen the face of a living warmonger [*Kriegsbrandstifter*]. Back home in the Soviet Union we don't have any of these types." To the audience's applause, Kataïev compared Lasky's "lies" to the methods of Goebbels.[65]

Lasky's speech also triggered a response by German intellectuals. During another one of the afternoon discussions, Harich brought up Lasky's speech. Without mentioning Lasky's name, Harich commented on the U.S. representative's closing remarks, which had been received with overwhelming audience applause. Harich did not share this approval: "It has been said this morning that the writer needs opposition, unconditionally, at all costs.... I disagree. In a place where positive, constructive, and progressive developments are unfolding, the writer needs to be supportive, and – under the condition that the state is a state of the people – he must also be state-affirming [*staatserhaltend*], if I'm allowed this term." Not only did Harich urge writers to support the Soviet state, he went on to attack U.S. occupation policies in Germany. If Lasky demanded opposition at all costs, Harich suggested that Lasky protest the fact that a "film based on a novel by [Communist writer] Anna Seghers could not be shown in Germany, that Sinclair Lewis's book could not be printed in Germany because it dealt with the Negro problem ... and that one of our most upright publicists, who has been in concentration camps for years,

---

[62] See *Tagesspiegel*, October 8, 1947; *Spandauer Volkszeitung*, October 8, 1947.
[63] See Scott-Smith, "'A Radical Democratic Political Offensive,'" 267–8.
[64] See Naimark, *The Russians in Germany*, 460; Giles McDonogh, *After the Reich: The Brutal History of the Allied Occupation* (New York: Basic Books, 2007), 224.
[65] *Erster Deutscher Schriftstellerkongreß*, 336.

The Limits of Humanism 151

has been deprived of his license without any justification.... It's deplorable how they use Metternich's methods of censorship and persecution to introduce democracy here. It won't work that way."⁶⁶ Harich earned strong applause for this mixture of Cold War defense of the Soviet Union and nationalist outrage over U.S. occupation policies.

Besides Kataïev's and Harich's explicit responses to Lasky's polemic, the congress went on with the discussion of more technical and practical questions on the status of writing and publishing in occupied and liberated Germany. However, it was the outbreak of the Cold War at the congress that dominated the coverage of the event, in the Western as well as in the Eastern occupation zones. While SMAD-licensed newspapers, such as the *Tägliche Rundschau*, sharply attacked Lasky's contribution as a deliberate provocation, the U.S.-licensed *Tagesspiegel* printed the speech almost in full length as an affirmation of Western cultural values.⁶⁷ The French-licensed *Kurier* made the strongest effort to cover the intellectual debates at the conference, but even this paper compared the congress with "Babylon."⁶⁸ The First German Writers' Congress's main objective – the restoration and demonstration of intellectual unity across East and West – had failed. As its only achievement the event could point to the passing of two unanimous resolutions – one against antisemitism and the other for the repatriation of exile intellectuals – but these voices of unity and reconciliation were drowned out by the noises of the Cold War.

The antisemitism resolution was introduced by writer and KPD functionary Hermann Duncker, who reflected in his speech on his experiences in U.S. exile: "My years in America have made a strong impression on me. When we got news about what was happening in Germany ... the most horrible things must surely have been the atrocities of antisemitism. And it was even worse when ... American friends showed us accounts of antisemitism flourishing again in Bavaria and other places."⁶⁹ Duncker's appeal for a resolution against antisemitism met with unanimous support and the discussion it triggered seemed to be free of the East–West differences that characterized interpretations of the Holocaust in the FRG and the GDR in later years.⁷⁰ Two days after Duncker's speech, the German-Jewish literary scholar Hans Mayer, whose family had been killed in the Holocaust, criticized that the resolution had faded into the background after the Lasky incident: "It has been disturbing for me to read parts

⁶⁶ Ibid., 350.
⁶⁷ See "Kulturelle Freiheit," *Tagesspiegel*, October 8, 1947.
⁶⁸ *Der Kurier*, October 9, 1947. See also Wende-Hohenberger, ed., *Der erste gesamtdeutsche Schriftstellerkongreß nach dem Zweiten Weltkrieg*, 95.
⁶⁹ *Erster Deutscher Schriftstellerkongreß*, 219.
⁷⁰ See Jeffrey Herf, *Divided Memory: The Nazi Past in the Two Germanys* (Cambridge, MA: Harvard University Press, 1997).

of the press coverage about our congress. I would have assumed that Duncker's request for us to take up the fight against antisemitism should have been the headline of all newspapers. ... But this was not the case."[71] Mayer's reproach was greeted with applause. Yet, even without the Cold War theme that overshadowed the congress, the reminder of the main victims of Nazism struck a contrasting note at an event that emphasized celebrations of German antifascist martyrdom and ended with open hostilities between the Nazis' vanquishers.

The End of the Kulturbund in the Western Zones

Arguably, the congress marked the end of the nonpartisan, pluralist movement for antifascist cultural renewal in Germany that spanned the occupation zones. Almost as if to signal the official end of this project, a "tormented" Günther Birkenfeld informed the congress participants on the very last evening of the event of the decision by the American and British occupation authorities to prohibit the Kulturbund's activities in their zones. This meant that the Kulturbund had to give up its main building at Schlüterstraße 45 in British-administered Charlottenburg and officially become a Soviet-zone, rather than an all-German organization.[72]

As Wolfgang Schivelbusch points out, the end of the Kulturbund in the Western zones was "the result of a complicated process desired and staged not only by the two Western powers."[73] At the center of the decision were the conflicting definitions of the Kulturbund's nature: for the Western Allies, it was a political organization that needed individual approvals in each of the occupation sectors. The Soviets, on the other hand, argued that it was a cultural organization, which meant that the Soviet license of May 1945 would still be valid in all four sectors. Although the Kulturbund's application for an American license was turned down in 1946, the U.S. Information Control Division assured general secretary Heinz Willmann that its activities were to be tolerated in the Western zones.[74] By October 1947, with the more confrontational stance adopted by their governments, the U.S. and British occupation authorities demanded a renewal of the Kulturbund's application. But at this point giving in to the Western demand would have seemed like a

---

[71] *Erster Deutscher Schriftstellerkongreß*, 415.
[72] Schivelbusch, *In a Cold Crater*, 98
[73] Ibid.
[74] See Office of Military Government, Berlin District, Information Control Division, gez. F. N. Leonard, Lt. Col. Chief of Division, June 17, 1946, SAPMO – BArch DY 27/1395, Blatt 4.

Soviet loss of face. As a result, the Kulturbund's officials were informed that their activities in the Western zones had to cease by November 1.

Schivelbusch maintains that the Soviets actually welcomed the Kulturbund's ban: "In the heightening cold war atmosphere, the Western powers' ban on the Kulturbund must, in terms of propaganda, have seemed more valuable to them than the organization itself was."[75] With this strategy the SMAD, perhaps for the last time, clashed even with the Communists in the Kulturbund's board. As late as September 1949 the SED's Willmann appealed to the SMAD officer of Berlin, Col. Yelisarov, for permission to reapply for a Western license: "The board of the Kulturbund in Berlin and its president, Johannes R. Becher, believe that we should submit an application and thus make a new contribution to normalize life in Berlin." Willmann also admitted that this would come with financial costs. The magistrate in the Western part of Berlin prohibited the use of schools and public buildings and of the city's billboards. Therefore, the Kulturbund would have to rent buildings and spend money on advertising: "Of course this would require that we receive a percentage of our revenue in Westmarks."[76] Willmann's request was denied, probably because of both political and financial reasons, but the exchange shows the extent to which the Kulturbund's objective of cultural renewal in East and West was incompatible with Stalinist Cold War strategies, rather than being a component of them.

Thus, it is highly symbolic that the news of the Kulturbund's end in the Western zones reached German intellectuals on the last day of a congress that had so strikingly revealed the limits of humanism and antifascist nonpartisanship. The Soviet delegation, predictably, denounced the Kulturbund ban as censorship of antifascist and democratic forces in the West. But the realization that the Kulturbund had now openly become a pawn in the rivalry between the Cold War superpowers dealt a huge blow also to those intellectuals, such as Friedensburg, who had become more skeptical toward the organization's aims. The reaction of the openly anti-Communist Birkenfeld demonstrates how much the Kulturbund, despite its obvious SED influence, was still a symbol for the idea of the "other Germany," the project of antifascist renewal. Birkenfeld delivered an emotional statement on the last day of the congress. First he emphasized that he understood politics in the spirit of "the great American democracy" – not "in the spirit of the great Eastern

---

[75] Schivelbusch, *In a Cold Crater*, 99.
[76] Letter of Heinz Willmann to the deputy Soviet commander of Berlin, Colonel Jelisarow, September 29, 1949, SAPMO – BArch DY 27/1395, Blatt 4.

democracy." However, the Kulturbund ban in the Western zones made him question these principles:

> I am not entitled to criticize a decree by the American military administration. But I believe as a German writer who tries to be a democrat I have a right to say the following. Like many of my friends I joined the Kulturbund with some hesitation. I knew then that most of the leadership had a political ideology that differed from mine, and although I knew that there were forces which strove for a partisan political influence, I joined the Kulturbund out of my deep conviction that we need to keep up the conversation with friends and colleagues who have different political principles.[77]

Birkenfeld was interrupted by sustained applause before he proceeded.

> We Germans don't have much more left than our language and our culture. At this congress I've gained the tragic and painful impression that we already no longer speak a common language and that the German language is on its way to split into two dialects, an eastern and a western one. For this very reason, out of this tragic realization, which torments me, I'm convinced that we need to keep talking.... I will stay in the Kulturbund ... until I no longer have the possibility to voice my opinion as free and honest as in my journal *Horizonte*.[78]

Half a year later, Birkenfeld cofounded a "Free Cultural League" "(Freier Kulturbund) in West Berlin. Two years later still, Birkenfeld was the head of the Berlin chapter of Lasky's CIA-financed Congress for Cultural Freedom.[79] In the first issue of this organization's journal, *Der Monat*, Birkenfeld portrayed the Cold War confrontation as "a new and perhaps final manifestation of the tenacious battle between Eastern submissiveness and Western love of freedom."[80] Depending on one's perspective, the "other Germany," the one representing German traditions of freedom and humanism, had moved either to the West or the East.

By 1946, the terms "humanism" and "cultural renewal" gradually became embedded in the growing East–West confrontation. At the same time, the intellectuals in the SBZ launched an attack against existentialist philosophy that broke up the intellectual unity between resistance traditions in the East and West. Unlike in the West, the Kulturbund and its publications questioned the moral authority of Sartre and Camus, and linked them to the passivity of intellectuals such as Jaspers and Heidegger in the face of the NS regime. Contrary to the major interpreters of cultural politics in the SBZ, though, this chapter has shown

---

[77] *Erster Deutscher Schriftstellerkongreß*, 417–18.
[78] Ibid.; see also *Der Kurier*, October 9, 1947.
[79] Schivelbusch, *In a Cold Crater*, 101–2.
[80] *Der Monat. Eine internationale Zeitschrift für Politik und geistiges Leben* 1, 1 (October 1948): 3.

that these shifts in discussions are not solely the result of a movement toward Stalinization that culminated in the anti-formalism campaigns of the early 1950s. Rather, the discussions on the Kulturbund board reflect, at least to a large part, the ongoing intellectual and moral struggle with the Nazi legacy. Even though shaped by Marxist historical materialism, attacks against Meinecke's *The German Catastrophe* critiqued the ideas of a general crisis of the West as moral failure to account for concrete German responsibilities. However, the context of the emerging Cold War made it increasingly difficult to distinguish these discussions from East–West politics.

The intertwined debates over the moral legacy of the Nazi years, the Communist critique of a perceived revival of antimodernist ideas, and Cold War politics also characterized the First German Writers' Conference. This congress was arguably the last attempt by a generation shaped by antifascism to stem the political division by intellectual unity. The four days of the congress encapsulated the debates on cultural renewal that had predominated since 1933 and linked it to the new political and moral issues of the post-1945 era. At the end of this process, the concept of an "other Germany" had lost much of its relevance unless employed in the context of the contrast between East and West. With the two German states adopting the political models of their respective client states, the intellectuals of the antifascist generation in the West turned to shaping the memory of the "other Germany," rather than to creating the politics of the Federal Republic. In the GDR, the entrenchment of the SED's power in the new state left no room for cultural politics in a different organization. As a consequence, the Kulturbund's career as an SED "mass organization" until 1989 was devoted to bourgeois cultural activities rather than to the revolutionary redefinition of German traditions that Becher and his Communist as well as liberal allies had envisioned in the ruins of 1945.

7 Mass Organization and Memory: Antifascist Humanism in Divided Germany, 1948 and Beyond

Shortly after the uprising of June 17, 1953, when the protests of workers at East Berlin's Stalinallee erupted, many East German intellectuals felt that they had to reiterate their loyalty to the three-and-a-half-year-old "workers and peasants' state." The Kulturbund, by then one of numerous "antifascist GDR mass organizations," issued a declaration stating that it upheld the leadership of the Socialist Unity Party (SED).[1] This declaration exposed antifascism's inability to bridge the gap between workers and party-affiliated intellectuals. The declaration of the Kulturbund – conceived during the Nazi dictatorship as a Popular Front coalition between Communist and non-Communist intellectuals – also revealed that by the early 1950s, antifascism in the East had become little more than a propagandistic term legitimizing the SED's rule.

In the same year, 1953, in the Federal Republic, author and former resistance activist Günther Weisenborn – a member of the Kulturbund's foundation in 1945 – published a volume dedicated to the memory of antifascism. Under the title *Der lautlose Aufstand* (*The Silent Revolt*), Weisenborn had compiled the histories and activities of German resistance groups since 1933. Embodying the spirit of the Popular Front antifascism of the 1930s, the volume chronicled the acts – and tragic failures – of organizations and individuals ranging from Catholics to Communists and from Wehrmacht colonels to Red Army collaborators. While the Federal Republic was poised to begin its economic miracle and assume its new political Cold War identity, the political and cultural ideas of antifascism – never more than vaguely formulated by intellectuals such as Weisenborn – had become a nostalgic project of remembering the "other Germany," the one that stood up against the Nazi dictatorship and represented the ideals of the classical German humanist tradition in the vein of Johann Wolfgang Goethe and Heinrich Heine.

---

[1] See "Erklärung des Kulturbundes zur loyalen Haltung der Intelligenz," Präsidialratssitzung vom 3. Juli 1953, Stiftung Archiv der Massenorganisationen im Bundesarchiv (BArch-SAPMO) DY 27/916, Präsidialratssitzungen 1953, Blatt 317.

The two developments in 1953 – the declaration of loyalty to the one-party state in the East and the remembrance of the anti-Hitler resistance as the foundation of the democratic West – mark the bookends of a development that led from the transformation of antifascism into a cultural movement to the entrenchment of the German division. After 1947, with the onset of the Cold War, the project of cultural renewal could not prevent the renewed breakup of political and intellectual unity in Germany. By 1949, the pre–World War II ideological concept of an "other Germany" became physical reality with the formation of two actual German states. "Renewal" in both German states did occur, but not under the premises of antifascist unity and its implicit cultural nationalism, but along liberal-capitalist or Soviet-Communist lines. With the cultural policies of both German states shaped by Cold War politics, the idea of antifascist humanism became largely irrelevant, relegated to quasi-bourgeois cultural activities in the GDR and to projects of antifascist remembrance in the Federal Republic.

This chapter traces the final stages in the demise of the pluralist elements in the "other Germany," a process that culminated in the expulsion of liberal Kulturbund founder Ferdinand Friedensburg and in the redefinition of the organization's main concept, humanist culture. By highlighting aspects of the biography of Günther Weisenborn, the Kulturbund member, resistance activist, and organizer of the ill-fated First German Writers' Congress, this chapter also analyzes the ideals of antifascist humanism and national cultural unity against the background of the political and personal identity of some of its participants. Weisenborn, as well as his fellow activist Alfred Kantorowicz, represents German intellectuals for whom antifascism was a source of political as well as aesthetic identity. Part of the same generation, they straddled the pre- and post-1945 periods as well as the boundaries of East and West at a time when the Cold War increasingly limited choices-and identities – on both sides. Both ultimately failed in their attempts to keep German cultural unity alive, not only because of the political pressures, but also because their vision of cultural nationalism found little appeal in the two new Germanies.

This chapter therefore contributes to recent research into the construction of national identities in the two early postwar German states. In a pioneering work, Jan Palmowski, complementing seminal studies on German concepts of *Heimat* by Celia Applegate and Alon Confino, has investigated "how nationhood and the imagination of the GDR were constructed and popularized."[2] While Palmowski's study demonstrates

---

[2] Jan Palmowski, *Inventing a Socialist Nation: Heimat and the Politics of Everyday Life in the GDR, 1945–90* (Cambridge: Cambridge University Press, 2009), 7. See also Mary

how the SED successfully created an interrelated sense of both *Heimat* (local identity) and nation for their new state, his work pays less attention to the pre-1945 identities that did not usher in the officially sanctioned nationalism of the workers' and peasants' state. This chapter argues that the all-German cultural nationalism espoused by the early Kulturbund left only traces in the GDR after 1948. Instead of a broad movement of cultural renewal, the humanist antifascism of the "other Germany" ushered in the depoliticized activities of the Deutscher Kulturbund from the early 1950s until the end of the GDR.

The Cold War and the Birth of "Real Humanism"

The failure to maintain – or restore – intellectual unity at the first writers' congress anticipated the open political confrontations of 1948. But, as the previous chapter has shown, concepts of German culture were not innocent victims of the Cold War politics of the West and East, but had brought their own divisive dynamics into the event. The congress was a focal lens that bundled and brought to the fore the themes of antifascist renewal, the self-understanding of the "other Germany" vis-à-vis the inner émigrés, the German image abroad, the struggle for unity, and – finally – the impotence and instrumentalization of humanist culture in the face of the Cold War. In November 1947, liberal intellectuals like Günther Birkenfeld and Ferdinand Friedensburg were still united with their Communist colleagues at a mass protest rally against the Kulturbund ban in the Western zones.[3] The rally took place at the site of the Kulturbund's inauguration, the broadcast center in the Masurenallee, now a Soviet enclave in the British sector. Friedensburg still tried to muster enough goodwill with the Americans to keep the Kulturbund as an East–West institution alive. His efforts were unsuccessful, partly because the SMAD had lost interest in a physical presence of the Kulturbund in the West. More importantly, cultural activities

---

Fulbrook and Andrew I. Port, eds., *Becoming East German: Socialist Structures and Sensibilities after Hitler* (New York: Berghahn, 2013). For the construction of postwar identities in East and West, see also Frank Biess, *Homecoming: Returning POWs and the Legacies of Defeat in Postwar Germany* (Princeton, NJ: Princeton University Press, 2009). For the concept of *Heimat* and the relationship between local identity and nationhood in Germany, see Celia Applegate, *A Nation of Provincials: The German Idea of* Heimat (Berkeley: University of California Press, 1990); Alon Confino, *The Nation as a Local Metaphor: Württemberg, Imperial Germany, and National Memory, 1871–1918* (Chapel Hill: University of North Carolina Press, 1997).

[3] See Karl-Heinz Schulmeister, *Auf dem Wege zu einer neuen Kultur: Der Kulturbund in den Jahren 1945–1949* (Berlin [East]: Dietz Verlag, 1977), 176–8; cf. Wolfgang Schivelbusch, *In a Cold Crater: Cultural and Intellectual Life in Berlin, 1945–1948*, trans. Kelly Berry; Berkeley: University of California Press, 1998), 100–1.

in the SBZ – such as the planning of the 1848 revolution's centenary events – had already shifted from the Kulturbund to the SED's own "cultural departments [*Kulturabteilungen*]" and "central cultural committees [*zentrale Kulturausschüsse*]."[4] Since December 1947, the SED had also begun to organize meetings and conferences of the writers in the party. At this time, Friedensburg's fellow Christian Democrats Ernst Lemmer and Jakob Kaiser had already defected to the West after refusing to be part of the SED-directed Volkskongreß (People's Congress).[5] But with or without non-Communist voices in its rank, the still officially nonpartisan Kulturbund had become more or less irrelevant for the cultural development of the SBZ. The project of antifascist political unity as a basis for cultural renewal, as it was envisioned by Friedensburg, but also, at least to a certain extent, by Becher, had become incompatible with the Soviet and SED's objective of establishing an East German state. While liberal and Communist intellectuals on the Kulturbund board viewed the organization as a vehicle to restore a cultural German unity that had been shattered during the 1920s and 1930s, the SED cadres that increasingly dominated cultural policies in the SBZ set out to turn antifascism and (socialist) humanism from pillars of the "other Germany's" unity to the cultural-ideological supplements for Germany's political division. By 1949, they had become tools in the construction of a specific East German national identity.[6]

The political antagonism between the SBZ and the Western zones exerted ever more influence over the Kulturbund's sense of its own mission. At its inception in 1945, the debates in the Kulturbund had centered predominantly on German intellectuals' attitude toward fascism and on individual behavior during the Third Reich. As has been shown, this was still true for the controversies between exiles and inner émigrés on the first day of the writers' congress on October 5, 1947. By 1948, not antifascist credentials, but intellectuals' position in the East–West conflict determined the Kulturbund's attitude toward its members. On September 7, 1948, the board passed a declaration that shifted the Kulturbund's focus from antifascism to pro-Soviet politics: "Participation in anti-Soviet

---

[4] See Gerd Dietrich, *Politik und Kultur in der Sowjetischen Besatzungszone Deutschlands (SBZ), 1945–1949. Mit einem Dokumentenanhang* (Bern, Switzerland: Peter Lang, 1993), 65–72, 112–13; Gerd Dietrich, ed., *Um die Erneuerung der deutschen Kultur: Dokumente zur Kulturpolitik, 1945–1949* (Berlin [East]: Dietz, 1983), 165–9.

[5] See Corey Ross, *The East German Dictatorship: Problems and Perspectives in the Interpretation of the GDR* (London: Oxford University Press, 2002), 100, n. 7.

[6] The East German Akademie der Künste (Academy of the Arts) is another cultural institution that evolved from the promotion of German unity to an SED tool to establish a GDR cultural identity; see Peter Davies, *Divided Loyalties: East German Writers and the Politics of German Division, 1945–1953* (London: Maney Publishing, 2000).

hate- and warmongering, i.e., activities that are also aimed against the cooperation of all cultural producers committed to democracy and freedom, are not compatible with membership in the Kulturbund."[7] The declaration's first and most prominent victim was Friedensburg, who up to this point had still attempted to negotiate between the Kulturbund and the Western Allies. A week after the board's declaration, the Berlin chapter of the Kulturbund decided to expel him, who "evidently in the course of the last few months has completely renounced his political position for the unity of Germany and Berlin, and for the peaceful understanding between the Allies. By participating in a campaign of hateful political instigation, the sole objective of which is the further poisoning of the political atmosphere and the finalization of the division of Germany, Dr. Friedensburg intentionally acted against the Kulturbund's principles."[8]

Friedensburg protested his expulsion on formal grounds, but the board confirmed the Berlin chapter's decision.[9] Like so many non-Communist – and Communist – Kulturbund founders before and after him, Friedensburg became part of West Berlin's political and intellectual scene. The historiographical literature has already sufficiently commented on Friedensburg's influence on the open-mindedness and pluralism of the early Kulturbund. His expulsion made obvious that the period of antifascist unity of Communist and liberal politicians had come to an end. However, the standard histories of the Kulturbund, which are more interested in its role in the prehistory of the GDR, tend to neglect the relationship between the Kulturbund and developments in the West. By the time Friedensburg was expelled, the Christian Democratic movement in the West was already dominated by the Western Allied-supported Konrad Adenauer and his circle. Friedensburg's willingness to confront the German past and keep up nonpartisan political dialogue with the Soviet Union without compromising his liberal principles seemed more attuned to the next generation's *Ostpolitik*. In 1948, however, Friedensburg's expulsion paved the way for a rewriting of the Kulturbund's foundation in the official GDR historiography, with

---

[7] "Gegen Antisowjet- and Kriegshetze. Entschließung des Präsidialrates des Kulturbundes zur demokratischen Erneuerung Deutschlands, 7. September, 1948," in Dietrich, *Politik und Kultur in der Sowjetischen Besatzungszone Deutschlands*, 332–3.
[8] "Ausschluß von Ferdinand Friedensburg aus dem Kulturbund. Beschluß der Landesleitung Berlin des Kulturbundes zur demokratischen Erneuerung Deutschlands, 14. September, 1948," in: Dietrich, *Politik und Kultur in der Sowjetischen Besatzungszone Deutschlands*, 334; see also Gerhard Wettig, ed., *Der Tjul'panov Bericht. Sowjetische Besatzungspolitik in Deutschland nach dem Zweiten Weltkrieg* (Göttingen: V&R unipress, 2012), 313.
[9] See Schivelbusch, *In a Cold Crater*, 102–3.

Friedensburg and his fellow Kulturbund cofounder Lemmer now cast as a "reactionary group" in the movement from the very beginning.[10]

It is significant that Friedensburg's expulsion was not initiated by the Kulturbund board, but by the Communist-dominated Berlin chapter. Yet, Becher, the Kulturbund president, seems not to have protested the expulsion of his Kulturbund cofounder, a man whose ideas on cultural renewal had been so similar to his own. This does not imply that Becher did not have any grievances. Nine months earlier, in December 1947, Becher had written a sharp complaint against the apparently deliberate SED policy of diminishing the Kulturbund's influence. In a letter to the party's Central Directorate [Zentralvorstand], Becher protested the Kulturbund's exclusion from the planning for the SED's Volkskongreß, and he expressed bitterness about Wilhem Pieck's remarks about Becher's alleged lack of "political work." Not for the first time, Becher found it difficult to reconcile his self-understanding as a poet with the demands of a Party functionary: "Because my special talent as a writer makes my inner self incapable of fulfilling the demands of political work as understood by Comrade Wilhelm Pieck, I will have to leave it to the Zentralvorstand to draw the consequences."[11] In 1949, in a more conciliatory tone and no longer threatening his resignation, Becher complained to Walter Ulbricht that the Kulturbund was not represented among the GDR delegation at a Stalin celebration in Moscow.[12] His disenchantment with the Party's dismissive attitude toward the Kulturbund did not prevent Becher from applying his special writer's talents for sycophantic poems celebrating Stalin, Ulbricht, and Pieck. In 1951, Becher completed the career from artist to functionary by becoming, until his death in 1958, the GDR's first minister of culture.[13]

After the debacle of the First German Writers' Congress, the concept of German humanism, which for more than a decade had kept the antifascist "other Germany" unified, underwent an evolution. It lost its open-ended character – and its complex status at the crossroads of national reformation, genuine attempts at coping with German

---

[10] See Schulmeister, *Auf dem Wege zu einer neuen Kultur*, 245, 215; see also Gerhard Schmidt, *Der Kulturbund zu Frieden and Demokratie, 1948/49. Teil 1* (Berlin [East]: Kulturbund der DDR, 1984), 96–9.

[11] "Johannes R. Becher an das Sekretariat des Zentralvorstandes der SED, 8. 12. 1947," in *Der gespaltene Dichter. Johannes R. Becher Gedichte, Briefe, Dokumente, 1945–1958* (Berlin: Aufbau Taschenbuch Verlag, 1991), 42–3.

[12] See "Johannes R. Becher an Walter Ulbricht, December 24, 1949," in *Der gespaltene Dichter*, 48.

[13] See Schiller, *Johannes R. Becher und die Krise des Kulturbundes*, for Becher's transition from poet to minister.

responsibility, and antifascist politics. During a discussion on the Kulturbund board in December 1946, Abusch had clung to his definition of humanism as "the humanism of Goethe, and that of Engels, and also that which the Church represents; the Kulturbund is the framework in which these three currents can come together to support the democratic renewal of our people."[14] Less than two years later, at the first Cultural Congress of the SED in May 1948, Anton Ackermann redefined humanism for the future GDR: "Marxism is the new, real humanism."[15] The new, real existing socialism about to emerge had found its cultural expression in a "real humanism" that left little room for Goethe, let alone the churches.

It also left no room for pluralist understandings of the arts and of aesthetics. By the early 1950s, the concept of humanism was squarely enlisted in the one-dimensional, Stalinist anti-formalism debate. A 1951 pamphlet by the Kulturbund's Saxony regional chapter proclaimed that "Art must be imbued with real humanism [*von echtem Humanismus durchdrungen*]." This brand of humanism was the answer to artistic ideals of "degeneration and decay [*Entartung und Zersetzung*]." Not surprisingly, these degenerate artistic ideals – "pathological, outside the norm, and contradictory to human nature" – thrived in "contemporary bourgeois American culture, which is shaped by the decay and the corrosion of imperialist society, and which is pathological and harmful to mankind and nation [*menschenfeindlich, volksfeindlich, und pathologisch*]."[16]

The striking use of National Socialist (NS) terminology in this pamphlet sheds light on the evolution of humanist tropes in the mid-twentieth century. In the 1930s, antifascist intellectuals had advanced a "militant humanism" that opposed the Nazi idea of German culture and tradition. By 1946–7, postwar humanism and existentialism came under attack by Communists, who argued that it diluted the antifascist notion of a specific German responsibility. With the Cold War out in the open, this critique ushered in the GDR's new, "real humanism," an understanding of culture – and a terminology to describe it – that seemed to have taken recourse to Goebbels's denunciations of "degenerate art."

---

[14] Präsidialratsitzung vom 6. Dezember 1946, SAPMO – BArch DY 27/908, Bl. 220, Bl. 238.
[15] "Marxistische Kulturpolitik. Rede Anton Ackermanns auf dem Ersten Kulturtag der SED in Berlin, 7. Mai 1948," in Dietrich, ed., *Um die Erneuerung der deutschen Kultur*, 266.
[16] Kulturbund zur demokratischen Erneuerung Deutschlands, Landesleitung Sachsen, *Kampf gegen den Formalismus in der Kunst und Literatur. Für eine fortschrittliche deutsche Kultur* (Dresden, n.d.[1951]), 11.

The Aesthetics of Antifascism

The looming breakup not only of German political unity, but also of the intellectual Popular Front was for many Kulturbund activists a deeply personal concern. Arguably, by the mid-1940s, a generation of German writers and intellectuals had derived not only their political beliefs, but their identity from the struggle against fascism. The multitude of literary-political journals in postwar Germany is a testimony to the personal commitment to antifascist unity felt by many of its founders. Even more than the Kulturbund's *Aufbau*, the Soviet-licensed journal *Ost und West*, published in Berlin since July 1947, tried to bridge the deepening rift between the occupation zones by emphasizing antifascist cultural renewal. The journal's founder and editor was Alfred Kantorowicz, who had participated in the struggle for the Saar as well as in the Spanish Civil War.[17] With the currency reform of 1948, *Ost und West*'s circulation sank more and more, first in the Western zones, then in the SBZ. Kantorowicz's request to the Party for financial subsidies was turned down. Unlike the Kulturbund's *Aufbau*, which had become increasingly anti-Western, *Ost und West* did no longer mesh with the SED's political directives. Unable to make up for mounting financial losses, Kantorowicz ceased the publication of *Ost und West* in December 1949. By then the formation of two German states had made his project obsolete in any case.[18]

Like Kantorowicz, Günther Weisenborn tried to transcend the division into East and West, and like Kantorowicz's, Weisenborn's biography reveals the strong conflation of personal identity, artistic self-definition, and political conviction among many of the Kulturbund activists who had spent the NS period as part of the "humanist front" and coalesced the identities of writers and resistance activists; few other political or aesthetic projects allowed intellectuals to merge artistic relevance with moral and political influence in the way that antifascism did. Weisenborn was born in the western German province of Westphalia in 1902 – Abusch was born in the same year, Kantorowicz in 1899. Focusing on their experiences during the Weimar period, Detlev Peukert has pointed out, some in this generation of Germans born around 1900 felt like theirs was a "superfluous generation." This generation, which included antifascists

---

[17] See Beate Ihme-Tuchel, "Alfred Kantorowicz" in Karl Wilhelm Fricke, Peter Steinbach, and Johannes Tuchel, eds., *Opposition und Widerstand in der DDR. Politische Lebensbilder* (München: C. H. Beck, 2002), 258–64; Ewald Birr, *Ost und West, Berlin 1947–1949. Bibliographie einer Zeitschrift* [Veröffentlichung der Akademie der Künste zu Berlin] (München: K.G. Saur, 1993); Alfred Kantorowicz, *Deutschland-Ost und Deutschland-West. Kulturpolitische Einigungsversuche und geistige Spaltung in Deutschland seit 1945.* [Sylter Beiträge 2] (Münsterdorf: Verlag Hansen & Hansen, n.d.).

[18] See Birr, *Ost und West*, 10–11.

such as Weisenborn and Abusch as well as some of the most fanatical Nazi careerists, e.g., Heinrich Himmler, were too young to be shaped by the *Fronterlebnis* (combat experience) that shaped their elders. Instead, in their twenties and thirties, the members of the "superfluous" generation underwent their formative political experiences during the crisis-filled and radicalized years of Weimar modernity, often under circumstances of economic and social powerlessness.[19] Peukert's thesis suggests that the rise of fascism gave many in this generation a sense of purpose and mission, either by actively participating in the National Socialist project or by actively opposing it.[20]

Of course the lack of World War I front experience was also shared by Becher, born in 1891 and a member of the generation that included Hitler and Ulbricht. However, as we have seen in Chapter 4, Becher's complicated biography seems to reveal much more difficulties in reconciling his identities of artist, communist functionary, and bourgeois Protestant. Weisenborn, too, did not seem to find his true calling until his career as a writer became intertwined with antifascist resistance. After what seems to have been an unsatisfying apprenticeship as a merchant, Weisenborn followed his interests and became a struggling writer, sympathizing with the communist left during the Weimar years, yet without becoming a Communist Party of Germany (KPD) functionary like Abusch and Becher.[21] The formative event of Weisenborn's life was his and his wife's Gestapo arrest in September 1942 for their affiliation with the Schulze-Boysen-Harnack resistance group (Rote Kapelle). In what must have been a characteristic document for oppositional artists in Nazi Germany, the manager of the stage that employed Weisenborn, Gustav Kiepenheuer, tried to defend his playwright by portraying him as a *Heimatdichter* after the Nazis' taste: "He is rooted in the soil of his Westphalian homeland [*Heimat*] and has never denied this harsh North German trait in his works. His works lack any corroding element; to the contrary, it is German to the bone, healthy, and possesses the positive vitality that is characteristic for a good race and an uncorrupted German

---

[19] See Detlev J. K. Peukert, *Die Weimarer Republik: Krisenjahre der klassischen Moderne* (Frankfurt a. M.: Suhrkamp, 1987), 30; see also Sean A. Forner, "Für eine demokratische Erneuerung Deutschlands: Kommunikationsprozesse und Deutungsmuster engagierter Demokraten nach 1945," *Geschichte und Gesellschaft* 33 (2007): 331, and footnote 11.

[20] For a classic sociological analysis of generational experience, see Karl Mannheim's "The Problem of Generations," in Kurt H. Wolff, ed., *From Karl Mannheim*. Second expanded edition. With an introduction by Volker Meja and David Kettler (New Brunswick, NJ: Transaction Publishers, 1993).

[21] Akademie der Künste Berlin (AdK Berlin), Nachlass (NL) Günther Weisenborn, 613.

mind."²² The NS judges were unconvinced, even though they spared him the death sentence. Instead, Weisenborn spent the next two and a half years in prison.²³

Even under harsh interrogation and torture, Weisenborn did not reveal any information about his friends to the Gestapo. His assessment by the Gestapo in August 1943 read: "Although he knew that his friend committed high treason, he did not report him. He repents the crime and makes a very good impression upon introduction." In the original of this document in Weisenborn's estate, the words "repents the crime" and "very" are crossed out in green ink.²⁴ It seems as if the faint trace of a Gestapo praise for the prisoner had to be edited because they would taint Weisenborn's unquestioned credentials as a Nazi resister who did not denounce his friends even in the face of torture and execution.

In 1945, the Red Army not only liberated Weisenborn from the *Zuchthaus* [prison] Luckau, but – as a confirmed antifascist – installed him as mayor of a cluster of small towns in the province of Brandenburg.²⁵ As mayor, Weisenborn founded a local antifascist committee (antifa) and presided over such activities as the arrest of fraudsters and former Nazis and the cleansing of school textbooks.²⁶ For Weisenborn, as for many other intellectuals of the "other Germany," organizations such as the Kulturbund held the promise to combine the political activism of the antifascist committees with an artist's emphasis on culture and aesthetic sensibilities. After all, for Weisenborn, who had used the pseudonym Christian Munk before the war, there were many similarities between the identities of authors and antifascist resisters, from the use of false names to the membership in tight-knit circles of likeminded associates. And already during his imprisonment, Weisenborn had resolved to survive and bear witness to the Nazi period in order to contribute to the German people's task of mourning (*Trauerarbeit*) after the war.²⁷ Weisenborn thus shared many of the Kulturbund's principles and objectives, and

---

²² Letter of Gustav Kiepenheuer, Bühnenvertriebs G.m.b.H to Kriminalrat Habecker, Geheime Staatspolizei, December 1, 1942, AdK Berlin, NL Weisenborn, 613 (biographical material).
²³ For autobiographical material on Günther and Joy Weisenborn's imprisonment, see also Günther Weisenborn and Joy Weisenborn, *Einmal laß mich traurig sein. Briefe, Lieder, Kassiber, 1942–1943* (Zürich: Arche, 1984).
²⁴ "Vermerk des Vorstandes des Zuchthauses Luckau, 16. Aug. 1943, AdK Berlin, NL Weisenborn, 613.
²⁵ Bescheinigung des Bürgermeisters von Luckau vom 2. Juli 1945 über Weisenborns Einsetzung als Bürgermeister der Gemeinden Langengrassau, Waltersdorf, Wittmannsdorf und Goßmar, AdK Berlin, NL Weisenborn, 613.
²⁶ "Tätigkeitsbericht der Gemeinde Langengrassau," AdK Berlin, NL Weisenborn, 613, Bl. 1 and Bl. 2.
²⁷ See Günther Weisenborn and Joy Weisenborn, *Einmal laß mich traurig sein*, 136.

Figure 8 Writer and resistance activist Günther Weisenborn (1902–69) in 1947. Weisenborn's biography reveals the strong conflation of personal identity, artistic self-definition, and political conviction among many of the Kulturbund activists who had spent the NS period as part of the "humanist front." Weisenborn ultimately failed in his effort to make the memory of antifascist resistance the foundation of a German postwar culture that would transcend the division into East and West. Ullstein bild via Getty Images.

he became one of its founding members. But Weisenborn continued to reside in West Berlin even though he tirelessly tried to prevent splits of cultural institutions such as the P.E.N. into East and West chapters. Throughout the rising tensions of the early Cold War, he kept his cultural ties with the intellectual scene in the East.[28]

From Renewal to Remembrance: The "Other Germany" in the Federal Republic

In West Germany, too, the project of cultural renewal had evolved. The year 1947, which marked the failure of Weisenborn's German Writers' Congress, also saw the birth of an informal circle of writers who were unconnected with the congress and the Kulturbund. The writers associated with the Gruppe 47 (Group 47) were not interested in restoring pre-1933 traditions of cultural reform, but in a radical break with them, often through the adoption of Anglo-American literary models.[29] Born between the outbreak of the First World War and the Great Depression, these writers' formative experiences occurred not in exile or resistance, but as young Wehrmacht draftees and Allied POWs. In the future Federal Republic, it was going to be writers such as Alfred Andersch and Heinrich Böll, with their American-influenced prose styles and their far-reaching critiques of ideologies, who would wield more cultural influence than Weisenborn or Kantorowicz, with their failed dreams of antifascist solidarity and German national unity. The generation of 1900, with its implicit German cultural nationalism, had been made superfluous again.[30]

Rendered useless as an instrument for cultural renewal, antifascism's main task now became the project of memorializing the "other Germany." It was no coincidence that a year after Kantorowicz's *Ost und West* journal ceased production, his memories of the Spanish Civil War were published by Aufbau as *Spanisches Tagebuch*. Where antifascism had failed to create unity between East and West, the memory of antifascist

---

[28] For Weisenborn's biography, see also Ernst Klee, *Das Kulturlexikon zum Dritten Reich. Were war was vor und nach 1945* (Frankfurt a. M.: S. Fischer, 2007), 652–3.

[29] For a basic introduction to the history of Gruppe 47, see, for example, Jost Hermand, *Kultur im Wiederaufbau. Die Bundesrepublik Deutschland 1945–1965* (München: Nymphenburger, 1986).

[30] This doesn't mean that this younger generation was completely absolved from criticism for its actions during and after the war. See, e.g., W. G. Sebald's polemics against Alfred Andersch in W. G. Sebald, *Luftkrieg und Literatur* (Frankfurt/Main: Fischer, 2001), 111–47. A more recent example of this generation's own need for *Vergangenheitsbewältigung* is of course the debate around Günter Grass's unintended – but until 2007 unacknowledged – membership in the Waffen SS.

heroism could still be used to inspire young readers in the antifascist workers' and peasants' state – and, later, the Western left. In the West, it was Weisenborn who became the dean and executor of antifascist testimonies. At the First Writers' Congress, Ricarda Huch, only weeks before her death, had asked Weisenborn to take over her project of collecting material and testimonies about the German anti-Nazi resistance. With his identities as writer and resistance activist so intertwined, Weisenborn was the logical choice as editor of the first comprehensive account of the German resistance, which was published as *Der lautlose Aufstand* (*The Silent Revolt*) in 1953. In his introduction Weisenborn explained the volume's title by the fact that knowledge about the German resistance had been intentionally kept from the world – not only by the Nazis, but also by the Allies, who suppressed all alternatives to their visions of a postwar order.[31] The book was meant finally to prove the existence of the "other Germany" to the world – almost a continuation of the exile struggles against "Vansittartism." Moreover, in the year when the June 17 uprising in East Berlin split the last vestiges of the former antifascist coalition, *Der lautlose Aufstand* united once more all the strands of antifascist resistance, from Christian and Jewish activists to the Communist underground to the officers of the Stauffenberg circle and other military and civilian oppositionists.

Weisenborn continued to make the memory of the resistance his central mission, not only lifting the "other Germany" out of its obscurity abroad, but also defending it against the charge that resistance to the Nazi regime – especially by its military officers – constituted high treason. In 1951, by now chief dramaturge of the Hamburger Kammerspiele, Weisenborn was involved in the production of a radio documentary on the resistance. For one of the segments of the show, Weisenborn sent a list of questions to Pastor Martin Niemöller, another icon of the anti-Hitler resistance. Weisenborn's questions reflect the extent to which the former representative of the "other Germany" did not feel at home in the early Adenauer republic: "Are the members of the resistance being respected? Are you forced to defend yourself and the resistance movement? Is there a need to educate the opponents of the resistance movement? Has the resistance movement benefited our people's standing [in the world]?"[32]

Weisenborn's memorialization of the resistance even found popular appeal when the playwright collaborated with Falk Harlan – his co-conspirator in the Rote Kapelle – on a feature film about Stauffenberg.

---

[31] Günther Weisenborn, ed., *Der lautlose Aufstand. Bericht über die Widerstandsbewegung des deutschen Volkes, 1933–1945*. Second edition (Hamburg: Rowohlt, 1953), 16–17.

[32] Günther Weisenborn, Brief an Martin Niemöller, 8. 6. 1951, AdK Berlin, NL Weisenborn, 1055.

Harlan directed the script by Weisenborn and the 1955 release was a commercial and critical success. Weisenborn's sketches for the script give evidence to the enduring presence of tropes of the "other Germany," for instance, the almost religious sense of a new beginning based on the sacrifices of German resisters: "The internal and external plot must be shaped by the *Leitmotif*, 'wherever there is danger, grow the forces that come to the rescue [*Wo aber Gefahr ist, wächst das Rettende auch*].' The healing power of the sacrifices reaches far into the future and helps to unearth buried values not only of the German people."[33]

At the same time the contrast between Stauffenberg, the main protagonist, and his main opponent, NS chief judge Roland Freisler, is painted with all the subtlety of the exile culture wars of the 1930s and 1940s. Stauffenberg is described as the "physical and intellectual heir to Gneisenau. Specimen of the soldier with artistic sensibilities and inherent nobility. Tall, thin, athletic, and with graceful movements. Strong, determined, and passionate ... a colonel who looks like a poet, with his pale face framed by dark hair, young but of tense determination, heavily wounded, but nevertheless in full possession of himself." Freisler, on the other hand, has "no trace of humanity in this reviling face with big and cunning eyes that are half covered by heavy eyelids ... nihilism personified."[34] The antifascist struggle was perhaps the last conflict with a moral clarity that allowed writers like Weisenborn the painting of such stark and distorted contrasts. At the same time, just as in the GDR, the language and the imagery of the antifascist culture wars apparently still informed Weisenborn's script, which depicted Stauffenberg as a Nordic "superman," and Freisler, undoubtedly one of the most reprehensible Nazi criminals, in a language that was itself reminiscent of NS rhetoric.

Cultural Renewal with and without Politics: The Kulturbund in the GDR

While Weisenborn and Huch evoked the antifascist solidarity of the Nazi years, in the GDR, many of the remaining antifascist friendships and alliances among Communists fell apart during the turbulent period from the June 17 uprising to the purges that choked the SED attempts at de-Stalinization in 1956.[35] Some of the internal clashes in the antifascist

---

[33] Günther Weisenborn, undated film sketch, AdK Berlin, NL Weisenborn, Bl. 1.
[34] Ibid., Bl. 1 and Bl. 2.
[35] See e.g., Fricke et al., eds. *Opposition und Widerstand in der DDR*; John C. Torpey, *Intellectuals, Socialism, and Dissent: The East German Opposition and Its Legacy* (Minneapolis: University of Minnesota Press, 1995), 22–56. For discussions on the Kulturbund board in the 1950s, see Magdalena Heider und Kerstin Thons, eds., *SED*

intelligentsia were less than heroic, even though they still engaged with debates on humanist German culture. In 1950, the antifascist literary scholar Hans Mayer, who had been a member of the British exile Freier Deutscher Kulturbund (Free German Cultural League [FDKB], see Chapter 2) during the war, tried to get Wolfgang Harich expelled from the Berlin Kulturbund. The reasons for Mayer's petition were not questions about Harich's antifascist integrity or his position in the Cold War (Harich was still a staunch defender of Stalin at this point), but unflattering reviews of Mayer's publications that Harich had penned in the *Tägliche Rundschau* and *Weltbühne*. Mayer was particularly irked by Harich's referring to him as a "Grünlich," a pompous and philistine impostor in Thomas Mann's novel *Buddenbrooks*. As a result, Mayer claimed that his own "social effectiveness [*soziale Wirksamkeit*]" as an intellectual had been compromised. Mayer also questioned whether Harich's Latin skills were sufficient to justify his employment as a philosophy lecturer at Berlin's Humboldt University.[36] In his official reply to the German Writers' Association, Harich used all his considerable sarcastic talents to make Mayer look even more ridiculous.[37] If the incident did not lead to serious consequences for Harich, it does demonstrate that by the early 1950s, humanist German literature and *Bildung* had changed from being a weapon in the struggle against fascism to a tool in petty quarrels about hurt professional and personal pride.

With the consolidation of the East German state, the Kulturbund's emphasis on democratic renewal seemed no longer necessary. In 1958, the year of Becher's death, the Kulturbund zur demokratischen Erneuerung Deutschlands was officially renamed Deutscher Kulturbund, an organization without any real influence on official cultural policy in the GDR. Becher's successor as minister of culture was Alexander Abusch, who, unlike Becher, never seemed to have felt any conflict between his aesthetic and intellectual sensibilities and firm enforcement of the Party line. Toning down the excesses of the anti-formalist campaign, under Abusch's influence, socialist humanism became a quasi-official GDR cultural doctrine, combining a critical interpretation of the German classics with dialectical-materialist Marxism.[38] For a more critical representative

---

und Intellektuelle in der DDR der fünfziger Jahre. Kulturbund Protokolle (Köln: Edition Deutschland Archiv, 1990).

[36] Hans Mayer, Antrag an den Vorstand des Deutschen Schriftstellerverbandes beim Kulturbund zur demokratischen Erneuerung zur Eröffnung eines Ehrgerichtsverfahren, SAPMO – BArch DY 27/3271.

[37] See Antwort Wolfgang Harich's vom 1.1.1951, SAPMO – BArch DY 27/3271.

[38] See, for instance, the collection of Abusch's later writings in Alexander Abusch, *Kulturelle Probleme des sozialistischen Humanismus. Beiträge zur deutschen Kulturpolitik, 1946–1961. Schriften, Bd. III* (Berlin: Aufbau Verlag, 1962).

Figure 9 Portrait of writer and philosopher Wolfgang Harich (1923–95) in 1947. As one of the youngest activists in the early Kulturbund circle, Harich early on became known as a rhetorical "firebrand." The philosopher's tendency to speak his mind contributed to his arrest and conviction during the SED purge of 1956. Even though Harich ultimately became a leading GDR dissident, in the early postwar years, he was a faithful follower of Stalin and did not shy away from fiercely attacking people who represented other beliefs.
Ullstein bild via Getty Images.

of the "other Germany," Alfred Kantorowicz, who fled to the West in 1957, Abusch was the embodiment of the despised political bureaucrat who sacrificed artistic principles as well as former antifascist comrades for SED party discipline.[39]

Becher and Abusch also presided over the transformation of the Kulturbund into a largely unpolitical and SED-led assortment of hobby clubs and organized leisure activities. During the intensification of the Cold War in 1949–50, the organization had lost 70,000 members. In an attempt to stem this development, the GDR's Economic Commission directed the Kulturbund in December 1949 to become "the central organizational framework for associations with cultural activities" and to "subsume them in new sections for nature and *Heimat* lovers, ornithologists and birders, philatelists and amateur photographers."[40] Membership in the Kulturbund rose by 50,000, and the SED had a mass organization that controlled the potential for opposition among idiosyncratic hobby groups that would otherwise not be interested in Party activities. Esther von Richthofen argues that the Kulturbund became an SED mass organization which – along with a host of other institutions of "cultural mass work" – served to "channel cultural life where possible to ensure that people do not engage in activities that could challenge or undermine the [Party's] leadership."[41] Accordingly, in a collection of lectures on different aspects of the Kulturbund, published in 2001, the last three of the eight contributions shed light on the "Kulturbund and Photography," "Philately in the Kulturbund between Indoctrination and Leisure Niche," and, last but not least, "The Esperanto Learners in the Kulturbund."[42]

Reformation in the GDR: The Wartburg Congress in 1954

Jan Palmowski dismisses the notion that the Kulturbund's provincial chapters were merely a "sphere of cultural banality in which politics had no place." He contends that these *Heimat*-related activities "could potentially enable the party to reach the majority of the population on

---

[39] See Fricke et al., eds., *Opposition und Widerstand in der DDR.*, 260.
[40] Quoted in Schiller, *Johannes R. Becher und die Krise des Kulturbundes*, 27.
[41] Esther von Richthofen, *Bringing Culture to the Masses: Control, Compromise and Participation in the GDR* (New York: Berghahn, 2009), 3, 2. For a broader analysis of the role of the Kulturbund and other mass organizations in the "contours of power" in the GDR, see Mary Fulbrook, *Anatomy of a Dictatorship: Inside the GDR, 1949–1989* (New York: Oxford University Press, 1995), 58–61; cf. Palmowski, *Inventing a Socialist Nation*.
[42] See *Heterogenität und Konsistenz. Zur Herausbildung und Entwicklung des Kulturbundes in der DDR* (Pankower Vorträge, Heft 30) (Berlin: "Helle Panke," 2001).

whom socialism alone had little impact."⁴³ There is no question that the activities of the post-1948 Kulturbund contributed to the GDR's long-term stability, even though, as Andrew I. Port has argued, "[m]any of the factors that may have accounted for the stability of the GDR were in themselves potentially destabilizing."⁴⁴

Arguably this holds true for the early Kulturbund's sense of cultural nationalism that found recourse not in local *Heimat* identities, but in the concepts of antifascist humanism and the tropes of the Protestant Reformation. The Wartburg Congress of 1954 might serve as a case in point.

While local Kulturbund chapters engaged in "bringing culture to the masses," the SED had begun to organize meetings and conferences of the writers in the party, since 1950 increasingly represented not by the SDA – another symbol of pre-1945 antifascist unity that had become irrelevant – but by the newly established Deutscher Schriftstellerverband (DSV) within the Kulturbund. Even more than the Kulturbund, the DSV, under Abusch's leadership, was little more than an extension of the SED's cultural department, especially after the purges of reform-minded functionaries in the mid-1950s. The DSV was inaugurated at the Second German Writers' Congress in July 1950, an event staged in direct response to Melvin Lasky's anti-Communist "Congress for Cultural Freedom" in West Berlin earlier that year.⁴⁵ The Second Writers' Congress had thus little in common with its predecessor's attempt to bridge the political divide with appeals to cultural unity, but was squarely grounded in the political dynamics of the Cold War. By the time of the Fourth German Writers' Congress in 1955, the official agenda did not include any reference to an all-German national literature. Rather, the congress was designed to "raise the ideological and artistic quality of our [i.e., the GDR's] literature, in order to make our literature an even more efficient means for the formation of our workers' consciousness (socialist education)."⁴⁶ For this purpose, the organizers did not appeal to Germany's pre-1933 traditions of classical humanism, but called for an "intensified effort" by GDR writers to "acquire and master the techniques of socialist realism."⁴⁷ The critiques of existentialism and modernism that had been one of the undertones of the First German Writers' Congress had

---

⁴³ Palmowski, *Inventing a Socialist Nation*, 7.
⁴⁴ Andrew I. Port, *Conflict and Stability in the German Democratic Republic* (Cambridge: Cambridge University Press, 2007), 5.
⁴⁵ See Carsten Gansel, *Parlament des Geistes: Literatur zwischen Hoffnung und Repression, 1945–1961* (Berlin: BasisDruck, 1996), 158, 161.
⁴⁶ ZK der SED, Abt. Kunst. Sekretariatsvorlage zum IV. Schriftstellerkongreß (June 11, 1955), published in Gansel, *Parlament des Geistes*, 342–5.
⁴⁷ Ibid., 343.

by then already deteriorated into the Stalinist campaign against "formalism" and "cosmopolitism."[48]

The vision underlying the First Writers' Congress – the vision of a regenerated humanist German culture that would provide national unity and counter political division – would remain an illusion. By the early 1950s, both antifascism and the staging of writers' congresses had become tools in the construction of a specific East German national identity. An exception to this development was the Wartburg Congress in July 1954. This meeting was initiated by Protestant pastor Otto Riedel with the authorization of Becher, then the GDR's first minister of culture. A member of the Confessing Church (Bekennende Kirche) during the Third Reich, Riedel envisioned a meeting of writers from East and West at the historical site for a manifestation of cultural unity. Riedel seemed concerned about the SED's involvement in his planned exchange of ideas that, according to a letter from Riedel to the DSV general secretary, was not supposed to be about "party-political speeches."[49] The conference was seen as a success; even though largely without the most prominent West German writers, at least there was no Lasky scandal at the Wartburg. The conference stood under the guiding principle of a *Bekenntnis der Teilnehmer* (confession of participants), signed in prominent places by such icons of antifascist resistance and exile, Anna Seghers and Alfred Kurella:

In the hour of German need [*Not*], we, German poets and writers, have met at the Wartburg to listen and talk to each other.

This is the place where Wolfram von Eschenbach and Walther von der Vogelweide sang,... where Luther created the German language, where a new tribe [*Geschlecht*] strove for a new fatherland.

We stand by the enduring forces of humanism and call on everybody of good will not to let up in their effort for a unified Germany.

...

Regardless of our political and ideological differences we jointly affirm the unity of our fatherland, which we will serve in peace.[50]

The language of the confession displayed all the hallmarks of the speeches at the First Writers' Congress. Its rhetoric of German martyrdom, the belief in the regenerative power of German culture, and its evocation of the Protestant Reformation as a symbol of German national unity and

---

[48] See Mathias Judt, ed., *DDR Geschichte in Dokumenten: Beschlüsse, Berichte, interne Materialien und Alltagszeugnisse* (Berlin: Ch. Links, 1998), 295ff.
[49] Pfarrer Riedel to DSV Secretary Gustav Just, March 3, 1954, quoted in Gansel, *Parlament des Geistes*, 227.
[50] "Wartburg-Treffen. Bekenntnis der Teilnehmer (Juli 1954)," published in Gansel, *Parlament des Geistes*, 406.

postwar renewal echoed Weisenborn's opening speech, "Von Tod und Hoffnung der Dichter," at the congress of 1947 (see Chapter 6). It is also strikingly reminiscent of Becher's more famous speech at the inauguration of the Kulturbund in June 1945, discussed in Chapter 4.[51]

The SED must have sensed that the Wartburg meeting's interpretation of German culture and, especially, its acknowledgment of – and exchange between – "political and ideological differences" constituted a potential threat. As a result, the DSV conferred the organization of the successor meeting to the East German CDU. The bloc party's general secretary, Gerald Götting, saw to it that "the next Wartburg circle was not to be conducted under Riedel's leadership." Under Götting's and the East CDU's direction, future Wartburg meetings would flout the GDR's purported tolerance of Christian artists and make sure that even the possibility of critical statements was avoided.[52] Thus, the all-German cultural nationalism of the early Kulturbund and the First German Writers' Congress lived only faintly in the SED-staged congresses that followed after 1950 or in the GDR's official memory culture that celebrated an exalted version of antifascism and communist resistance.[53] As for Germany's humanist tradition, SED cultural policy soon – for example, at the Schiller anniversary of 1955 – used Weimar as the cultural heritage of a "socialist national culture" in the GDR.[54] During the last two decades of the GDR, the activities of the Nationale Forschungs- und Gedenkstätten der klassischen deutschen Literatur in Weimar (NFG) represented Weimar humanism less as a symbol for all-German traditions, but the GDR's alternative to an ostensibly Americanized and materialist consumer culture in the West.[55]

However, the appeal of "cultural renewal" seemed to survive decades of GDR stagnation and the fall of the Wall. None of the dissident and oppositional activities that led to the implosion of the GDR in 1989 originated in the Deutscher Kulturbund, and as late as October 1989 the board rejected all demands for social reforms. However, with a new leadership since November, the Kulturbund gained representation at the Round Table negotiations of fall 1989. Here, the Kulturbund tried

---

[51] See Deutscher Kulturbund, Manifest und Ansprachen von Bernhard Kellermann [et al.] gehalten bei der Gründungskundgebung des Kulturbundes zur demokratischen Erneuerung Deutschlands am 4. Juli 1945 im Haus des Berliner Rundfunks (Berlin: Aufbau Verlag, n. d.).
[52] Gansel, *Parlament des Geistes*, 228.
[53] See Ross, *The East German Dictatorship*, 176–82.
[54] See Gunther Mai, "Sozialistische Nation und Nationalkultur" in Lothar Erhlich and Gunther Mai, eds, *Weimarer Klassik in der Ära Honecker* (Köln: Böhlau, 2001), 29–76.
[55] See Lothar Erhlich, Gunther Mai, and Ingeborg Cleve, "Weimarer Klassik in der Ära Honecker," in Ehrlich and Mai, eds., *Weimarer Klassik in der Ära Honecker*, 18.

to define itself, once again, as an *Erneuerungsbewegung* (movement of renewal). In a flyer of autumn 1989, the Kulturbund voiced demands such as "freedom of the arts and sciences," the "ecological reconstruction of [our] society," and an "end of the further decay of humanist and moral values."[56] In a memo to its members from December 1989, the similarity to the language of 1945 is even more striking: "With our people's revolutionary uprising for freedom, democracy, and honesty, the Kulturbund has arrived at a watershed.... Our people have been lied to and cheated by the leadership of the SED and the state. Anger, bitterness, deep disappointment, and outrage are spreading.... The profound political, economical, ecological, and spiritual-cultural crisis of our country can only be solved by [the cooperation of] all political forces and people of good will.... *What this country needs most of all is an intellectual-cultural renewal*" [emphasis added].[57] The Kulturbund contributed little to this renewal other than the recycled tropes of 1945, but it survived the *Wende* as a public association (*eingetragener Verein*) of hobby clubs – from dialect associations to breeders of pet fish – run by unpaid volunteers.[58]

The nonviolent mass demonstrations of 1989 had little to do with the period of antifascist mobilization. As John Torpey argued, in 1989, only parts of the GDR dissident intelligentsia still clung to visions of a reformed but socialist East German state that would offer an alternative – an "other Germany"? – to both the SED's bureaucratic monopoly of power and to West Germany's capitalist culture of "materialism" and its "ritualized and episodic plebiscites of 'party democracy.'"[59] A few weeks after the collapse of the Third Reich in June 1945, Becher and his Kulturbund colleagues boldly proclaimed a second German Reformation under the vague ideal of a socialist humanism. Traces of this vision might still have been present during the last days of the SED regime, not within the by then irrelevant Kulturbund, but among dissident intellectuals. For example, during a mass demonstration on East Berlin's Alexanderplatz on November 4, 1989, writer Christa Wolf urged listeners of her speech to "Imagine there was socialism and nobody left."[60]

For intellectuals such as Christa Wolf and Stefan Heym, but also for younger civil rights activists such as the New Forum's Bärbel Bohley, it was especially the GDR's perceived antifascist legacy that was worth

---

[56] Kulturbund Flugblatt, Herbst 1989, SAPMO – BArch DY 27/2869.
[57] Rundschreiben des Kulturbunds der DDR an seine Mitglieder, Dezember 1989, SAPMO – BArch DY 27/2869.
[58] See www.kulturbund.de/#, accessed February 2, 2009.
[59] Torpey, *Intellectuals, Socialism, and Dissent*, 172.
[60] Quoted in ibid., 155. Wolf's question is an allusion to the popular German peace movement slogan, "Imagine that there was war and nobody went."

preserving.[61] It was a sign of the SED's enduring success in portraying itself as the antifascist "other" German state, an appeal that is only insufficiently explained by the historiographical term "foundation myth," with its implications of a purely instrumental rationality. Yet, this success was confined to some GDR intellectuals – and to some of the West German student protesters of the 1960s. For the masses of GDR voters at the elections of 1990, antifascism was not a strong enough alternative to the promises of a capitalist consumer society and national unification under West German terms.

The end of the SED regime in 1990 opened up a wide-ranging discussion about the role of intellectuals in the GDR and their relationship to the Party. Posthumously, Johannes R. Becher became one of the most prominent embodiments of a GDR intellectual whose compliance with the SED supported a dictatorial political system. Many debates ensued about the removal of Becher's considerable presence in East German public life, e.g., through the renaming of streets, schools, and other institutions once named after the first GDR minister of culture. But despite his official role in the SED regime, Becher still enjoyed respect even among dissident intellectuals such as Walter Janka and Hans Mayer.[62] In a letter to a high school that was named after Johannes R. Becher but was considering to change its name, Janka – along with Harich one of the victims of the SED purge of 1956 – defended Becher by pointing out the poet's frequent support for opposition intellectuals *from within*.[63] It is unclear whether Janka was aware of the irony with which he defended the antifascist exile poet and Kulturbund founder, using the same arguments members of the inner emigration in Nazi Germany after 1933 had mustered on their behalf. Almost a half century after the dramatic inauguration of the Kulturbund at the Berliner Masurenallee, the question of how to represent the "other Germany" was still wide open.

---

[61] Ibid., 135–9.
[62] See Schiller, *Johannes R. Becher und die Krise des Kulturbundes*, 47.
[63] Letter from Walter Janka to Johannes R. Becher Oberschule in Berbisdorf, n.d., SAPMO – BArch DY 27/2869.

Conclusion: From the Saar to Salamis

During the mid-1930s in Europe, especially after the defeat of the antifascist Popular Front in the Saar referendum, German intellectuals in opposition and exile turned to the idea of humanist culture. A concept that had traditionally been debated among a politically rather detached academic *Bildungsbürgertum* became an ideological and rhetorical tool to counter the racialized NS cultural vision and to hold together Popular Front coalitions between communist and liberal intellectuals. The recourse to the classical Weimar tradition of Goethe and Schiller combined with the Weimar Republic's legacy of politicized culture. This concept of an "other Germany" yielded little political success against the SS and Gestapo, but it spawned a thriving scene of pluralist cultural-political discussion groups and journals that provided the seeds for the rudimentary early postwar public sphere in all four occupation zones.

The dynamics of exile and of Communist-dominated Popular Front communities that were only loosely controlled by Moscow produced a blend of traditional bourgeois cultural activities, the attempted mobilization for a democratic renewal, and critical intellectual inquiries into the German past and collective responsibilities for the rise and the crimes of the Nazi regime. At the same time, the role and moral status of the more passive opposition within Germany – the representatives of the "inner emigration" – complicated the definition of the "other Germany" already during the war and set the stage for conflicts after the war had ended. Moreover, as the power of the Nazi regime waned and the extent of its crimes became more widely known, the "other Germany's" cultural nationalism also became a defense against the doctrine of "Vansittartism" – sweeping condemnations of German national character and Allied conflations of German Nazis and antifascists.

The breakdown of the NS regime and the period of revolutionary upheaval in 1945 made evident that the concept of antifascist mobilization – temporarily resuscitated by the short-lived "antifa" movement – did not offer an alternative to the political postwar order the Allied occupation powers and most Germans had envisioned. Instead, the antifascist exile communities' emphasis on *cultural* renewal continued in organizations such as the Kulturbund zur Demokratischen Erneuerung Deutschlands, which took up multiple strands of twentieth-century German aesthetic movements and social reform ideas, and fused them with the KPD's conscious efforts to legitimize and increase its political influence over the intellectuals in the Soviet Occupation Zone (SBZ).

During the consolidation of the SBZ, the Kulturbund initially provided an example of liberal and communist cooperation in the common project of denazifying German culture and reeducating the population. However, even without the increasingly obvious and well-documented communist instrumentalization of antifascism, the concept of cultural renewal suffered under the strains of its own vagaries and ambiguities. Did the discourse of the "other Germany" restore the intellectual unity that had fallen apart in 1933 or did it give moral superiority to the exiles over the inner émigrés? Was the effort at cultural renewal compatible with the reintegration of public figures who had not explicitly spoken out or acted against the NS dictatorship? And how could the project of "cleansing" German culture work in practice without continuing established practices such as censorship, the use of Nazi-tainted language of disinfection and contamination, and the forced activism of a population that seemed to turn its back to the mobilizing politics of the prewar period?

As the discussions on the Kulturbund board showed, demands to politicize the Kulturbund and prevent the project of cultural reform from petering out in trivial bourgeois activities accompanied, and might even have aided, the Communist tactic of streamlining the antifascist organization's leadership. This constitutes an important addition to our understanding of the Stalinization of East Germany, countering narratives of a passive liberal acquiescence to a carefully planned Communist takeover. Liberals such as the Christian Democrat Ferdinand Friedensburg were not naïve about their precarious situation and their limited space for political maneuvers in the SBZ, but they shared a sincere interest in cultural renewal and a critique of German traditions with KPD representatives such as Johannes R. Becher and Alexander Abusch.

After 1946, the antifascist unity in the Kulturbund and in occupied Germany in general broke apart. However, the discussions on the Kulturbund board and in its publications demonstrate that the clash between liberal and communist concepts of democracy was intertwined with different interpretations of German history and with conflicting approaches of coming to terms with it. Liberal interpretations – e.g., by Friedensburg and the West German historian Friedrich Meinecke – that situated the NS period in a general "crisis of Western thought" came under attack by communist intellectuals who stressed the material and economic context of German fascism. With the rise of Cold War tensions, this communist critique was extended to existentialism and humanism in general, thereby creating a rift in the intellectual resistance traditions in East and West that prefigured the Moscow-orchestrated anti-formalist campaign of the late 1940s and early 1950s.

The First German Writers' Congress in 1947 was the last gasp of antifascist intellectual unity. Its spectacular failure exposed not only the impotence of intellectuals in the face of the Cold War politics of the Allies – the standard historiographical interpretation – but all the unresolved conflicts, vagaries, and ambiguities that had accompanied the concepts of "cultural renewal," "antifascist humanism," and the "other Germany" since their first employments in the struggle against Hitler's Germany. The Cold War did not "defeat" the "other Germany"; it highlighted how malleable the concept was by redefining it in terms of the East–West conflict. It underscored that there had never been one monolithic "other Germany," but a fluctuating procession of "other Germanies" that various intellectual and historical actors adapted to evolving political circumstances.

Seen in this light, the history of cultural renewal in Germany in the mid-twentieth century can easily be read as a narrative of failure. The idealistic dream of a humanist German tradition that would resist Nazi inhumanity and would resurrect a democratic, tolerant, and unified nation out of the ruins of the war ended as either the GDR's crude rhetorical weapon in the Cold War or in the petty bourgeois club activities of the Esperanto learners and pet breeders in the depoliticized Kulturbund after 1950. However, with all its ambiguities and unresolved issues, the construct of an "other Germany," with all its Reformation-derived quasi-nationalistic rhetoric was also an early component of the distinct postwar German memory culture known as *Vergangenheitsbewältigung*. The official GDR historiography undoubtedly lacked the self-critical openness of the Federal Republic's public sphere since the 1960s. Most strikingly, the GDR's exclusive emphasis on material and economic factors and its moral condemnation of capitalism consistently ignored or downplayed the significance of Nazi racial thought and the significance of the Holocaust. Yet, as Gregory P. Wegner points out, at least until the 1960s, accounts of the "complicity of some German industrial concerns in the Nazi policy of mass extermination" were more likely to be found in GDR secondary school history books than in West Germany, or, for that matter, the United States.[1] If the official antifascism of the SED had its ideological distortions and blind spots, so too had the liberal

---

[1] Gregory P. Wegner, "The Legacy of Nazism and the History Curriculum in the East German Secondary Schools," *The History Teacher* 25, 4 (August 1992): 479.

historiography and idealist humanism that Meinecke promulgated in the West – although many would argue with John Torpey's sweeping claim that "the Germans in the GDR nurtured a deeper historical consciousness than their compatriots in the Federal Republic.[2]

The point of this study was not, however, to weigh the contributions or moral flaws of the Federal Republic against those of the GDR – there are enough Cold War histories to keep score. My aim was to show that both *Vergangenheitsbewältigung* and Stalinization are more complex and interconnected than many histories of the immediate postwar period have taken into consideration. The ill-fated history of the Kulturbund in particular demonstrated the interaction between sincere attempts at coming to terms with the past and the cynical political manipulation of antifascist principles. Moreover, the history of the "other Germanies" demonstrates that the calls for cultural renewal and national rebirth did not suddenly emerge in a mythical zero hour in 1945, but have long roots in the complicated mass politics of the twentieth century. Fascism itself, according to Roger Griffin, "is a form ... of modern, mass politics which draws its ideological cohesion and mobilizing force from the vision of imminent national rebirth." Destruction and moral decay presage "a new life, a new creation."[3] Ironically, the same can be said about the antifascist calls for a cultural renewal after the catastrophe of World War II. The often nationalist or culturally conservative background of many of the antifascist Kulturbund founders, as well as the striking – and disturbing – continuation of Nazi rhetoric in the process of "cleansing" German culture points to common historical roots.

This is not to say that twentieth-century fascists and antifascists were cut from the same cloth. To the contrary, it can be argued that Germany's twentieth-century tradition of cultural renewal not only made its intellectuals receptive to authoritarian movements, but also prepared the country for addressing the mistakes of the past and – at least in the West – to effect a largely successful democratic and liberal transformation.[4] While the often anti-modern and illiberal prewar visions of cultural renewal

---

[2] John C. Torpey, *Intellectuals, Socialism, and Dissent: The East German Opposition and Its Legacy* (Minneapolis: University of Minnesota Press, 1995), 8. Apart from the fact that this statement is hard to prove empirically, the comparatively high acceptance of right-wing extremism in the East after 1989 supports the opposite argument, namely, that the GDR's educational policies were seriously lacking.
[3] Roger Griffin, "Revolution from the Right: Fascism," in David Parker, ed., *Revolutions and the Revolutionary Tradition in the West, 1560–1991* (London: Routledge, 2000), 187, 192.
[4] For a detailed recent analysis of this transformation, cf. Konrad H. Jarausch, *After Hitler: Recivilizing Germans, 1945–1995*, trans. Brandon Hunziker (Oxford: Oxford University Press, 2006).

helped bring about the disastrous and genocidal Nazi new order, intellectuals after 1945 were able to continue discourses that entailed the self-scrutiny of one's national past. This tradition of demanding a reformation of cultural traditions might have also prepared German intellectuals for critically assessing their nation's responsibilities.[5] The fact that in the East the antifascist mastering of the German past boosted the SED dictatorship only underscores the volatility and complexity of cultural renewal in twentieth-century Germany.

At the center of this study's narrative was the Kulturbund's adoption of what I called the dual legacy of Weimar: the recourse to the traditional "Weimar humanism" of Goethe and Schiller blended with the politicized cultural mass politics of the Weimar Republic. Thus, instead of a century neatly divided in two halves by the year 1945, the roughly two decades from the mid-1930s to the mid-1950s emerged as a period of transition in attitudes toward political and cultural mobilization. In 1935, a majority of Germans in the Saar region – and presumably many more in Germany proper – seemed to have embraced the Nazi vision of a thoroughgoing national "rebirth" – however ignorant or skeptical many ordinary Germans were of some of this vision's details and methods. In contrast, by 1953, the workers in East Berlin did not rise up for a utopian program of cultural-political reformation, but for the reduction of production norms and more democratic elections. The same, more tangible demands were central to the majority of the participants of the 1989 mass demonstrations that contributed to the end of the GDR.

Does this mean that the tropes of cultural renewal and the "other Germany" have dissipated in a reunified, liberal republic? It could be argued that the discourse continues in different forms. While the political constellations of the 1930s and the Cold War are fading, cultural debates about the war's representation and its significance for German national identity have continued into the twenty-first century. Echoes of the "other Germany's" reaction to the Allied wartime doctrine of "Vansittartism" reverberated, for instance, in attacks on "the enduring summary equation of Germans and Nazis attaching to the war generation in Germany and, if fuzzily but not therefore less potent, to all Germans in the United States."[6] While Abusch, Weisenborn, and other antifascist intellectuals

---

[5] As Timothy Garton Ash argues, West Germany's post-1945 tradition of *Vergangenheitsbewältigung* also prepared a unified Germany better than other post-Communist countries to confront and "master" its Communist past, specifically the legacy of the Stasi (state security) activity. See Timothy Garton Ash, "The Stasi on Our Minds," *New York Review of Books*, May 31, 2007.

[6] Dagmar Barnouw, *The War in the Empty Air: Victims, Perpetrators, and Postwar Germans* (Bloomington: Indiana University Press, 2005), 24.

of the 1940s and 1950s tried simultaneously to critique the German past and enshrine the memory of the antifascist "other Germany," at the beginning of the twenty-first century a heated debate and an influential and diverse body of literature and other cultural productions spun around the experiences of the victims of Allied fire bombings, post-Yalta expulsions, and mass rapes.[7] And just as the memory of antifascism was instrumentalized by the Stalinist left, the debate on German victimization – like all victimization debates – has displayed the potential of being politically abused, this time by the old and new extreme right.

While refutations of sweeping and undifferentiated attitudes toward German history seem to resume the "other Germany's" defense of pre-Nazi German traditions during the war, critiques of postwar Germany's "culture of remorse" also challenge the key demands of the movement for antifascist cultural renewal: the insight into the political and moral catastrophe of the Nazi regime as a stepping stone for a self-critical reflection on national traditions in order to build a more liberal and humane society. Thus, the memory of Nazi crimes, however painful and burdensome, is inexorably linked to a national identity and democratic political culture in Germany. This line of argument – arguably the implication of the Kulturbund's vision of cultural renewal – has been most vocally represented in postwar Germany by Jürgen Habermas, who holds that "German citizens had to ... rediscover the muted legacy of humanism and the Enlightenment in their own traditions.... The Federal Republic has become politically civilized only to the degree that the obstacles to our perception of a heretofore unthinkable breach in civilization have been swept away. We had to learn to publicly confront a traumatic past."[8] Habermas's allusion to the "legacy of humanism in Germany's traditions" and his urge to undertake a "reflection on the incomprehensible" has strong echoes of the Kulturbund discussions of the 1940s, a sign that

---

[7] Among the most influential publications, including fiction, literary criticism, autobiography, and historical documentary, of the past decade are W. G. Sebald, *Luftkrieg und Literatur. Mit einem Essay zu Alfred Andersch* (Munich: Hanser, 1999) [Engl. transl. *On the Natural History of Destruction* (New York: Random House, 2003)]; Jörg Friedrich, *Der Brand. Deutschland im Bombenkrieg, 1940–1945* (Berlin: Propyläen, 2003) [Engl. transl. *The Fire: The Bombing of Germany, 1940–1945* (New York: Columbia University Press, 2006)]; see also several recent popular TV documentaries and shows. Important English-language publications discussing German suffering in a nuanced way are Norman M. Naimark, *The Russians in Germany: A History of the Soviet Zone of Occupation, 1945–1949* (Cambridge, MA:Harvard University Press, 1995), 400–8; Atina Grossman, *Jews, Germans, and Allies: Close Encounters in Occupied Germany* (Princeton, NJ: Princeton University Press, 2007); Giles MacDonogh, *After the Reich: The Brutal History of the Allied Occupation* (New York: Basic Books, 2007).

[8] Jürgen Habermas, "1989 in the Shadow of 1945: On the Normality of a Future Berlin Republic," in *A Berlin Republic: Writings on Germany. Die Normalität einer Berliner Republik*, trans. Steven Rendall (Lincoln: University of Nebraska Press, 1997), 163–4.

the larger themes of Germany postwar renewal survived the Stalinization of this organization.

The difficulty of neatly juxtaposing a Germany of victims to one of perpetrators, or an unconditionally "good," humanist tradition to another tradition that stands for dictatorship and barbarity, is exemplified by the case of Günter Grass, whose novel *Crabwalk* in 2002 painted a differentiated picture of the link between German suffering and moral failure, and the necessity to remember both. A few years after the publication of *Crabwalk*, Grass's belated admission of his own involuntary youthful membership in the Waffen SS compromised for many commentators the Nobel Prize winner's heretofore significant contributions to postwar Germany's cultural renewal and *Vergangenheitsbewältigung*.[9] The stark moral black-and-white contrast implied by the idea of an "other Germany" clearly has its limits, even without the influence of Stalinists.

And yet the painting of a stark moral contrast might be the lasting historical legacy of the antifascist movement today, not only in Germany, but in the West at large. The cultural impact of the antifascists of the 1930s and 1940s has for many decades contributed to discrediting fascism as a viable political doctrine for all but the fringes of European societies. Moreover, as the vaguely religious tones of the Kulturbund's project of reformation had already indicated in 1945, in the secularized postwar West, "fascism" provides moral categories of good and evil in popular culture as well as in international politics. As a result, the ideological use of the memory of fascism has not ended with the fall of Soviet communism.[10] Neither has the political instrumentalization of Germany's and Europe's cultural traditions: In the second decade of the twenty-first century, in the wake of demographic changes and new global explosions of violence, German streets, especially in parts of the former GDR, gave birth to movements that attempt to mobilize for the alleged representation and the defense of the *Abendland* (occident) but have little in common with either the cosmopolitanism of classical Weimar humanism or the Kulturbund founders' commitment to a tolerant German society.

---

[9] See Günter Grass, *Im Krebsgang. Eine Novelle* (Göttingen: Steidl, 2002) [Engl. transl. *Crabwalk* (Orlando: Harcourt, 2002)]. For an exhaustive documentation of the different aspects of the Grass debate, see Martin Körbel, ed., *Ein Buch, ein Bekenntnis. Die Debatte um Günter Grass' "Beim Häuten der Zwiebel"* (Göttingen: Steidl, 2007).

[10] See, for example, the fuzzy as well as historically questionable use of the term "Islamofascism" in the context of early twenty-first-century neoconservative U.S. Middle East policies. For a discussion of this topic, see Robert O. Paxton, *The Anatomy of Fascism* (New York: Vintage, 2004), 203–5. For a new interpretation of fascism in Germany, see also Geoff Eley, *Nazism as Fascism: Violence, Ideology, and the Ground of Consent in Germany, 1930–1945* (Milton Park, UK: Routledge, 2013).

Conclusion

At a time when the resurgence of right-wing populism – not only in Europe but also in the United States – evokes memories of the rise of fascism, the twentieth-century dynamics of antifascism, humanism, and cultural renewal still have lessons to teach. In a novel by the Spanish writer Javier Cercas, the first-person narrator and protagonist, a middle-aged, liberal-progressive journalist, researches the life and the role of the poet Rafael Sánchez Mazas, one of the founders of the fascist Falange movement. Against his expectations, the protagonist – who is also a failed novelist – finds much to admire in Sánchez Mazas's political-aesthetic vision of cultural renewal. Influenced by the ideas of Oswald Spengler and José Ortega y Gasset, as well as by Lenin, Sánchez Mazas created the Falange movement to fend off "egalitarian barbarism" and "preserve civilization by force" – the modern heir to the ancient Greek soldiers who ensured the survival of Western civilization.[11] Only in the end does the narrator come to the unequivocal conclusion that it was not Sánchez Mazas's movement that was the equivalent of the soldiers of Salamis – the saviors of the foundation of Western civilization and humanism – but the many nameless and often deeply flawed and unheroic men and women in Europe who took up the cause of antifascism.

The antifascist German intellectuals discussed in these pages would surely have concurred with this conclusion. But the fascist poet Sánchez Mazas, who became the minister of culture in Franco's government, also exhibits remarkable parallels to the German poet Johannes R. Becher, the Kulturbund president who became the minister of culture for the SED regime. It reminds us of the appeal, the risks, and the potential of politics that pursue the ideal of cultural renewal, whether before or after 1945. As the experience of postwar Germany has shown, the idea of renewing cultural traditions can both legitimize authoritarian regimes and democratize former dictatorships. In the twenty-first century, politics and culture will continue to interact in ways that will defy easy and unambiguous categorization. This makes it worthwhile to pay further attention to the experiences, failures, and successes of the various "other Germanies" of the past century.

---

[11] Javier Cercas, *Soldiers of Salamis*, trans. Anne McLean (New York: Bloomsbury, 2001), 77.

Bibliography

Archival Sources

Akademie der Künste, Berlin (AdK Berlin)
  Nachlass Günther WeisenbornNachlass Johannes R. Becher
Institut für Zeitungsforschung, Dortmund
Stadtarchiv Duisburg (Sta DU)
  OB Akte Weitz (1945)
Stiftung Archiv der Parteien und Massenorganisationen der DDR im Bundesarchiv (SAPMO – Barch)
  DY 27 – Kulturbund zur demokratischen Erneuerung Deutschlands
  SgY 30 – Sammlung Antifaschistische Ausschüsse und Komitees

Selected Newspapers and Periodicals

Aufbau
FDKB Nachrichten (London)
Freies Deutschland/Alemania Libre (Mexico City)
La Otra Alemania/Das Andere Deutschland (Buenos Aires)
Merkur
Der Monat
Ost und West
Pariser Tageszeitung
Tagesspiegel (Berlin)
Tägliche Rundschau (Berlin)
Die Weltbühne

Literature Cited

Abusch, Alexander. *Ansichten über einige Klassiker.* Berlin (East) and Weimar: Aufbau, 1982.
Der Deckname. Memoiren. Berlin (East): Dietz, 1984.
Entscheidung unseres Jahrhunderts. Beiträge zur Zeitgeschichte, 1921 bis 1976. Berlin (East): Aufbau, 1977.

"Gibt es eine besondere deutsche Krise?" (1947) in *Kulturelle Probleme des sozialistischen Humanismus. Beiträge zur deutschen Kulturpolitik, 1946–1961*. Schriften, Band III. Berlin (East): Aufbau-Verlag, 1962.

Der Irrweg einer Nation. Berlin: Aufbau, 1946.

Literatur im Zeitalter des Sozialismus: Beiträge zur Literaturgeschichte 1921 bis 1966. Schriften, Band II. Berlin (East): Aufbau, 1967.

Ackermann, Anton. "Das Nationalkomitee 'Freies Deutschland' – miterlebt und mitgestaltet." In Heinz Voßke, ed., *Im Kampf bewährt. Erinnerungen deutscher Genossen an den antifaschistischen Widerstand v on 1933 bis 1945*. Berlin (East): Dietz Verlag, 1977, 277–331.

Agethen, Manfred, Eckhard Jesse, and Ehrhart Neubert, eds. *Der missbrauchte Antifaschismus. DDR-Staatsdoktrin und Lebenslüge der deutschen Linken*. Freiburg: Herder, 2002.

Alexander Abusch: Bildnis eines Revolutionärs. Freunde und Genossen über ihre Begegnungen mit Alexander Abusch in fünf Jahrzehnten. Berlin (East): Aufbau, 1972.

Andreas-Friedrich, Ruth. *Battleground Berlin: Diaries 1945–1948*. Translated by Anna Boerresen. New York: Paragon, 1990.

Applebaum, Anne. *Iron Curtain: The Crushing of Eastern Europe, 1944–1956*. New York: Doubleday, 2012.

Applegate, Celia. *A Nation of Provincials: The German Idea of Heimat*. Berkeley: University of California Press, 1990.

Badstübner, Rolf et al. *Deutsche Geschichte, Band 9. Die antifaschistisch-demokratische Umwälzung, der Kampf gegen die Spaltung Deutschlands und die Entstehung der DDR von 1945 bis 1949*. Berlin (East) and Cologne: Pahl-Rugenstein, 1989.

Barnouw, Dagmar. *The War in the Empty Air: Victims, Perpetrators, and Postwar Germans*. Bloomington and Indianapolis: Indiana University Press, 2005.

Becher, Johannes R. *Deutsches Bekenntnis. Fünf Reden zu Deutschlands Erneuerung*. Third, extended edition. Berlin: Aufbau Verlag, 1946.

Der gespaltene Dichter. Gedichte, Briefe, Dokumente, 1945–1958. Berlin: Aufbau Taschenbuch Verlag, 1991.

Lyrik, Prosa, Dokumente: Eine Auswahl. Wiesbaden: Limes Verlag, 1965.

Beevor, Anthony. *The Fall of Berlin 1945*. New York: Viking, 2002.

Behrens, Alexander. *Johannes R. Becher: Eine politische Biographie*. Cologne: Böhlau Verlag, 2003.

Berendsohn, Walter A. *Die humanistische Front. Einführung in die deutsche Emigranten-Literatur. Erster Teil: Von 1933 bis zum Kriegsausbruch 1939*. Zürich: Europa Verlag, 1946.

Die humanistische Front. Einführung in die deutsche Emigranten-Literatur. Zweiter Teil: Vom Kriegsausbruch 1939 bis Ende 1946. Worms, Germany: Verlag Georg Heintz, 1976.

Bessel, Richard. *Germany 1945: From War to Peace*. New York: HarperCollins, 2009.

Betts, Paul and Greg Eghigian, eds. *Pain and Prosperity: Reconsidering Twentieth-Century German History*. Stanford, CA: Stanford University Press, 2003.

Biess, Frank. *Homecoming: Returning POWs and the Legacies of Defeat in Postwar Germany*. Princeton, NJ: Princeton University Press, 2009.

Birr, Ewald. *Ost und West, Berlin 1947–1949. Bibliographie einer Zeitschrift.* Veröffentlichung der Akademie der Künste zu Berlin. Munich: K. G. Saur, 1993.

Blackbourn, David and Geoff Eley. *The Peculiarities of German History: Bourgeois Society and Politics in Nineteenth-Century Germany.* Oxford: Oxford University Press, 1984.

Boterbloem, Kees. *The Life and Times of Andrei Zhdanov, 1896–1948.* Montreal & Kingston: McGill-Queen's University Press, 2004.

Brandt, Peter. *Antifaschismus und Arbeiterbewegung. Aufbau – Ausprägung – Politik in Bremen 1945/46.* Hamburger Beiträge zur Sozial- und Zeitgeschichte, Band XI. Hamburg: Hans Christians Verlag, 1976.

Brinson, Charmion and Richard Dove. *Politics by Other Means: The Free German League of Culture in London, 1939–1946.* London: Valentine Mitchell, 2010.

Broszat, Martin, Klaus-Dietmar Henke, and Hans Woller, eds. *Von Stalingrad zur Währungsreform: Zur Sozialgeschichte des Umbruchs in Deutschland.* Quellen und Darstellungen zur Zeitgeschichte. Herausgegeben vom Institut für Zeitgeschichte, Band 26. R. Oldenbourg Verlag: Munich, 1988.

Cercas, Javier. *Soldiers of Salamis.* Translated by Anne McLean. New York: Bloomsbury, 2001.

Clark, Mark W. *Beyond Catastrophe: German Intellectuals and Cultural Renewal after World War II, 1945–1955.* Lanham, MD: Lexington Books, 2006.

Confino, Alon. *The Nation as a Local Metaphor: Württemberg, Imperial Germany, and National Memory, 1871–1918.* Chapel Hill: University of North Carolina Press, 1997.

"Telling about Germany: Narratives of Memory and Culture," *Journal of Modern History* 76 (June 2004): 389–416.

Connelly, John. *Captive University: The Sovietization of East German, Czech, and Polish Higher Education, 1945–1956.* Chapel Hill: University of North Carolina Press, 2000.

Curtius, Ernst Robert. *Deutscher Geist in Gefahr.* Stuttgart: Deutsche Verlagsanstalt, 1932.

Curtius, Ludwig, "Die Antike Kunst und der Moderne Humanismus," *Die Antike* 3 (1927). Reprinted in Oppermann, ed., *Humanismus,* 49–65.

Danyel, Jürgen, ed. *Die geteilte Vergangenheit: Zum Umgang mit Nationalsozialismus und Widerstand in beiden deutschen Staaten.* Zeithistorische Studien, Vol. 4. Berlin: Akademie Verlag, 1985.

Davies, Peter. *Divided Loyalties: East German Writers and the Politics of German Division, 1945–1953.* London: The Modern Humanities Research Association and the Institute for Germanic Studies, University of London, 2000.

Deák, István, Jan T. Gross, and Tony Judt, eds. *The Politics of Retribution in Europe: World War II and Its Aftermath.* Princeton, NJ: Princeton University Press, 2000.

Deutscher Kulturbund. *Manifest und Ansprachen von Bernhard Kellermann [et al.] gehalten bei der Gründungskundgebung des Kulturbundes zur demokratischen Erneuerung Deutschlands am 4. Juli 1945 im Haus des Berliner Rundfunks.* Berlin: Aufbau Verlag, n.d.

Diehl, James M. *Paramilitary Politics in Weimar Germany*. Bloomington: Indiana University Press, 1977.
Dietrich, Gerd. *Politik und Kultur in der Sowjetischen Besatzungszone Deutschlands (SBZ), 1945–1949*. Bern: Peter Lang, 1993.
Dietrich, Gerd, ed. *Um die Erneuerung der deutschen Kultur. Dokumente zur deutschen Kulturpolitik, 1945–1949*. Berlin (East): Dietz, 1983.
Diner, Dan. "On the Ideology of Antifascism." Translated by Christian Gundermann. "Legacies of Antifascism." *New German Critique*, 67 (Winter 1996): 123–32.
Drachkovitch, Milorad M. and Branko Lazitch, eds. *The Comintern: Historical Highlights. Essays, Recollections, Documents*. Published for the Hoover Institution on War, Revolution, and Peace, Stanford University, Stanford, California. New York: Frederick A. Praeger, 1966.
Dwars, Jens-Fietje. *Abgrund des Widerspruchs: Das Leben des Johannes R. Becher*. Berlin: Aufbau-Verlag, 1998.
Erbe, Günter. *Die Verfemte Moderne: Die Auseinandersetzung mit dem "Modernismus" in der Kulturpolitik, Literaturwissenschaft und Literatur der DDR*. Opladen: Westdeutscher Verlag, 1993.
Ehrenburg, Ilya. *We Will Not Forget*. Information Bulletin, Embassy of the Union of Soviet Socialist Republics, Washington, DC, Special Supplement, June 1944.
einer neuen Zeit Beginn: Erinnerungen and die Anfänge unserer Kulturrevolution, 1945–1949. Herausgegeben vom Institut für Marxismus-Leninismus beim ZK der SED und vom Kulturbund der DDR. Berlin and Weimar: Aufbau Verlag, 1981.
Eley, Geoff. *Forging Democracy: A History of the Left in Europe, 1850–2000*. New York: Oxford University Press, 2002.
 Nazism as Fascism: Violence, Ideology, and the Ground of Consent in Germany, 1930–1945. Milton Park: Routledge, 2013.
Erhlich, Lothar and Gunther Mai, eds. *Weimarer Klassik in der Ära Honecker*. Köln: Böhlau, 2001.
Erhlich, Lothar and Gunther Mai, Gunther Mai, and Ingeborg Cleve, "Weimarer Klassik in der Ära Honecker," in Ehrlich and Mai, eds., *Weimarer Klassik in der Ära Honecker*, 7–28.
Erster Deutscher Schriftstellerkongreß. 4.–8. Oktober 1947. Edited by Ursula Reinhold, Dieter Schlenstedt, and Horst Tanneberger. Berlin: Aufbau, n. d.
Eschenburg, Theodor. *Geschichte der Bundesrepublik Deutschland, Band 1. Jahre der Besatzung 1945–1949*. Stuttgart: Deutsche Verlagsanstalt, 1983.
Evans, Richard J. *The Coming of the Third Reich*. New York: Penguin, 2003.
 Fabian Tracts, Volume 7 (Nos. 223–261), 1928–1944. Nendeln/Liechtenstein: Kraus Thomson, 1969.
Faye, Emmanuel. *Heidegger: The Introduction of Nazism into Philosophy in Light of the Unpublished Seminars of 1933–1935*. Translated by Michael B. Smith. New Haven, CT: Yale University Press, 2009.
Fillafer, Franz Leander and JürgenOsterhammel. "Cosmopolitanism and the German Enlightenment," in Smith, ed., *The Oxford Handbook of Modern German History*, 119–43.

Flanagan, Clare. "Political Myth and Germany 1945–1949." *German Life and Letters* 57, 1 (January 2004): 111–25.
Forner, Sean A. "Für eine demokratische Erneuerung Deutschlands: Kommunikationsprozesse und Deutungsmuster engagierter Demokraten nach 1945." *Geschichte und Gesellschaft* 33 (2007): 228–57.
German Intellectuals and the Challenge of Democratic Renewal: Culture and Politics after 1945. Cambridge: Cambridge University Press, 2014.
"Reconsidering the 'Unpolitical German': Democratic Renewal and the Politics of Culture in Occupied Germany." *German History* 32, 1 (March 2014): 53–78.
Frei, Norbert, ed. *Hitler's Eliten nach 1945*. München: dtv, 2003.
Fricke, Karl Wilhelm, Peter Steinbach, and Johannes Tuchel, eds. *Opposition und Widerstand in der DDR. Politische Lebensbilder*. Munich: C. H. Beck, 2002.
Friedmann, Germán C. *Alemanes antinazis en la Argentina*. Buenos Aires: Siglo ventiuno, 2010.
Friedrich, Jörg. *Der Brand. Deutschland im Bombenkrieg, 1940–1945*. Berlin: Propyläen, 2003.
Fritzsche, Peter. *Rehearsals for Fascism: Populism and Political Mobilization in Germany*. New York: Oxford University Press, 1990.
Fulbrook, Mary. *Anatomy of a Dictatorship: Inside the GDR, 1949–1989*. New York: Oxford University Press, 1995.
German National Identity after the Holocaust. Cambridge: Cambridge University Press, 1988.
The People's State: East German Society from Hitler to Honecker. New Haven, CT, and London: Yale University Press, 2005.
Fulbrook, Mary., and Andrew I. Port, eds., *Becoming East German: Socialist Structures and Sensibilities after Hitler*. New York: Berghahn, 2013.
Gallus, Alexander. "'Intellectual History' mit Intellektuellen und ohne sie: Facetten neuerer geistesgeschichtlicher Forschung." *Historische Zeitschrift*, 288, 1 (2009): 139–50.
Gansel, Carsten. *Parlament des Geistes: Literatur zwischen Hoffnung und Repression, 1945–1961*. Berlin: BasisDruck, 1996.
Gerhardt, Uta. *Soziologie der Stunde Null. Zur Gesellschaftskonzeption des amerikanischen Besatzungsregimes in Deutschland, 1944–1945/1946*. Frankfurt am Main: Suhrkamp, 2005.
Gimbel, John. *The American Occupation of Germany: Politics and the Military, 1945–1949*. Stanford, CA: Stanford University Press, 1968.
Glaser, Hermann. *The Rubble Years: The Cultural Roots of Postwar Germany, 1945–1948. [Kulturgeschichte der Bundesrepublik Deutschland]*. New York: Paragon, 1986.
Gollancz, Victor. *Shall Our Children Live or Die? A Reply to Lord Vansittart on the German Problem*. London: Victor Gollancz, 1942.
Grass, Günter. *Im Krebsgang. Eine Novelle*. Göttingen: Steidl, 2002.
Grieder, Peter. *The German Democratic Republic*. Basingstoke: Palgrave Macmillan, 2012.
Griffin, Roger. "Revolution from the Right: Fascism," in David Parker, ed., *Revolutions and the Revolutionary Tradition in the West, 1560–1991*. London and New York: Routledge, 2000, 185–201.

Grossmann, Atina. *Jews, Germans, and Allies: Close Encounters in Occupied Germany*. Princeton, NJ: Princeton University Press, 2007.
Grunenberg, Antonia. *Antifaschismus: Ein deutscher Mythos*. Reinbek: Rowohlt, 1993.
Habermas, Jürgen. "1989 in the Shadow of 1945: On the Normality of a Future Berlin Republic," in *A Berlin Republic: Writings on Germany. Die Normalität einer Berliner Republik*. Translated by Steven Rendall. Lincoln: University of Nebraska Press, 1997.
Hagen, William W. "Master Narratives beyond Postmodernity: Germany's 'Separate Path' in Historiographical-Philosophical Light." *German Studies Review* XXX, 1 (February 2007): 1–32.
Hake, Sabine. *Topographies of Class: Modern Architecture and Mass Society in Weimar Berlin*. Ann Arbor: University of Michigan Press, 2008.
Haynes, Mike and Jim Wolfreys, eds., *History and Revolution: Refuting Revisionism*. London and New York: Verso, 2007.
Heider, Magdalena. *Politik – Kultur – Kulturbund. Zur Gründungs- und Frühgeschichte des Kulturbundes zur demokratischen Erneuerung Deutschlands 1945–1954 in der SBZ/DDR*. Cologne: Verlag Wissenschaft und Politik, 1993.
Heider, Magdalena, and Kerstin Thöns, eds. *SED und Intellektuelle in der DDR der fünfziger Jahre. Kulturbund Protokolle*. Köln: Edition Archiv Deutschland, 1990.
Heineman, Elizabeth. "The Hour of the Woman: Memories of Germany's 'Crisis Years' and West German National Identity." *American Historical Review* 101, 2 (April 1996): 354–95.
Heinz, Joachim. "Sozialdemokratie und Kommunisten 1933 bis 1945 im Saarland. Ein Überblick," in Hermann und Bauer, eds., *Widerstand, Repression und Verfolgung*, 185–211.
Herf, Jeffrey. *Divided Memory: The Nazi Past in the Two Germanys*. Cambridge, MA: Harvard University Press, 1997.
Hermand, Jost. *Culture in Dark Times: Nazi Fascism, Inner Emigration, and Exile*. Translated by Victoria W. Hill. New York: Berghahn, 2013.
 Kultur im Wiederaufbau: Die Bundesrepublik Deutschland, 1945–1965. Munich: Nymphenburger, 1986.
Herrmann, Hans-Christian, and Ruth Bauer, eds. *Widerstand, Repression und Verfolgung. Beiträge zur Geschichte des Nationalsozialismus an der Saar*. St. Ingbert: Röhrig Universitätsverlag, 2014.
Heterogenität und Konsistenz. Zur Herausbildung und Entwicklung des Kulturbundes in der DDR. Pankower Vorträge, Heft 30. Berlin: "Helle Panke," 2001.
Hoffmann, Stefan-Ludwig. "Germany Is No More: Defeat, Occupation, and the Postwar Order," in Smith, ed., *The Oxford Handbook of Modern German History*, 593–614.
Horn, Gerd-Rainer. *European Socialists Respond to Fascism: Ideology, Activism, and Contingency in the 1930s*. New York: Oxford University Press, 1996.
Ihering, Herbert. *Der Kampf ums Theater*. Dresden: Sybillen Verlag, 1922.
 Der Kampf ums Theater und andere Streitschriften 1918 bis 1933. Berlin (East): Henschelverlag Kunst und Gesellschaft, 1974.
Institut für Marxismus-Leninismus beim Zentralkomitee der SED. *Geschichte der deutschen Arbeiterbewegung, Band 6: Von Mai 1945 bis 1949*. Berlin (East): Dietz, 1966.

Jacobs, Nicholas. "Trials and Triumphs of East German Publishing." *New Left Review* I/231 (September–October 1998): 146–51.
Jaeger, Werner. "Antike und Humanismus," Rede zur Eröffnung der Tagung "Das Gymnasium," Berlin, April 1925. Reprinted in Oppermann, ed., *Humanismus*, 18–32.
Jäger, Manfred. *Kultur und Politik in der DDR, 1945–1990*. Köln: Edition Deutschland Archiv, 1995.
James, Harold. "Review: The Prehistory of the Federal Republic." *Journal of Modern History* 63, 1 (March 1991): 99–115.
Jarausch, Konrad H. *After Hitler: Recivilizing Germans, 1945–1995*. Translated by Brandon Hunziker. Oxford: Oxford University Press, 2006.
Jarausch, Konrad H., ed., *Dictatorship as Experience: Towards a Socio-cultural History of the GDR*. New York: Berghahn, 1999.
Jarausch, Konrad H., and Michael Geyer. *Shattered Past: Reconstructing German Histories*. Princeton, NJ: Princeton University Press, 2003.
Jarausch, Konrad H., and Hannes Sigrist, eds. *Amerikanisierung und Sowjetisierung in Deutschland, 1945–1970*. Frankfurt: Campus, 1997.
Judt, Mathias, ed. *DDR Geschichte in Dokumenten: Beschlüsse, Berichte, interne Materialien und Alltagszeugnisse*. Berlin: Ch. Links, 1998.
Kahn, Arthur D. *Experiment in Occupation. Witness to the Turnabout: Anti-Nazi War to Cold War*. University Park: Pennsylvania State University Press, 2004.
Kantorowicz, Alfred. *Deutschland-Ost und Deutschland West. Kulturpolitische Einigungsversuche und geistige Spaltung in Deutschland seit 1945*. Sylter Beiträge 2. Münsterdorf: Verlag Hansen & Hansen, n. d.
Kießling, Friedrich. "Westernisierung, Internationalisierung, Bürgerlichkeit? Zu einigen jüngeren Arbeiten der Ideengeschichte der alten Bundesrepublik." *Historische Zeitschrift*, 287 (2008), 2: 363–89.
Kießling, Wolfgang, ed,. *Alemania Libre in Mexico. Band 1. Ein Beitrag zur Geschichte des antifaschistischen Exils (1941–1946)*. Berlin (East): Akademie Verlag, 1974.
Alemania Libre in Mexico. Band 2. Texte und Dokumente zur Geschichte des antifaschistischen Exils 1941–1946. Berlin (East): Akademie Verlag, 1974.
Klee, Ernst. *Das Kulturlexikon zum Dritten Reich. Were war was vor und nach 1945*. Frankfurt a. M.: S. Fischer, 2007.
Kleßmann, Christoph. *Die doppelte Staatsgründung. Deutsche Geschichte 1945–1955*. Göttingen: Vandenhoek & Ruprecht, 1982.
Klönne, Arno. "Die gebrochene Tradition: Arbeitermilieu und gewerkschaftliche Organisation im Ruhrgebiet nach 1945," in Jan-Pieter Barbian and Ludger Heid, eds., *Zwischen Gestern und Morgen: Kriegsende und Wiederaufbau im Ruhrgebiet*. Essen: Klartext Verlag, 1995, 136–44.
Kocka, Jürgen, ed. *Historische DDR-Forschung: Aufsätze und Studien*. Berlin: Akademie Verlag, 1993.
Koepnick, Lutz. "Culture in the Shadow of Trauma?" in Smith, ed., *The Oxford Handbook of Modern German History*, 711–13.
Kolb, Eberhard. *Die Arbeiterräte in der deutschen Innenpolitik 1918–1919*. München: Ullstein, 1978.
Kölbel, Martin. *Ein Buch, ein Bekenntnis: Die Debatte um Günter Grass' "Beim Häuten der Zwiebel."* Göttingen: Steidl, 2007.

Koshar, Rudy. *From Monuments to Traces: Artifacts of German Memory, 1870–1990*. Berkeley: University of California Press, 2000.

Kroll, Thomas. *Kommunistische Intellektuelle in Westeuropa: Frankreich, Österreich, Italien und Großbritannien im Vergleich (1945–1956)*. Cologne: Böhlau Verlag, 2007.

Kulturbund zur demokratischen Erneuerung Deutschlands. *Um Deutschlands neue Kultur. Aufruf und Ansprachen gehalten bei der Gründungskundgebung des Kulturbundes zur demokratischen Erneuerung Deutschlands für die Provinz Sachsen am 14. Oktober 1945 in Halle (Saale)*. Halle: Akademischer Verlag Halle, 1946.

Kulturbund zur demokratischen Erneuerung Deutschlands, Landesleitung Sachsen. *Kampf gegen den Formalismus in der Kunst und Literatur. Für eine fortschrittliche deutsche Kultur*. Dresden, n.d. [1951].

Kurella, Alfred. *Der Mensch als Schöpfer seiner Selbst: Beiträge zum sozialistischen Humanismus*. Berlin (East): Aufbau, 1961.

Lamberti, Marjorie. "German Antifascist Refugees in America and the Public Debate on 'What Should Be Done with Germany after Hitler,' 1941–1945" *Central European History* 40, 2 (June 2007): 279–305.

Leonhard, Wolfgang. *Child of the Revolution*. Translated by C. M. Woodhouse. London: Ink Links, 1979.

Die Revolution entlässt ihre Kinder. Cologne: Kiepenheuer & Witsch, 1955.

Lepenies, Wolf. *The Seduction of Culture in German History*. Princeton, NJ: Princeton University Press, 2006.

Loth, Wilfried. *Stalin's Unwanted Child: The Soviet Union, the German Question and the Founding of the GDR*. Translated by Robert F. Hagg. New York: St. Martin's Press, 1998.

MacDonogh, Giles. *After the Reich: The Brutal History of the Allied Occupation*. New York: Basic Books, 2007.

Mai, Gunther. "Sozialistische Nation und Nationalkultur," in Erhlich and Mai, eds., *Weimarer Klassik in der Ära Honecker*, 29–76.

Maier, Charles. *The Unmasterable Past: History, Holocaust, and German National Identity*. Cambridge, MA: Harvard University Press, 1988.

Mannheim, Karl. "The Problem of Generations," in Kurt H. Wolff, ed. *From Karl Mannheim*.

Mazower, Mark. *Dark Continent: Europe's Twentieth Century*. New York: Vintage, 1998.

McCormick, John P., ed. *Confronting Mass Democracy and Industrial Technology: Political and Social Theory from Nietzsche to Habermas*. Durham, NC: Duke University Press, 2002.

McDermott, Kevin, and Jeremy Agnew, *The Comintern: A History of International Communism from Lenin to Stalin*. Houndmills: Macmillan, 1996.

McLellan, Josie. *Antifascism and Memory in East Germany: Remembering the International Brigades 1945–1989*. Oxford: Clarendon Press, 2004.

Meinecke, Friedrich. *Werke, Band VIII*. In *Autobiographische Schriften*. Edited by Eberhard Kessel. Stuttgart: K. F. Koehler Verlag, 1969.

Merl, Andreas. "'... sich selbst auf dem Altare des Vaterlandes zu opfern' – Zum vorauseilenden Gehorsam der Saarländer 1933 bis 1935," in Herrmann and Bauer, eds., *Widerstand, Repression und Verfolgung*, 125–148.

Mitscherlich, Alexander and Margarete Mitscherlich. *The Inability to Mourn: Principles of Collective Behavior* (1967). Preface by Robert Jay Lifton. Translated by Beverley R. Placzek. New York: Grove Press, 1975. [*Die Unfähigkeit zu trauern: Grundlagen kollektiven Verhaltens.* Munich: Piper, 1967.]

Moeller, Robert G. "Germans as Victims?: Thoughts on a Post–Cold War History of World War II's Legacies." *History & Memory* 17, 1/2 (2005): 147–94.

"Sinking Ships, the Lost *Heimat* and Broken Taboos: Günter Grass and the Politics of Memory in Contemporary Germany," *Contemporary European History* 12, 2 (2003): 147–81.

War Stories: The Search for a Usable Past in the Federal Republic of Germany. Berkeley: University of California, 2001.

"What Did You Do in the War, *Mutti*? Courageous Women, Compassionate Commanders, and Stories of the Second World War," *German History* 22, 4: 563–94.

Moses, A. Dirk. *German Intellectuals and the Nazi Past*. New York: Cambridge University Press, 2007.

Mosse, George L. *The Crisis of German Ideology: Intellectual Origins of the Third Reich*. New York: Grosset & Dunlap, 1964.

The Nationalization of the Masses: Political Symbolism and Mass Movements in Germany from the Napoleonic Wars Through the Third Reich. New York: Howard Fertig, 1975.

Müller, Jan-Werner. *Another Country: German Intellectuals, Unification and National Identity*. New Haven, CT: Yale University Press, 2000.

Mosse, George L., ed. *Memory and Power in Postwar Europe: Studies in the Presence of the Past*. Cambridge: Cambridge University Press, 2002.

Naimark, Norman M. *The Russians in Germany: A History of the Russian Zone of Occupation, 1945–1949*. Cambridge, MA: The Belknap Press of Harvard University Press, 1995.

Niethammer, Lutz. *Entnazifizierung in Bayern: Säuberung und Rehabilitierung unter amerikanischer Besatzung*. Frankfurt am Main: Fischer, 1972.

Niethammer, Lutz, ed. *"Hinterher merkt man, daß es richtig war, daß es schiefgegangen ist." Nachkriegserfahrungen im Ruhrgebiet*. Lebensgeschichte und Sozialkultur im Ruhrgebiet, 1930 bis 1960, Band 2. Berlin: J. H. W. Dietz, 1983.

"Die Jahre weiß man nicht, wo man die heute hinsetzen soll." Faschismuserfahrungen im Ruhrgebiet Lebensgeschichte und Sozialkultur im Ruhrgebiet 1930 bis 1960, Band 1. Berlin: J. H. W. Dietz Nachf., 1983.

"Wir kriegen jetzt andere Zeiten." Auf der Suche nach der Erfahrung des Volkes in nachfaschistischen Ländern. Lebensgeschichte und Sozialkultur im Ruhrgebiet, 1930 bis 1960, Band 3. Berlin: Verlag J. H. W. Dietz Nachf., 1985.

Ulrich Bosdorf, and Peter Brandt, eds. *Arbeiterinitiative 1945. Antifaschistische Ausschüsse und Reorganisation der Arbeiterbewegung in Deutschland*. Wuppertal: Peter Hammer Verlag, 1976.

Nivens, Bill, ed., *Germans as Victims: Remembering the Past in Contemporary Germany*. Houndmills: Palgrave, 2006.

Nolan, Mary. "Antifascism under Fascism: German Vision and Voices." *New German Critique*, 67 (Winter 1996): 33–55.

Olick, Jeffrey K. *In the House of the Hangman: The Agonies of German Defeat, 1943–1949.* Chicago and London: University of Chicago Press, 2005.
Oppermann, Hans, ed. *Humanismus.* Darmstadt: Wissenschaftliche Buchgesellschaft, 1970.
Ott, Hugo. *Martin Heidegger: A Political Life.* Translated by Allan Blunden. New York: Basic Books, 1993.
Palmier, Jean-Michel. *Weimar in Exile: The Antifascist Emigration in Europe and America.* Translated by David Fernbach. London: Verso, 2006.
Palmowski, Jan. *Inventing a Socialist Nation: Heimat and the Politics of Everyday Life in the GDR, 1945–90.* Cambridge: Cambridge University Press, 2009.
Paxton, Robert O. *The Anatomy of Fascism.* New York: Vintage, 2004.
Peukert, Detlev J. K. *Die Weimarer Republik. Krisenjahre der klassischen Moderne.* Frankfurt a. M.: Suhrkamp, 1987.
Pietsch, Hartmut. *Militärregierung, Bürokratie und Sozialisierung. Zur Entwicklung des politischen Systems in den Städten des Ruhrgebietes 1945 bis 1948.* Duisburger Forschungen: Schriftenreihe für Geschichte und Heimatkunde Duisburgs, 26. Band. Duisburg: Walter Braun Verlag, 1978.
Pike, David. *The Politics of Culture in Soviet-Occupied Germany, 1945–1949.* Stanford, CA: Stanford University Press, 1992.
Port, Andrew I, "The Banalities of East German Historiography," in Fulbrook and Port, eds., *Becoming East German*, 1–30.
  Conflict and Stability in the German Democratic Republic. Cambridge University Press, 2007.
  "Democracy and Dictatorship in the Cold War: The Two Germanies, 1949–1961," in Smith, ed., *The Oxford Handbook of Modern German History.*
Pritchard, Gareth. *The Making of the GDR, 1945–53: From Antifascism to Stalinism.* Manchester and New York: Manchester University Press, 2000.
Rabinbach, Anson. *In the Shadow of Catastrophe: German Intellectuals between Apocalypse and Enlightenment.* Weimar and Now: German Cultural Criticism, 14. Berkeley: University of California Press, 1997.
Rathgeb, Eberhard, ed. *Die engagierte Nation: Deutsche Debatten 1945–2005.* Munich: Hanser, 2005.
Reichel, Peter. *Vergangenheitsbewältigung in Deutschland: Die Auseinandersetzung mit der NS-Diktatur in Politik und Justiz.* München: Beck, 2001.
Richthofen, Esther von. *Bringing Culture to the Masses: Control, Compromise and Participation in the GDR.* New York: Berghahn, 2009.
Riedel, Volker. *Freies Deutschland. México 1941–1946.* Mit einem Vorwort von Alexander Abusch. Berlin (East): Aufbau Verlag, 1975.
Ringer, Fritz K. *The Decline of the German Mandarins: The German Academic Community, 1890–1933.* Cambridge, MA: Harvard University Press, 1969.
Röder, Werner. *Die deutschen sozialistischen Exilgruppen in Großbritannien 1940–1945. Ein Beitrag zur Geschichte des Widerstandes gegen den Nationalsozialismus.* Schriftenreihe des Forschungsinstituts der Friedrich-Ebert-Stiftung, Band 58. Bonn-Bad Godesberg: Verlag Neue Gesellschaft, 1973.
Ross, Corey. *The East German Dictatorship: Problems and Perspectives in the Interpretation of the GDR.* London: Oxford University Press, 2002.
Roth, Karl Heinz and Angelika Ebbinghaus, eds. *Rote Kapellen – Kreisauer Kreise – Schwarze Kapellen. Neue Sichtweisen auf den Widerstand gegen die NS-Diktatur 1938–1945.* Hamburg: VSA, 2004.

Sayner, Joanne. "Communicating History: The Archived Letters of Greta Kuckhoff and Memories of 'Red Orchestra,'" in Fulbrook and Port, eds., *Becoming East German*, 79–98.

SBZ Handbuch. Staatliche Verwaltungen, Parteien, gesellschaftliche Organisationen und ihre Führungskräfte in der Sowjetischen Besatzungszone Deutschlands 1945–1949. Edited by Martin Broszat and Hermann Weber. Im Auftrag des Arbeitsbereiches Geschichte und Politik der DDR an der Universität Mannheim und des Instituts für Zeitgeschichte München. Munich: R. Oldenbourg, 1990.

Schiller, Dieter. *Johannes R. Becher und die Krise des Kulturbunds, 1949–1951. Drei Studien*. Hefte zur DDR-Geschichte, 63. Berlin: Helle Panke, 2000.

Schissler, Hanna, ed. *The Miracle Years: A Cultural History of West Germany, 1949–1968*. Princeton, NJ: Princeton University Press, 2001.

Schivelbusch, Wolfgang. *In a Cold Crater: Cultural and Intellectual Life in Berlin, 1945–1948*. Translated by Kelly Berry. Berkeley: University of California Press, 1998.

Schmidt, Gerhard. *Der Kulturbund zu Frieden und Demokratie, 1948/49. Teil 1 und Teil 2*. Berlin (East): Kulturbund der DDR, 1984.

Schock, Ralph, ed. *Haltet die Saar, Genossen! Antifaschistische Schriftsteller im Abstimmungskampf 1935*. Berlin: J.H.W. Dietz Nachf., 1984.

Schoenhals, Kai P. *The Free German Movement: A Case of Patriotism or Treason?* New York: Greenwood Press, 1989.

Schöpflin, George. *Politics in Eastern Europe, 1945–1992*. Oxford: Blackwell, 1993.

Schuler, Friedrich. *Mexico Between Hitler and Roosevelt: Mexican Foreign Relations in the Age of Lázaro Cárdenas, 1934–1940*. Albuquerque: University of New Mexico Press, 1999.

Schulmeister, Karl-Heinz. *Auf dem Wege zu einer neuen Kultur: Der Kulturbund in den Jahren 1945–1949*. East-Berlin: Dietz Verlag, 1977.

Scott-Smith, Giles. "'A Radical Democratic Political Offensive': Melvin J. Lasky, *Der Monat*, and the Congress for Cultural Freedom." *Journal of Contemporary History* 35, 2 (April 2000): 263–80.

Sebald, H. G. *Luftkrieg und Literatur. Mit einem Essay zu Alfred Andersch*. Frankfurt/M.: Fischer Taschenbuch, 2001.

Seton-Watson, Hugh. *The East European Revolution*. Third edition. New York: Frederick A. Praeger, 1956.

Smith, Helmut Walser, "When the Sonderweg Debate Left Us," *German Studies Review* XXXI, 2 (May 2008): 225–40.

The Oxford Handbook of Modern German History. New York: Oxford University Press, 2011.

Spranger, Eduard. *Der Anteil des Neuhumanismus an der Entstehung des deutschen Nationalbewußtsein*. Festrede zur Reichsgründungsfeier der Friedrich-Wilhelms-Universität zu Berlin am 18. Januar 1923. Berlin: Norddeutsche Buchdruckerei und Verlagsanstalt, 1923.

"Die Bedeutung der wissenschaftlichen Pädagogik für das Volksleben" (1920) in *Kultur und Erziehung. Gesammelte pädagogische Aufsätze*. Third Edition. Leipzig: Quelle & Meyer, 1925.

"Goethe und die Metamorphose des Menschen" (1924). In *Kultur und Erziehung*.

Das humanistische und das politische Bildungsideal im heutigen Deutschland. Berlin: Ernst Siegfried Mittler und Sohn, 1916.

Spriano, Paolo. *Stalin and the European Communists.* Translated by Jon Rothschild. London: Verso, 1985.

Stalinism Revisited: The Establishment of Communist Regimes in East-Central Europe. Edited by Vladimir Tismaneanu. Budapest: Central European University Press, 2009.

Stenzel, Julius. "Die Gefahren Modernen Denkens und der Humanismus," *Die Antike* 4 (1928). Reprinted in Oppermann, ed., *Humanismus*, 85–110.

Stern, Fritz. *The Politics of Cultural Despair: A Study in the Rise of the Germanic Ideology.* Berkeley: University of California Press, 1961.

Suckut, Siegfried. *Die Betriebsrätebewegung in der Sowjetisch Besetzten Zone Deutschlands (1945–1948). Zur Entwicklung und Bedeutung von Arbeiterinitiative, betrieblicher Mitbestimmung und Selbstbestimmung bis zur Revision des programmatischen Konzeptes der KPD/SED vom "besonderen deutschen Weg zum Sozialismus."* Frankfurt/Main: Haag und Herchen, 1982.

Témoigner entre histoire et mémoire. Revue pluridisciplinaire de la Fondation Auschwitz Bruxelles, No104 (July–September 2009): L'Antifascisme revisité. Histoire – idéologie –mémoire. Paris: Éditions Kimé, 2009.

Thacker, Toby. *Music after Hitler, 1945–1955.* Aldershot: Ashgate, 2007.

Torpey, John C., *Intellectuals, Socialism, and Dissent: The East German Opposition and Its Legacy.* Minneapolis: University of Minnesota Press, 1995.

Traverso, Enzo. *Á feu et à sang: de la guerre civile européenne, 1914–1945.* Paris: Stock, 2007.

——— "The New Anti-Communism: Rereading the Twentieth Century," in Mike Haynes and Jim Wolfreys, eds., *History and Revolution: Refuting Revisionism.* London and New York: Verso, 2007, 138–55.

Ueberschär, Gerd R. *Für ein anderes Deutschland. Der deutsche Widerstand gegen den NS-Staat 1933–1945.* Frankfurt a. M.: Fischer Taschenbuch Verlag, 2006.

Unser Kampf gegen Hitler. Protokoll des Ersten Landeskongresses der Bewegung "Freies Deutschland" in Mexico. Mexico City: Alemania Libre, 1943.

Vansittart, The Rt. Hon. Lord. *Lessons of My Life.* New York: Knopf, 1943.

Vasile, Christian. "Propaganda and Culture in Romania at the Beginning of the Communist Regime," in *Stalinism Revisited*, 367–99.

Vogt, Timothy R. *Denazification in Soviet-Occupied Germany: Brandenburg, 1945–1948.* Cambridge, MA: Harvard University Press, 2000.

Voßke, Heinz, ed., *Im Kampf bewährt. Erinnerungen deutscher Genossen an den antifaschistischen Widerstand von 1933 bis 1945.* Berlin (East): Dietz Verlag, 1977.

Wagner, Peter. *A Sociology of Modernity: Liberty and Discipline.* London: Routledge, 1994.

Wegner, Gregory P. "The Legacy of Nazism and the History Curriculum in the East German Secondary Schools." *The History Teacher*, 25, 4 (August 1992).

Wehler, Hans-Ulrich. *Deutsche Gesellschaftsgeschichte. Band 1: Vom Feudalismus des alten Reiches bis zur defensiven Modernisierung der Reformära, 1700–1815.* München: C. H. Beck, 1987.

——— *Deutsche Gesellschaftsgeschichte. Band 2: Von der Reformära bis zur industriellen und politischen "Deutschen Doppelrevolution", 1815–1845/49.* München: C. H. Beck, 1987.

Deutsche Gesellschaftsgeschichte. Band 3: Von der "Deutschen Doppelrevolution" bis zum Beginn des Ersten Weltkrieges, 1849–1914. München: C. H. Beck, 1995.
Deutsche Gesellschaftsgeschichte. Band 4: Vom Beginn des Ersten Welkriegs bis zur Gründung der beiden deutschen Staaten, 1914–1949. München: C. H. Beck, 1995.
Weisenborn, Günther, ed. *Der lautlose Aufstand. Bericht über die Widerstandsbewegung des deutschen Volkes, 1933–1945*. Second edition. Hamburg: Rowohlt, 1953.
Weisenborn, Günther, and Joy Weisenborn. *Einmal laß mich traurig sein. Briefe, Lieder, Kassiber, 1941–1943*. Zürich: Arche, 1984.
Wende-Hohenberger, Waltraud, ed. *Der erste gesamtdeutsche Schriftstellerkongreß nach dem Zweiten Weltkrieg im Ostsektor Berlins vom 4. bis 8. Oktober 1947*. Frankfurt am Main: Peter Lang, 1988.
Wettig, Gerhard, ed. *Der Tjul'panov Bericht. Sowjetische Besatzungspolitik in Deutschland nach dem Zweiten Weltkrieg*. Göttingen: V&R unipress, 2012.
Wienand, Christiane. "Remembered Change and Changes of Remembrance: East German Narratives of Anti-fascist Conversion," in Fulbrook and Port, eds., *Becoming East German*, 99–118.
Wickberg, Daniel. "Intellectual History vs. the Social History of Intellectuals." *Rethinking History* 5:3 (2001): 383–95.
Wilkinson, James D. *The Intellectual Resistance in Europe*. Cambridge, MA: Harvard University Press, 1981.
Williams, Rhys. "'Das sichtbare und das unsichtbare deutsche Vaterland.' Die Zeitschrift Das Innere Reich," in Hermann Haarmann, ed., *Heimat, liebe Heimat. Exil und innere Emigration (1933–1945)*. Berlin: Bostelmann & Siebenhaar, 2004, 93–105.
Willmann, Heinz. "Das sowjetische Volk war uns immer Freund und Helfer," in Voßke, ed., *Im Kampf bewährt*, 377–415.
Winter, Jay. *Sites of Memory, Sites of Mourning: The Great War in European Cultural History*. New York: University of Cambridge Press, 1995.
Wolff, Kurt H, ed. *From Karl Mannheim*. Second expanded edition. With an introduction by Volker Meja and David Kettler. New Brunswick, NJ: Transaction Publishers, 1993.
Women under the Swastika. London: Free German League of Culture in Great Britain, 1942.
Wurm, Carsten. *Der frühe Aufbau-Verlag 1945–1961. Konzepte und Kontroversen*. Wiesbaden: Verlag O. Harrassowitz, 1996.

Index

Abusch, Alexander, 4–5, 18, 19, 32, 131, 137, 139, 141, 162, 163, 164, 170, 172, 173, 179, 183
   Der Irrweg einer Nation, 53, 92, 123, 131
   early life, 32–5
   as Kulturbund ideological coordinator, 128, 136
   in Mexican exile, 44, 46
   reaction against Vansittartism, 51–2
Academy of the Arts, 77
Academy for Musical Arts of Berlin, 112
Ackermann, Anton, 78, 79, 93, 96, 162
Action Committee for Reconstruction (Aktionsausschuß für Wiederaufbau), 58
Adenauer, Konrad, 66, 160, 168
agitprop (agitation and propaganda), 7, 73
Alemania Libre. *See Freies Deutschland/Alemania Libre*
Allied Control Council (ACC), 99
Alltagsgeschichte, 15, 17
Andersch, Alfred, 167
Andreas-Friedrich, Ruth, 83, 95
Angriff, 27, 28
anti-cosmopolitan. *See also* anti-formalism campaign
anti-cosmopolitan campaign, 19
Antifaschistisches Aktionskomitee (Afa), 59, 61
antifascist committees (antifas), 17, 18, 54–67, 165, 178
anti-formalism campaign, 19, 135, 139, 155, 162, 170, 174, 180
antisemitism, 45, 47, 104, 133, 151, 152
Aragon, Louis, 140
Aufbau, 19, 43, 53, 73, 88, 91, 103–5, 104n103, 109, 111, 115, 117, 119, 120, 121, 125, 131, 132, 133, 134, 135, 135n18, 146, 163
   KGF publication, 59, 62, 64, 65
Aufbau Verlag (publishing house), 103, 110, 123, 132, 167

Aufruf, 27
Avila Camacho, Manuel, 46

Bach, Johann Sebastian, 83, 92
Bauhaus, 1
Bavaria, 59, 116, 151
Bebel, August, 50
Becher, Johannes R., 2, 3, 4, 18, 19, 24, 27, 33, 44, 82–4, 86, 93, 99, 103, 104, 111, 113f5, 115–16, 117–19, 120, 121–5, 126, 127, 128, 129, 131, 137, 153, 155, 159, 161, 164, 174, 175, 176, 179, 185
   "Becher circle" in Dahlem, 78–80
   biographical and artistic background, 88–93
   election as Kulturbund president, 95–8
   as GDR minister, 170–2
   memorialization in the GDR, 177
Beethoven, Ludwig van, 2, 44, 82
Bekennende Kirche. *See* Confessing Church
Bennedik, Bernhard, 94, 112, 115, 119, 120, 121, 122, 123, 132
Berendsohn, Walter A., 30, 35
Berlin, 1–2, 3, 4, 5, 18, 33, 43, 45, 53, 72, 73, 77, 81–2, 84, 85, 86, 91, 93–4, 97–8, 99, 105, 112, 115–16, 118, 121, 122, 123, 124, 125, 126, 129, 132, 137, 139, 140, 141, 148, 150, 153, 154, 156, 160–1, 163, 167, 168, 170, 173, 176, 182, 183n8
   Charlottenburg, 1, 81, 99, 152
   Dahlem, 79, 80, 93, 117
Berliner Zeitung, 81
Bewegung Freies Deutschland (BFD), 43–5, 46–9, 55
Birkenfeld, Günther, 139, 148, 149, 152, 153, 154, 158
Black Record, 50, 51
Bloch, Ernst, 4n7
Bohley, Bärbel, 176

201

Bohner, Theodor, 120, 123
Böll, Heinrich, 167
Brandenburg, 118, 165
Braun, Max, 26
Brecht, Bertolt, 13n35, 35, 88, 149
Bremen, 59, 62
British Occupation Zone, 115
Buenos Aires, 40, 42
Burckhardt, Jacob, 31

Camus, Albert, 135, 154
Cárdenas, Lazaro, 43, 46, 47
Carossa, Hans, 41
Central Cleansing Committee for the Eradication of Fascist Literature (Zentraler Säuberungsausschuß zur Ausmerzung der faschistischen Literatur), 112–14
Cercas, Javier, 185
Chopin, Frederic, 73
Christian Democratic Union (CDU), 4, 80, 109, 110, 111, 114, 117, 118, 120, 122, 123, 126, 127, 128, 175
Churchill, Winston, 50, 109n6, 117
co-determination, 57
Cold War, 2, 3, 5, 10, 13n33, 15, 17, 19, 56, 58, 73, 75, 92, 96, 109, 129, 130, 136, 137, 147, 151, 152, 153, 154, 155, 156, 157, 158, 162, 167, 170, 172, 173, 180, 181, 182
Communist Information Bureau (Cominform), 137
Communist International (Comintern), 6, 29, 33
Communist Party of Germany. *See* KPD
Confessing Church, 80, 174
Congress for Cultural Freedom, 148n56, 148n57, 154, 173
Copenhagen, 35
Cultural League for the Democratic Renewal of Germany. *See* Kulturbund zur demokratischen Erneuerung Deutschlands
cultural nationalism, 5, 10, 14, 15, 16, 92, 130, 143, 157, 158, 167, 173, 175, 178
Curtius, Ernst Robert, 31, 32
Curtius, Ludwig, 31

D'Annunzio, Gabriele, 114
Dachau, 59, 145
Dahn, Felix, 114
Dahrendorf, Gustav, 94, 120, 121
Das Andere Deutschland. See La Otra Alemania

Das Innere Reich, 72
de Rougemont, Denis, 133
denazification, 56, 58, 66, 115
Deutsche Demokratische Partei (DDP), 80
Deutsche Verwaltung für Volksbildung (DVV), 111, 128
Deutsche Volkszeitung, 99
Deutscher Kulturbund, 170, 175
Deutscher Schriftstellerverband (DSV), 173, 174, 175
Dilschneider, Otto, 80, 83, 94, 95, 103, 109, 115, 116, 123, 126, 131, 132
Dimitrov, Georgi, 29
Dirks, Walter, 73, 115
Döblin, Alfred, 140
Duisburg, 58
Duncker, Hermann, 151, 152
Dymshits, Alexander, 99, 137, 150

Ehrenburg, Ilya, 76
Eisenstein, Sergei, 149
Engels, Friedrich, 44, 47, 95, 131, 162
Enlightenment, 9, 37, 78, 121, 183
Erpenbeck, Fritz, 79
Europäische Hefte, 27
European Writers' Association, 41
existentialism, 135, 135n20, 147, 154, 162, 173, 180
expressionism, 2, 4, 23, 82, 86, 88, 89, 103, 121

Fallada, Hans, 97, 131
Federal Republic of Germany (FRG), 11, 57, 116, 151, 155, 156, 157, 167, 180, 181, 183
Feuchtwanger, Lion, 27, 29
Fichte, Johann Gottlieb, 52
First German Writers' Congress, 10, 14, 19, 136, 151, 157, 161, 167, 168, 173, 174, 175, 180
First World War, 7, 30, 79, 86, 89, 167
Fourth German Writers' Congress, 173
Fraenkel, Heinrich, 50
Frankfurt, 79, 115
Frankfurter Hefte, 73
Free German Cultural League (Freier Deutscher Kulturbund, FDKB), 37–40, 44, 78, 170
Freie Deutsche Kulturgesellschaft (Free German Cultural Association), 115
Freies Deutschland/Alemania Libre, 18, 42–6, 51, 53
Freiheitsaktion Bayern (FAB), 59
French Occupation Zone, 65

Index

Friedensburg, Ferdinand, 3, 4, 19, 80, 94, 110, 112–14, 115, 116–17, 120, 122–3, 125–7, 128, 132, 140, 153, 157, 158–9, 160–1, 179
Furet, François, 5
Furtwängler, Wilhelm, 97, 131

Gegenangriff, 28
Gera, 59
German Communist Party. *See* KPD (Kommunistische Partei Deutschlands)
German Democratic Republic (GDR), 2, 4–5, 6, 7, 11, 12, 14–16, 18, 33, 37, 56, 81, 88, 92, 93, 104, 111, 130, 136, 151, 155, 156, 157, 158, 160, 161, 162, 169, 170–4, 175, 176–7, 180, 181, 182, 184
Gestapo (Geheime Staatspolizei), 35, 47, 164, 165, 178
Goebbels, Joseph, 1, 7, 24, 27, 28, 31, 35, 36, 38, 41, 49, 50, 51, 52, 53, 99, 150, 162
Goethe, Johann Wolfgang, 3, 9, 10, 20, 24, 31, 32, 38, 44, 46, 47, 49, 50, 73, 78, 82, 85, 95, 101, 102f4, 103, 104, 131, 132, 133, 134, 143, 156, 162, 178, 182
Goethegemeinden, 134
Gollancz, Victor, 50
Gorki, Maxim, 91
Götting, Gerald, 175
Grass, Günter, 184
Grenzland, 28
Gross, Babette L., 28
Grossek, Melchior, 94, 122
Gruppe 47, 167
Gysi, Klaus, 93, 96, 115, 116, 117, 118, 123, 124, 125

Habermas, Jürgen, 183
Hanstein, Wolfram von, 118
Harich, Wolfgang, 4, 94, 95, 97, 135, 145, 146, 150, 151, 170, 171f9, 177
Harlan, Falk, 168, 169
Hauptmann, Gerhart, 97, 98, 103, 131
Havemann, Robert, 123
Heidegger, Martin, 23, 31, 88, 135, 154
Heidelberg, 79, 115, 116
Heine, Heinrich, 3, 8, 10, 38, 44, 101, 156
Heinrich-Heine Club, 43–5, 78
Herder, Johann Gottfried, 9, 31, 32, 46, 52, 131
Heuss, Theodor, 66, 115, 116
Heym, Stefan, 176

Hitler, Adolf, 8, 25, 27, 31, 36, 38, 40, 42, 47, 48, 49, 58, 59, 78, 82, 86, 92, 120, 133, 134, 141, 143, 145, 149, 157, 164, 168, 180
Hitler-Stalin Pact, 10, 29, 37
Hofer, Carl, 93, 94, 109
Hofmann, Paul, 110
Hölderlin, Friedrich, 9, 24, 25, 30, 31, 38, 44, 78
Holocaust, 13, 13n34, 151, 180
Honecker, Erich, 26n11
Horizonte, 139, 154
Huch, Ricarda, 5, 48, 140, 141, 142f7, 144, 150, 168, 169
humanism
  as scholarly ideal, 30–2
humanist front, 10, 11, 30, 163, 166f8
Humboldt, Alexander von, 46
Humboldt, Wilhelm von, 31, 52, 85, 170
Husserl, Edmund, 23, 24
Hutten, Ulrich von, 60

Ihering, Herbert, 87, 88, 89, 94, 112, 126, 128
inner emigration, 19, 32, 72, 94, 95, 96, 98, 133, 135, 140, 144, 146, 148, 149, 177, 178
inner émigrés, 4, 13, 19, 41, 48, 94, 97, 130, 131, 135, 144, 145, 147, 158, 159, 179
inner exile, 5, 41, 144. *See* inner emigration
International Congress for the Defence of Culture, 9
Iron Curtain, 6, 14, 109, 115

Jacob, P. Walter, 42
Jaeger, Werner, 30
Jahn, Hans, 42
Janka, Walter, 95n74, 177, 177n63
Jaspers, Karl, 13n35, 140, 146, 154
Jena, 33, 59
Joint Chiefs of Staff Directive 1067 (JCS 1067), 60
June 17 uprising, 156, 168, 169
Jünger, Ernst, 10, 114, 135, 146
Jungmann, Erich, 47

Kahn, Arthur D., 57, 58
Kaiser, Jakob, 159
Kammer der Kulturschaffenden, 111
Kampfbund für deutsche Kultur, 11, 24, 30
Kampfgemeinschaft gegen den Faschismus (KGF), 59, 62, 64
Kant, Immanuel, 9, 37, 46, 78, 95

Kantorowicz, Alfred, 19, 27, 144, 145, 157, 163, 167, 172
Kataïev, Valentin, 136, 150, 151
Kellermann, Bernhard, 93, 94, 95, 96
Kerr, Alfred, 27, 37
Kisch, Egon erwin, 44
Klemperer, Viktor, 104
Kogon, Eugen, 73
KPD, 3, 4, 5, 6, 12, 14, 19, 26, 29, 32, 33, 37, 39, 43, 45, 46, 51, 54, 55, 56, 58, 63, 64, 72, 75–6, 78, 79, 84, 87, 91, 93, 96–7, 106, 110, 111, 117, 119, 121, 123, 124, 125, 128, 129, 151, 164, 179
Kracow, 32
Kuckhoff, Adam, 145
Kuckhoff, Greta, 145
Kuczynski, Jürgen, 37
Kulturbund zur demokratischen Erneuerung Deutschlands, 1–5, 10, 11, 13–15, 17, 18–20, 72–5, 79–80, 87, 91, 129, 131–2, 133, 134–5, 141–3, 146–7, 163, 165–7, 179, 180, 181–2, 183–5
  agenda and early activities, 93–8
  charter committee meeting, 93–8
  "cultural cleansing" activities, 109–14
  discussions of federalism, 114–18
  end of license in Western zones, 152–5
  as GDR mass organization, 156, 169–73, 175–7
  historiography, 71
  inauguration, 80–4
  lack of political mobilization, 118–23
  organizer of the First German Writers' Congress, 137–40
  role of earlier reform ideas, 84–6, 87–8
  "Sovietization", 107–9, 123–8, 157–62
Kurella, Alfred, 32, 35, 174

La Otra Alemania/Das Andere Deutschland, 40–2
Langgässer, Elisabeth, 144–5
Lasky, Melvin J., 136, 148–51, 154, 173, 174
Lassalle, Ferdinand, 52
Leipzig, 54, 55, 59, 75
Lemmer, Ernst, 94, 109, 110, 111, 112, 114, 117, 126, 127, 128, 159, 161
Leonhard, Hans, 129
Leonhard, Wolfgang, 137
Lessing, Gotthold Ephraim, 8, 9, 20, 31, 33, 38, 39, 78, 103, 121
Lewis, Sinclair, 150
Liebknecht, Karl, 91

Lommer, Horst, 104
London, 38, 50, 52
Löwenstein, Hubertus Prinz zu, 27
Lukács, Georg, 4n7, 24, 103, 104
Luther, Martin, 7, 24, 101–3, 121, 141, 174
Luxemburg, Rosa, 91

Mainz, 58
Mann, Heinrich, 27, 29, 77, 79, 103
Mann, Klaus, 25, 27, 29, 30, 115
Mann, Thomas, 9, 13n35, 24, 25, 30, 38, 49, 49n43, 77, 79, 97, 98, 140, 170
Mannheim, Karl, 20n47, 164n20
Marshall Plan, 137
Marx, Karl, 7, 10, 24, 30, 46, 47, 95, 131
mass mobilization, 10, 11, 14, 15, 17, 32, 45, 55
Mayer, Hans, 151, 170, 177
Mazzini, Guiseppe, 48, 49
Mecklenburg-Vorpommern, 119
Meinecke, Friedrich, 13n35, 53, 84n42, 133–4, 155, 179, 181
Mendelsohn, Moses, 33
Merker, Paul, 44, 45, 47, 51
Merkur, 133
Mexico City, 18, 40, 43, 46, 47, 78, 132
modernism, 1, 139, 173
Monat, 154
Montevideo, 40
Moscow, 4, 5, 28, 32, 37, 45, 55, 57, 78–9, 80, 84, 94, 110, 123, 127, 161, 178, 180
Mühlen, Norbert, 27, 28
Munich, 59, 61, 89
Münzenberg, Willi, 28, 29, 33

National Committee for a Free Germany. *See* Nationalkomitee Freies Deutschland
National Socialism, 1, 7, 39, 50, 51, 52, 59, 61, 83, 96, 104, 133, 145
National Socialist German Workers' Party (NSDAP), 23
Nationale Forschungs- und Gedenkstätten der klassischen deutschen Literatur in Weimar (NFG), 175
Nationalkomitee Freies Deutschland (NKFD), 32, 52, 54, 55–6, 59, 75, 78
Nazism. *See* National Socialism
New Forum (Neues Forum), 176
Niekisch, Ernst, 4n7, 147
Niemöller, Martin, 80, 168
Nietzsche, Friedrich, 8, 24, 31, 44, 47, 101
Nuremberg, 32, 33
Nuremberg Trials, 66, 119, 120

Index

Office of Strategic Studies (OSS), 57, 58
Ortega y Gasset, José, 147, 185
Ost und West, 163, 167
Ostpolitik., 160
Ould, Hermon, 143

Paris, 8, 9, 25, 28, 29, 30, 32, 43, 46, 124, 139
Pariser Tageblatt, 35
Partisan Review, 148
Pieck, Wilhelm, 76, 77, 78, 161
Piscator, Erwin, 10, 27, 88
Plivier, Theodor, 38, 94
Poelzig, Hans, 1
Poljakow, Wladimir, 35
Popovič, Jovan, 143
Popular Front, 9, 10, 18, 26, 43, 45, 46, 49
Potsdam Conference, 99
Prague, 29
Protestant Reformation, 105, 141
Protestantism, 2, 3, 8, 14, 18, 74, 80, 83, 91, 92, 94, 101, 105, 115, 141, 143, 173, 174

Red Army, 14, 55, 56, 56n5, 57, 59, 156, 165
Reformation, 14, 60, 74, 92, 101, 143, 173, 174, 176, 180
Reformpädagogik, 85, 86
Reichsbanner, 64
Reinhardt, Ernst. *See* Abusch, Alexander
Renn, Ludwig, 44, 47, 48, 51
Richter-Schoch, Eva, 145
Riedel, Otto, 174, 175
Rosenberg, Alfred, 11, 24, 30
Rote Fahne, 33, 35, 46, 49, 124
Rote Kapelle, 164, 168
Roter Frontkämpferbund, 64
Ruhr, 58, 63

Saar referendum, 9, 18, 25–9, 35, 37, 52, 55, 80, 163, 178, 182
Sánchez Mazas, Rafael, 185
Sartre, Jean-Paul, 135, 154
Saxony, 118, 162
Schiller, Friedrich, 8, 9, 10, 24, 32, 35, 38, 49, 60, 60n23, 78, 103, 132, 175, 178, 182
Schirmer, Walter, 94
Schlamm, Willi, 27
Schmid, Carlo, 65, 66
Schnog, Karl, 145
Schulze-Boysen-Harnack group. *See* Rote Kapelle
Schumacher, Kurt, 76, 77

Schutzverband deutscher Autoren (SDA), 137, 139, 140, 173
Schutzverband deutscher Schriftsteller (SDS), 27, 29, 77, 137
Second German Writers' Congress, 173
Second World War. *See* World War II
Seghers, Anna, 5, 27, 35, 44, 48, 48f2, 94, 150, 174
Silesia, 98
Sintenis, Renée, 94
Social Democracy, 27, 28, 32, 50, 52, 58, 75, 129
Social Democratic Party in Exile (SoPaDe), 29
Social Democratic Party of Germany (SPD), 29, 63, 64, 65, 75, 76, 94, 117, 125, 129
socialist humanism, 12, 20, 25, 30, 32, 37, 71, 73, 74, 76, 97, 108, 131, 132, 170, 176
socialist realism, 135n20, 173
Socialist Unity Party (SED), 4, 11, 14, 16, 19, 20, 56, 71, 75, 93, 108, 117, 124, 125, 127, 128, 137, 139, 153, 155–6, 158, 159, 161, 162, 163, 169, 172, 173, 174, 175, 176, 177, 180, 182, 185
Soviet Military Administration in Germany (SMAD), 2, 67, 75, 79, 80, 81, 97, 99, 100, 111, 112, 124, 127, 129, 137, 139, 148, 150, 151, 153, 158
Soviet Occupation Zone (SBZ), 4, 10, 14, 15, 18, 56, 67, 71, 74, 75, 80, 100, 107, 108, 114, 115, 116, 118, 125, 127, 129, 134, 137, 150, 154, 159, 163, 179
Sovietization, 75, 76, 101, 107, 107n2, 125, 128. *See* also Stalinization
Spanish Civil War, 9, 43, 145, 163, 167
Spartakus uprising, 33
Spengler, Oswald, 185
Spranger, Eduard, 30, 85, 86, 87, 89, 94
Stahlhelm, 64
Stalin, 5, 16, 28, 51, 56, 73, 76, 79, 117, 137, 161, 170
Stalingrad, 55
Stalinism, 6, 14
Stalinization, 6, 14, 107, 107n1, 137, 155, 169, 179, 181, 184
Stauffenberg, Claus von, 57, 168, 169
Steinbeck, John, 140, 148
Stenzel, Julius, 31
Stoph, Willi, 33, 33n42
Stout, Rex, 50
Stroux, Johannes, 93, 94, 115, 126
Supreme Headquarters of the Allied Expeditionary Forces (SHAEF), 57, 58

Tagesspiegel, 151
Tägliche Rundschau, 151, 170
Tagore, Rabindranath, 30
Tchaikovsky, Pjotr, 2, 73, 82
Thuringia, 59
Tjulpanov, Sergei, 99, 100n93, 127
Toller, Ernst, 27, 29
totalitarianism, 9n19, 15, 16, 20, 39, 64, 122, 149
Truman Doctrine, 137
Truman, Harry S., 117

Ulbricht, Walter, 56, 77, 78, 79, 123, 161, 164
United States, 180, 182
Unity Front (*Einheitsfront*), 26, 28, 29

Vansittart, Lord Robert, 50–1, 53
Vansittartism, 18, 50, 53, 60, 168, 178, 182
Vergangenheitsbewältigung, 12, 13, 59, 74, 180, 181, 182n5, 184
Versailles Treaty, 25, 86
Vishnevski, Vsevolod, 136, 147, 148
Völkischer Beobachter, 27
Volksfront. *See* Popular Front

Wandel, Paul, 111
Wartburg Congress, 172, 173, 174
Wegener, Paul, 82, 94, 111, 116
Wehler, Hans-Ulrich, 16
Wehner, Herbert, 26n11
Weimar, 41, 175

classical period, 8, 10, 31, 41, 175, 178, 182, 184
republican period, 1, 7, 10, 23, 24, 31, 33, 61, 64, 73, 74, 84, 94, 117, 124, 126, 163, 164, 178, 182
Weisenborn, Günther, 4, 19, 104, 137, 139, 141–4, 145, 148, 149, 156, 157, 163–9, 166f8, 175, 183
Weltbühne, 53, 129, 146, 170
West Germany. *See* Federal Republic of Germany (FRG)
Westland, 28
Westphalia, 163
White Rose, 57
Wiegler, Paul, 112
Wilhelmine Empire/period, 7, 33, 84, 85, 89, 134
Willmann, Heinz, 79, 80, 81, 93, 96, 118, 121, 122, 152, 153
Winckelmann, Johann Joachim, 31, 32
Wolf, Christa, 176
woman of the rubble, 65
works councils, 57, 63
World War I, 25, 30, 33, 86, 87, 91, 106n108, 164. *See also* First World War
World War II, 8, 25, 57, 86, 108, 157, 181
Wuppertal, 62

Yalta Conference, 120, 121, 183

Zhdanov, Andrei, 73, 137, 139
Zuckmayer, Carl, 87

CPSIA information can be obtained
at www.ICGtesting.com
Printed in the USA
LVHW092200030619
620048LV00022B/1175/P